D1288177

WITHDRAWN

End of Watch

End of Watch _____

Utah's Murdered Police Officers, 1858–2003

Robert Kirby

The University of Utah Press
Salt Lake City

The Defiance House Man colophon is a registered trademark of the University of Utah Press. It is based upon a four-foot-tall, Ancient Puebloan pictograph (late PIII) near Glen Canyon, Utah.

09 08 07 06 05 04
5 4 3 2 1

Library of Congress Cataloging-in-Publication Data

Robert Kirby, 1953–
  End of watch : Utah's murdered police officers, 1858–2003 / Robert Kirby
        p. cm.
Includes bibliographical references (p.) and index.
  ISBN 0-87480-783-2 (hardcover : alk. paper)
  1. Police murders—Utah—History. 2. Police—Utah—Biography. I. Title.
  HV8145.U8K57 2004
  364. 152'3'0922792—dc22

2003022619

Book design by Richard Firmage

Frontispiece: Salt Lake City police officers drill in the jail yard, July 16, 1909, under the direction of Chief S. A. Barlow (center, front row). Three of these officers would be murdered in the line of duty. Sergeant Henry Johnston (back row, first from the right), Patrolman Tommy Griffiths (back row, second from the right), and Sergeant Nephi Pierce (to the left of Barlow, back row). (Photograph courtesy of Utah State Historical Society)

If you ever
fought traffic in the rain,
sleep and fear in the hour of the dead,
or tears at a bagpipe's skirl,
this is for you
and for the next to fall.

Contents

Preface _____

My name is etched into the low blue-gray marble wall of the National Law Enforcement Officers Memorial in Washington, D.C. "Robert L. Kirby" is one of more than fifteen thousand names of American police officers killed in the line of duty.

The name on panel 56 E, line 6 actually belongs to a Chickasaw County, Mississippi, deputy sheriff, one of several things he and I shared, including a similar age, education, and interest in law enforcement. We began our police careers within a year of each other. Deputy Kirby and I performed the usual police duties small communities require: long hours of traffic enforcement, accident investigations, business checks, domestic disputes, barking dogs, stretches of boredom punctuated by occasional bursts of terror. We could have been twins in more than just name. We were in fact brothers.

Although we never met, Kirby and I were both police officers on the morning of December 1, 1981, when he paid the terrible price that resulted in our name being placed on the memorial. While serving a routine domestic assault warrant on a man in the small, quiet town of Van Vleet, Kirby was shot with a .30-06 rifle. His death was not instantaneous. Backup officers later found his body facedown in a field one hundred fifty yards from the initial scene, where his killer had pursued and shot him four more times. The assailant was convicted and sent to prison.

The name on the memorial reveals nothing about what happened to Kirby other than the fact that he was just one of 202 officers killed that year in America. But it serves as a chilling reminder that it could have been me. It almost was.

A former police officer, I am the son of a retired police officer. My brothers are police officers, as are the majority of my closest friends. At one time or another all of us have come closer to an eternal association with that low marble wall than we care to remember. Those of us who barely survived attempts on our lives carry the marks of those searing moments when the outcome could have gone either way. Three years before Deputy Kirby was murdered, I narrowly escaped having my brains blown out by a man I detained for attempting to steal a vehicle. The incident, similar to hundreds encountered daily by police officers across America, goes unrecognized today by anyone other than those closest to me.

I began my law enforcement career when I was hired by the Grantsville Police Department in the spring of 1978, one of three police officers in that rural west-desert town. Back then, agencies had a grace period of eighteen months before the law obligated them to send new officers to the police academy, so my transition from unemployed carpenter to police officer consisted of little more than a change of clothes.

After a couple shifts spent riding with an experienced officer—a cursory examination to see if I was stupid or clumsy enough to shoot myself—I was on my own. The first arrest I made, which did not occur for another two months, illustrates just how unprepared I was to protect and serve. One afternoon I followed a drunk driver as he ran through three stop signs before I finally realized that something was amiss. The subsequent traffic stop necessitated a phone call to the local service station where the police chief worked part time. He came to the scene in his coveralls, administered the field sobriety tests, and explained how to arrest the driver.

Four months later, I approached a man attempting to drive away in a vehicle that I knew didn't belong to him. While I was questioning him inside my patrol car, the suspect struck me on the head and grabbed for my pistol. We fought over the gun for a small eternity, taking turns pointing the muzzle at each other. I finally managed to subdue him in the only way I knew how at the time: I beat him unconscious.

My wife learned of the incident from concerned neighbors. When she asked about it, I downplayed the danger. I told her that police work in Utah was not dangerous compared to that in places like Los Angeles or New York. It was the first of many white lies I told her as a police officer. The following month, on a lonely road near Panguitch, Utah Highway Patrol Trooper Lynn Pierson was shot to death during a traffic stop.

Graduating from Peace Officer Standards and Training classes in April 1979, I was hired by the Springville Police Department. Winds of change were gusting across America. The training and safety of police officers had become imperative. The 1970s were a terrible time for law enforcement. Of the five worst years for police deaths in America, four are from this decade (1974, 271 deaths; 1973, 260 deaths, 1971, 238 deaths; and 1975, 230 deaths). The toll in recent years would not approach these numbers again until the tragedy of September 11, 2001, when seventy police officers died in the terrorist attack on the World Trade Center, adding their names to those officers killed that year throughout the rest of country.

I left police work for journalism in 1989. It was a difficult choice. Police work indelibly stamps those who do it for any length of time. Frankly, I wasn't sure I could do anything else. But there were things I wanted to say about the public that might not be appreciated by my superiors—pointed things the public needed to know about those whose lot it is to protect them, most often from themselves.

Although television and Hollywood have long proved America's morbid fascination with police work, most people have little concept of the true workings of the profession. They understand the dangers only in the abstract. Certainly, people realize that police officers can be killed and wounded; but it is the inability to predict the manner and source of the threat that weighs most heavily on the psyche of police officers, prompting them toward a fatalism that extracts a heavy psychic and emotional toll.

I once watched a television talk show about the psychological impact law enforcement can have on those who do it, specifically the elevated rates of divorce, alcoholism, and suicide among police officers. The host was interviewing two police officers, who were explaining how hard it was to cope with constant life-and-death decisions, when a peeved woman in the audience demanded to know why police officers deserved more understanding from the public just because they had a tough job. After all, her husband was a doctor who also dealt with life-and-death decisions every day, and he wasn't crazy. (This might be a good place to mention the elevated rates of divorce, substance abuse, and suicide among America's doctors; but I lack both the time and the inclination.)

I believe that the woman failed to understand what was being discussed, specifically *whose* life and *whose* death? It certainly wasn't her husband's. If two hundred patients sat up in their hospital beds and shot or stabbed their doctors every year, America soon would have a new batch of laws designed solely to protect doctors.

If the public fails to appreciate the nature of the danger, they are even more oblivious to the source. One morning I stopped a young couple for speeding through a school zone. When I approached the car, I remained behind the driver's window, as I had been trained to do. This maneuver enables a police officer to see into the car and observe the occupants' hands, while making it somewhat more difficult for the driver to turn and shoot him. But it also forces less criminally inclined drivers to turn uncomfortably and look back at the officer. Later, while signing his citation, the man grumbled about what he considered a lack of courtesy. He pointed to the front fender of his car and asked why I couldn't stand "up there" where he could see me better. When I tried to explain, he sneered and accused me of being a poor judge of character.

A widespread public misconception is that police officers become cynical because they deal only with the worst kinds of people, that such people are readily identifiable by the way they look. Like the Beagle Boys from the Donald Duck cartoons, don't criminals tiptoe about in thin black masks and striped shirts? The truth is that police officers contend with everyone at their worst moments, and that is why Utah's police killers range from hardened criminals to a bank vice president.

This book was conceived after I left law enforcement. In the summer of 1993, I chanced upon the headstone of William J. Strong in the Provo City Cemetery. The century-old inscription read in part, "Who met his death while on duty as a city officer." Standing beside Strong's grave, I flashed back to those brutal moments when I fought a deranged man for possession of my gun. I knew nothing about Strong except that his last conscious thoughts were of his family and his duty, and a terrible regret that he had failed both.

When I located the graves of three other police officers within sight of Strong's, nothing on their headstones spoke to what the men had been or done, nor to what at various times must have been singular tragedies for the communities they served. Attempting to learn more, I was surprised to find little available information. Published histories of Provo, rich in detail on matters of business, church, and education, contain almost no mention of those who died to help make such things possible.

Eventually, I found the location of Strong's home and walked the route he took that summer night in 1899 when he was shot to death by a transient. It was the beginning of a decade-long search for the identities and stories of other forgotten Utah police officers, men whose commitment to a profession took them places few others dared go. Since the arrival of the Mormon pioneers in 1847, fifty-six Utah police officers have been murdered in the line of duty. A similar number died in rescue attempts, training accidents, traffic collisions, airplanes crashes, and injuries suffered in assaults.

Locating the fallen was not easy; and determining what happened to them was even more difficult. In most cases there are no archived police reports to dig through, no musty records waiting for researchers to reexamine the minutiae of old crimes. Standardized police reporting is a relatively recent invention. Yet even when police reporting came into practice, it failed to preserve the meticulously gathered information for long. Old police files are routinely destroyed after sufficient time is deemed to have passed. For more than a century, a vast and incredibly rich portion of Utah's history has literally gone up in smoke.

What I did learn over the years was often contrary to traditional or popular views. There may have been a "Wild, Wild West" in the 1800s, a time when lawmen faced vicious killers in quick-draw street encounters, but Utah police deaths do not reflect this Hollywood stereotype. Of the fifty-six officers murdered during the past 146 years, 40 percent fell in the thirty-year period between 1895 and 1925, a time when officers rode horseless carriages and trolleys more often than mustangs.

Most of those killed were older than I expected. Law enforcement was once a second profession, something men did after the rigors of mining and farming became too much for them. The average age of officers murdered before 1900 is 47.7 years. Not until 1922 was an officer in his twenties murdered. The trend continued through that century, until the police profession began to attract younger men. Even so, the average age of murdered Utah police officers is 41.5 years.

Many victims succumbed due in part to a lack of training. Utah did not have a mandatory police academy until 1967, and even then recruits were not required to attend it before going out on patrol. It took the 1974 murder of Utah Highway Patrol Trooper William Antoniewicz, shot to death just six months after he was hired, for Utah to begin a serious albeit ponderous move toward training police officers *before* sending them out to do their jobs. Even so, it wasn't until 1987 that this training became mandatory.

Officers reading these accounts today will note glaring procedural errors that contributed to tragic outcomes, things rookie officers today understand long before they go out on patrol. This experience is hard won and therefore should not be taken for granted. In many cases it is born of the blood shed by those who went before us.

If not particularly unkind to its fallen officers, Utah's history has largely been indifferent to them. Many fallen Utah officers would be nameless but for the fatal bit parts they played in overly romanticized tales of banditry. History aficionados can easily recount the deeds of Butch Cassidy's Hole-in-the-Wall gang, but few even know the name of Grand County Sheriff Jesse Tyler, murdered by one of them.

Oral family history also was frequently misleading and distracting. Though sometimes insightful, more often than might be expected, oft-polished family legends failed to match established accounts. To give one example, shortly before this work was completed, a man in Canada wrote asking for information about an ancestor who his family claimed was once "High sheriff of Utah and head of the State Police," a man active in putting an "end to a reign of terror in the State" when he was shot and killed by rustlers in 1890. Eventually, I determined that the ancestor in question had once been a deputy U.S. marshal but in fact was shot and killed during a drunken argument with a friend in an Ogden saloon.

In order to make the work manageable, it soon became necessary to determine its scope: specifically, who in fact was a police officer. Since 1847, dozens of security guards, night watchmen, posse members, mine guards, private detectives, and special officers have been murdered. Tragic though these deaths were, the men were not professional police officers, public servants answering directly to constitutionally elected officials rather than private enterprise. Sometimes it was difficult to distinguish between the two. Most notable among these was Charles C. Riley, employed by a Salt Lake neighborhood as a special officer and murdered in 1909 by a robbery suspect he was escorting to the police station house. Today, Riley's name appears on the granite memorial in front of the Salt Lake City Police Department, which "adopted" him for the service he rendered.

In some cases, sentiment more than fact has added to memorials the names of officers not killed in the line of duty. In 1969, for example, Utah Highway Patrol Trooper Charles Warren was shot and badly wounded near Springville while attempting to arrest a man in a stolen car. Warren's name appears on the police memorial in the state capitol, and on the National Law Enforcement Officers Memorial in Washington, D.C. This despite the fact that, although permanently confined to a wheelchair by his wounds, Warren lived another twenty-four years, was promoted to sergeant, and eventually retired before dying from complications of pneumonia.

In the end, those whose stories are told here met the following criteria:

• They were armed and sworn professional police officers employed and directed by government agencies.

• They died within a short time of wounds suffered by deliberate acts while in the performance of their official duties.

• Their assailants, when captured, were charged with and/or prosecuted for murder.

There undoubtedly are mistakes in this work. Collected primarily from microfilmed news reports of their time, many stories are factual only insofar as those whose job it was to report the events could make them, and my own ability to research them. In some cases, particularly those where the suspect was also killed, the only accounts of the crime remaining today are these news stories. The earliest official police report available for research was the federal investigation into the 1967 murder of Ute Tribal Officer Adolph Bush, and it contained so few similarities to the sparse news accounts of his death that I wondered if they pertained to the same incident.

When forced to rely primarily on news accounts, I tried to ascertain what happened by comparing the reports from all available newspapers. During the early part of the last century, Salt Lake City had as many as four daily newspapers in operation at the same time, and they were fiercely competitive. If one paper printed something that was not accurate, the others were more than eager to point that out to their own readers.

This work is not intended as a minute examination of what transpired, something that for many cases would merit an entire book. In some instances it already has, most notably two infamous stand-offs: the 1913 Highland Boy Mine siege precipitated by the deaths of Bingham Marshal William Grant and Salt Lake County deputies Otto Witbeck and Nephi Jensen, and the 1988 Singer/Swapp cult standoff resulting in the death of Utah Department of Corrections Lieutenant Fred House.

What I have tried to do is identify who the slain officers were, where and how they died, and provide some element of insight into the scope of each tragedy. It was a labor of love, an attempt to keep my brothers and sisters from becoming simply more faceless names on a somber memorial.

There were times when the grim ironies of this work became almost more than I could bear. The most poignant of these occurred in January 2003, at a time when I thought the manuscript was finished. Its seeds were sown nearly two decades before. Serious considerations about leaving law enforcement began for me in 1986. During that summer a young couple just out of the military moved in across the street from my home in Springville. The husband, a likeable enough man, stopped me one day as I got into my patrol car for work. David said he was interested in becoming a police officer, something he had always wanted to do. He asked me for advice. I don't recall what I told him, but considering my frame of mind at the time I doubt that I encouraged him.

After a few months David found another job and moved away. But the pull law enforcement has on some people is strong. The next time I saw David Jones was seventeen years later, when his face appeared on an evening news braodcast announcing his murder in the line of duty as a Garfield County deputy sheriff.

Finally, I must say that this is not a particularly pleasant work. There are no happy endings, no satisfying social judgments made. It is a subject that promises only continued pain. There is a price free societies must pay to keep the lights on. And so, tragic though this book may seem, the greater tragedy is that it will ever remain a work in progress.

Robert L. Kirby
Springville, Utah
March 2, 2003

Acknowledgments

This work would not have been possible without the following:

Irene, who suffered me through both the doing and the telling.

Salt Lake City Police: Lieutenant Steve "Duffy" Diamond (retired) and Captain Judy Dencker for their tireless efforts to preserve that department's law enforcement heritage.

Utah Department of Corrections: Joe Borich, Officer Sonny Dyle, and Officer Jesse Beales.

My parents, Bob and Eris Kirby, who provided countless hours and miles of the best kind of research assistance—diligent and free.

Jeff Grathwohl, director and senior editor for the University of Utah Press, who patiently waited for me to finish, then helped make sense of it all with very little shouting.

Utah Peace Officers Association: in particular Brigitte Dawson.

Utah Highway Patrol: Sergeant Lee Perry and Sergeant Les Langford. And Trooper William Antoniewicz—whose presence kept the work going when I faltered.

Steven Lund, whose great-grandfather is listed among the fallen.

Fellow time traveler Robert Carter, Springville.

Utah State Archives and Records Service.

Utah State Historical Society.

Family and friends of the fallen, who graciously resurrected the worst moments of their lives to help me tell the stories as accurately as possible.

Utah newspaper reporters, past and present.

The *Salt Lake Tribune*: particularly editors James Shelledy, Peg McEntee, Tim Fitzpatrick, and Terry Orme, who faced the daunting task of turning an old street monster into a functional journalist.

Finally, the nameless volunteers at the Utah County Family History Center at Brigham Young University, who for years changed hundreds of dollars into photocopier dimes, one dollar at a time.

End of Watch

Chapter 1

1858–1899

The first recorded line-of-duty law-enforcement death in Utah occurred six years after the arrival of the Mormon pioneers, members of the Church of Jesus Christ of Latter-day Saints (LDS), who first settled the region. Salt Lake County Deputy Rodney Badger drowned April 29, 1853, in the Weber River while trying to rescue a stranded immigrant family.

It would be another forty years before the next accidental death of a police officer. During this time the dangers of law enforcement stemmed more from homicide than from accident. However, the future rise of technology, particularly in transportation, would greatly increase the accidental-death risk for police officers.

Law enforcement during this early period was unsophisticated, the line between apprehension and punishment of criminals often becoming blurred. As Linda Sillitoe wrote in *A History of Salt Lake County*, during the first decade of settlement in the Salt Lake Valley, the governing council "ruled that 'no person shall ride or drive through the Forts or their lanes faster than a slow trot under a penalty of $1.00 for each offense.' To handle speeders, thieves, and rowdies, the council appointed a public complainer to act as both police and prosecutor. Offenders were fined or whipped, but there was no jail." In some cases, rather than prompting the building of jails and hiring of guards, the hard-labor sentences of convicted criminals were auctioned to the highest bidder, who would then put the criminals to work at whatever needed doing.

By the late 1800s, however, even small communities were attempting to professionally equip police departments. In 1883 the Ephraim City Council in Sanpete County ordered "some weapons of deffence [*sic*] in the shape of 2 derringers and 4 clubs and also some marks of distinguishing the officers in the shape of stars or buttons also two jail locks" (Ephraim City Council Minutes, 6 January 1883).

Wages for officers were notoriously low. In some cases, particularly

3

in smaller communities, the only compensation officers received for the risk they assumed was a remission of their taxes. Turnover was understandably high, but dedicated professionals still managed to get the job done.

The Salt Lake City police department set the standard for law enforcement during these early years. By the end of the century the department had a uniformed patrol force, detectives, motorcycles, a photo lab, and the latest in forensic methods. But there was still a long way to go.

William Cooke
Salt Lake City Police Department
October 18, 1858

In terse script, entry 925 of the Salt Lake City Register of Deaths records the death of Utah's first murdered police officer: "Shot by a gentile [a non-Mormon] while on duty as a policeman."

Born August 28, 1803, in Pollington, England, William Cooke and his wife, Sarah Anne Sutton, immigrated to America in 1828. The family originally settled in North Carolina before moving to Iowa. In the spring of 1852, the Cookes were living in Dubuque when "California fever" struck. Cooke and his eldest married son, William, purchased several wagons and contracted to deliver twelve men to Sacramento. Along with six children and a daughter-in-law, the family said goodbye to their friends and set out for the West.

The Cookes arrived in the Salt Lake Valley that summer and, like many road-weary travelers, decided to winter over. After securing a place for his family to live, William continued on with his contract passengers to California, where he eventually found work managing a farm. During their time apart, Sarah converted to Mormonism, thus tying the family firmly to Utah.

Exactly when Cooke returned to Utah, or when he converted to his wife's new faith, is not known. However, by 1854 he was serving a Mormon mission in Australia, where he established various branches of the faith in the gold mining camps of the Wellington district. Cooke remained in Australia until 1856, when he returned to Utah. Records show that he and Sarah were sealed together in the church's Endowment House in 1857.

In 1858, Cooke's primary job was as night manager of the city jail, a position that soon earned him the attention and enmity of the local criminal element. Eleven years after the arrival of the Mormon pioneers, the City of the Saints was a community under siege. A mere forty officers patrolled the streets of the city, their beats a thin skirmish line against a growing population of footpads, thieves, killers, prostitutes, and whiskey peddlers. The problem was particularly bad during the fall and winter months, when large numbers of mountain men, teamsters, and hunters descended on the town for shelter from the winter. Other factors divided the growing community. Mormons despised the army and federal authorities sent to watch them, while gentiles hated the Mormon police force.

On September 11, 1858, George A. Smith wrote to a friend about Salt Lake's ill-famed Whiskey Street: "The Headquarters of rowdyism is on East Temple St. There have been two murders in a week, and several men badly wounded." The problem eventually became so bad that Brigham Young finally asked Salt Lake City leaders to increase the size of the police force to two hundred officers. Sickened by the increasing crime rate—and perhaps because a hint from Young was almost equivalent to a command—city commissioners complied without a single dissenting vote. On September 16, 1858, the new officers gathered in the livery stable of the Lion House where they were sworn in. During his remarks to the new officers, Young acknowledged that Salt Lake's crime problem was not solely a gentile one, and even apologized for the criminal behavior of many young Latter-day Saints.

Captain Jesse Gove wrote of Whiskey Street's reaction to the reinforced police department. "After dark no Gentile walks the streets alone. Everyone, night and day, is armed to the teeth. Daily we expect to hear of a row."

During this difficult time, Cooke was frequently the target of abuse and ambushes. Periodically, mobs attempted to storm the jail in an effort to free comrades locked inside. The jail, originally the home of Joseph L. Schofield, was located at approximately 130 East 100 South. Purchased by the city two years prior to Cooke's death, it had been converted into police headquarters and a jail. A *Harper's Weekly* article called it a "wretched mud hovel" guarded constantly by "eight men." But mild-mannered Cooke was on duty alone the night of October 12.

On that night, Edward Davidson and Peter Goodridge were incarcerated in the jail. The two men had considerable freedom inside the jail while awaiting their appearance before the justice of the peace. The morning following their arrest, two friends, Nathan D. Foster and a man named Ingham, came to visit them in jail. After looking over the conditions of the jail, Foster told Davidson and Goodridge that they were fools for remaining in such a flimsy "caliboos." Foster left and returned a short time later with a key. After experimenting and discovering that it actually fit the lock on the door, Foster tried to give the key to Goodridge. When Goodridge refused it, Foster stuffed the key into Davidson's pocket. Possibly because the guards had treated them well neither Davidson nor Goodridge was inclined to escape, preferring instead to take their chances with the judge. As soon as Foster left, they handed the key over to the officer on guard.

Cooke arrived for his tour of duty that afternoon. Shortly after 3:00 p.m., Foster and Ingham returned to the jail for another visit. With them was a man named McDonald, a belligerent teamster recently arrived in Salt Lake City with a wagon train. For a time, prisoners and visitors sat around the fire talking.

First Salt Lake City Calaboose (Jail)

The first jail in Salt Lake City as it appeared in *Harper's Weekly*, November, 1858. Cooke was gunned down just inside the front door. The structure, located on the southeast corner of State Street and 100 South, was formerly the home of Joseph L. Schofield. (Utah State Historical Society)

Eventually, Ingham asked Cooke for permission to go and buy some oysters to cook over the fire. Cooke agreed. Ingham left and returned with the oysters, some crackers, and a bottle of liquor. The prisoners cooked the oysters in a kettle over the fire and then took them outside to eat. Cooke, Goodridge, and McDonald were still inside the jail when McDonald abruptly drew his pistol and pointed it at Goodridge, telling him to leave. Thinking that McDonald was joking, Goodridge declined with a laugh. Cursing, McDonald then pointed his gun at Cooke and told the officer to stand aside.

"He [McDonald] told Mr. Cooke to let me out or he would shoot him," Goodridge testified later. "Mr. Cooke said he could not do it, that he was a policeman and on duty, and would not let me out. With that, McDonald shot Mr. Cooke and at the same moment, jumped out of doors and ran."

McDonald may have been a poor shot, or perhaps intended to merely incapacitate Cooke by shooting him in the leg. In either case, the bullet struck Cooke in the right thigh, shattering the femur. Prisoners caught the wounded officer as he fell, lowering him to the ground and putting a coat under his head. Cooke told the prisoners that his leg was broken and asked them not to escape.

The fifty-five-year-old Cooke was taken to his home in Salt Lake City's Fourteenth Ward, where he languished in agony for nearly a week, succumbing to his wounds on October 18. Two days following his death, the *Deseret News* published the sad news: "We regret to learn that Mr. Wm. Cooke, policeman, who was shot by a ruffian ... died on Monday evening last about 7 o'clock, at his own residence after six days suffering which he bore with great patience and fortitude."

In a letter to T.B.H. Stenhouse, a resident of Salt Lake City wrote of the event: "The death of Wm. Cooke, policeman, who was unprovokedly murdered while in the discharge of his duty, threw a gloom over the citizens, as it made them to feel bitterly the effects of the sad change which had been the result of Mr. [President] Buchanan's policy of civilizing Utah."

Justice of the Peace Jeter Clinton conducted a coroner's inquest in the Cooke home on the evening of Cooke's death. Both Goodridge and Davidson testified that McDonald had deliberately shot Cooke from a distance of about three feet and then fled the scene before the arrival of other officers.

Following the shooting, Ingham was immediately captured and jailed. Although McDonald managed to elude officers and get out of Utah, he outlived Cooke by only a few days. Together with Foster he made good his escape from the city, traveling east toward Fort Bridger, where they hoped to pose as teamsters from Camp Floyd until the spring. Edwin P. "Scottie" Jones, a Salt Lake mail carrier whose route took him east from Utah, spread the news and a description of Cooke's killer to those he passed, unaware that McDonald was behind him traveling in the same direction. When McDonald learned that Jones was spreading the word ahead, he vowed to kill the mail carrier as soon as they met.

The fateful meeting occurred near Fort Bridger a few days later, on October 21. Having learned that McDonald was at Black's Fork, Jones traded routes with a westbound carrier near Green River, Wyoming, and hastened back to find the killer. McDonald was gambling with friends when Jones rode up. As Jones dismounted, McDonald drew his pistol and fired. The bullet passed through the collar of Jones's shirt but didn't spoil the mail carrier's aim. (Another account claims that Jones was actually wounded by McDonald's shot.) Drawing his own pistol, Jones shot McDonald in the throat. Not content with McDonald merely being dead, Jones also scalped him. The bloody act angered those present, and Jones was forced to leave the area in a hurry. Before leaving, however, he gave his grisly trophy to a friend for safekeeping. After a brief investigation, McDonald's body went into a nameless grave.

Two weeks after the death of her husband, Sarah Ann Cooke received $150 from the Salt Lake City Council for the immediate care of her children. She later earned a living as a teacher of vocal and instrumental music. Numbered among her students were many of Salt Lake City's elite, including children of Brigham Young. Sarah also became an accomplished actress, performing in dramas throughout the region. On December 11, 1866, the city council appropriated $2,000 to the matter of finding the Cookes a home. Brigham

Sarah Cooke successfully sued Brigham Young to keep the home he gave her following the murder of her husband. (Utah State Historical Society)

Young either directly gave to Sarah or sold to the city council a small home located on the current site of the Salt Palace, a fact that eventually led to a bitter lawsuit between the two.

In the years following her husband's death, Sarah gradually became disenchanted with Mormonism, and her relationship with Brigham Young deteriorated as a result. In 1866, Young attempted to sell her home to someone else. Believing the home was hers, Sarah sued him in civil court. The case dragged on for seven years and reached the territorial supreme court. Meanwhile, Sarah left the Mormon faith and became a leader in the Women's National Anti-Polygamy Society. She was a principal in aiding Ann Eliza Young's flight from Brigham Young and Utah, when the famous "twenty-seventh wife" wanted a divorce from the Mormon Church leader. On August 17, 1878, Sarah became the "first person to win a civil judgment against Brigham Young" when the Utah Territorial Supreme Court upheld her case. Young did not live to see it, however, having died the previous year.

Considered a matriarch of the anti-polygamy movement and a founding member of Utah's theatre, Sarah Cooke died August 7, 1885, and is buried beside her husband in the Salt Lake City Cemetery.

William Rufus Story

United States Marshal
May 2, 1870

William Rufus Story was born on March 31, 1839, in Miegs County, Ohio. On February 24, 1862, Story enlisted in Battery B, Second Illinois Light

Deputy United States Marshal William R. Story survived the Civil War only to die while attempting to arrest a murder suspect in Grantsville. (Story Lodge, Utah Masons)

Artillery, at St. Joseph, Missouri, eventually receiving a promotion to captain. During the Civil War, Battery B served primarily in western Tennessee and northern Mississippi, participating in the battles of Shiloh and Corinth. On his twenty-seventh birthday, Story mustered out of the army and, like many young veterans at loose ends, headed west. He arrived in Utah in 1866 and found work as a civilian employee of the military. A saddler by trade, Story lived and worked at Camp Douglas. He continued to reside there after his appointment on an unknown date as a deputy U.S. marshal.

Story's best friend during this time was fellow army veteran Ira M. Swartz, a clerk in the quartermaster department at Camp Douglas. The two men were members of the Wasatch Lodge of Free and Accepted Masons and were frequent visitors to Salt Lake City. On April 30, 1870, Story and Swartz registered at the Salt Lake House, unaware that their friendship was soon to end.

Joseph F. Carrigan also came to Salt Lake City on April 30. A deputy sheriff from Nevada, Carrigan was looking for Albert H. Haws, a man wanted for a murder committed in that territory the previous fall. Carrigan had information that Haws was living in Grantsville.

Initially, Carrigan approached Utah Governor John W. Shaffer for assistance in apprehending Haws and holding him until the governor of Nevada could formally request extradition. Shaffer wrote out an executive order directing Tooele County Sheriff Thomas Tanner to arrest Haws. "It has been thought best that the warrant should be put in your hands," Shaffer wrote to Tanner, "deeming you the proper officer to arrest and bring to this city the criminal who is charged with a most foul murder, of which there was abundant evidence submitted to the Judge before issuing his writ."

Although the writ was addressed to Tanner, Carrigan apparently had second thoughts about involving the Tooele sheriff, perhaps because there was a $1,500 reward for the arrest of Haws. At some point prior to leaving Salt Lake City, Carrigan connected with Story, whose federal arrest powers perhaps convinced Carrigan that it wasn't necessary to trouble Tanner.

On May 1, Carrigan and Story left Salt Lake City and traveled to Grantsville by buggy, where they spent the night at the home of Edward Hunter, Jr. At 7:00 o'clock the following morning, they asked for directions to the home where Haws lived with his wife. Even though Haws had lived in Grantsville only since the previous fall, many in the community already avoided him. Short and powerfully built, Haws "had the look of a desperado" and was viewed as a man capable of committing any deed. His companion was "a woman such as a man of his character might be expected to consort with."

When they arrived, Story and Carrigan located Haws working in his yard. Taking out their pistols, the two officers informed Haws of the warrant and told him that he was under arrest. Haws cooperated with the officers, raising his hands in surrender. Story took out a pair of handcuffs, while Carrigan continued to cover Haws. "Gentlemen, you have got me," Haws reportedly said. "Let me get some things before you take me off."

Story refused and was in the process of handcuffing his prisoner when Haws suddenly shoved him away and grabbed Carrigan's pistol. The weapon discharged as it was torn from the deputy's hand, the bullet grazing Haws across the abdomen but leaving him otherwise unhurt. Shouting for his wife to bring his pistols, Haws exchanged shots with Story. Both men fired twice. Story missed, but Haws's bullets struck the marshal in the chest, one in the left breast and the other under his left arm, killing him.

Unarmed, Carrigan chose the only reasonable course of action. He broke and ran as Haws repeatedly fired at him. One of the bullets passed harmlessly through his coat sleeve. Carrigan didn't stop running until he arrived at the home of Riley Judd, an acquaintance of Story's. After telling Judd what happened, he and Judd armed themselves and returned to the Haws home. By then, however, Haws had already made good his escape. There was nothing left for the two men to do but carry Story's body to the Grantsville social hall, where they spread the news.

Posses immediately set out after Haws. Judd and Carrigan led one; Sheriff Tanner formed another when news of the killing reached him in Tooele. Captain Samuel Woolley and John W. Cooley led other posses. From Lehi, Porter Rockwell and a group of men started in the direction of Simpson Springs, where it was believed Haws might go preparatory to striking out for California.

In fact, however, Haws was much closer to home. After the gunfight in his yard, the killer rode away from Grantsville carrying four pistols, two of his own and those belonging to Carrigan and Story. He stopped briefly at the home of an acquaintance, where he borrowed yet another gun, saying that he wanted to shoot some rabbits. Thus armed, Haws rode to South Willow Canyon, where he stopped for the night at the home of one of his wife's relatives.

Before arriving at the home, Haws made a fateful mistake. Encountering a herd boy during his flight from town, Haws sent him with a message to his wife instructing her where to meet him. Haws threatened the boy's life if he betrayed him to the law. Returning to town, the boy met Haws's stepson and gave him the message, which the stepson passed on to his mother. As Haws's wife prepared to join her husband in South Willow Canyon, the stepson told another sibling about the meeting. This particular sibling had no love for Haws and immediately gave the information to lawmen, who then prevented Mrs. Haws from leaving. A second posse started in the direction of the meeting place, eventually arriving at Haws's temporary hideout, where they spotted his unsaddled horse tethered outside. Knowing that a family was inside the home with the killer, the posse elected not to attack, preferring instead to surround the home and wait until Haws departed.

At first light on May 3, Haws stuck his head out and spotted the posse hiding in the surrounding brush. Knowing that they wouldn't shoot for fear of hitting the home's occupants, Haws carefully maneuvered his horse in front of the door. Throwing a saddle on the horse, he quickly mounted and spurred his horse up the canyon, with the posse close on his heels.

The chase continued for three miles. Two of the posse members were better mounted than Haws and began to gain on him. In an attempt to lose them, Haws tried steering his horse down a steep ridge. When it balked, he jumped off and began to run but lost his footing and fell heavily, disappearing into some brush near the creek.

The posse surrounded the area and waited for reinforcements from Grantsville. A company of men, including Woolley and Cooley, arrived and plans were made to go in after the killer. Grantsville resident Festus Sprague accompanied Cooley, while Emanuel Bagley followed Woolley. The rest of the posse formed a skirmish line to prevent Haws from escaping once he was flushed out of hiding.

Creeping into the brush along a cow path, Sprague and Cooley found Haws waiting for them. The killer fired first, hitting Sprague in the chest. Sprague managed to return fire once before falling mortally wounded. Standing behind Sprague, Cooley raised his gun, but it misfired. Furious, he resorted to throwing rocks at Haws, one of which struck the killer in the face. Hearing the shots, the rest of the posse converged on the scene. Bagley spotted Haws taking aim at Cooley again. He snapped off a shot that struck the killer in the side and undoubtedly saved Cooley's life. The rest of the posse then opened up on

Marshal Story's grave in the Fort Douglas
Cemetery. (Author)

Haws, shooting him full of holes. A coroner's examination later showed that
one of the many bullets broke Haws's neck.

Even though Haws was dead, the Grantsville posse still wasn't out of danger.
As the killer fell, the posse converged on him. William Averill spotted a pistol
in Haws's lap and grabbed it, only to discover that Haws had cocked and
rigged the pistol to his belt with a string. When Averill grabbed the gun by the
barrel and pulled it, the weapon fired and sent a bullet through his wrist and
into the hip of a Montana man named Pagett who was in Grantsville to buy
cattle and had volunteered for posse duty.

On May 3, while Haws was being riddled by the posse, Story was buried at
the Fort Douglas Cemetery in a ceremony conducted by the Masons, of which
he was a member in high standing. What happened to Haws's body is not
known. Sprague was buried in Grantsville.

When the smoke cleared, Carrigan was excoriated by Salt Lake City
newspapers, both for running away when Story was killed and for not contacting
local authorities to assist in the initial arrest. They accused Carrigan of allowing
the reward offered for Haws to affect his judgment. "Carrigan's conduct in
this dreadful transaction exposes him to severe animadversion and
condemnation. Had he pursued the course, which as an officer from Nevada
coming into a neighboring territory he should have done, we are morally certain
that Haws could have been captured without the loss of life."

Carrigan wasn't the only one who felt the media's lash. Brigham Young
was condemned for not appearing in Story's funeral procession, a cortege that
included the territorial governor, U.S. court judges, and other officials. It was
also noted that the only flag flying at half-staff in Salt Lake City was the one
in front of the Masonic Hall.

Today, the Masonic lodge in Provo, Story Lodge No. 4, is named after the
first federal officer killed in Utah.

Albert Hastings Bowen

Provo City Police Department
October 16, 1873

On a quiet autumn evening in 1873, the city of Provo lost both its innocence and its chief of police. Newspapers throughout Utah carried the news: "Murder at Provo. Chief of Police Bowen Shot by a Rough, Who Escapes."

Albert Orlando Hastings Bowen was the first police officer in Utah County to lose his life in the line of duty. He was born July 22, 1829, to Israel and Charlotte Durham Bowen in Bethany, New York. The family joined the LDS Church and lived for a time in Nauvoo, eventually being driven with the rest of the church members out of that city and into Iowa. Bowen was part of the early migration to Utah, and he is mentioned as a member of Captain Howard Stansbury's exploration of the Great Salt Lake in 1849–50. In 1853, he married Catherine Stoker in Kanesville, Iowa. The couple immigrated to Utah, settling in Provo, where Bowen reportedly started the town's first pottery business. Appointed as the city's police chief, Bowen was widely respected, and it seemed inconceivable to most citizens that anyone would want to kill him, much less someone who knew him.

Despite a predominant Mormon culture, Provo was home to a large number of saloons in 1873. In some parts of town alcohol flowed about as freely as water, requiring the constant attention of the police department. According to editorials that appeared in the *Salt Lake Tribune* following Bowen's death, it was precisely the nature of this attention that caused Bowen's death. Editorials claimed that Provo officers had in the past "used too freely the billy and the brass knuckles, and used them when there was no excuse for so doing." This alleged brutality aroused "the intense feeling of indignation which anti-Mormons have long felt at the outrages perpetrated upon them under cover of law by the Provo police." The editorials were quick to point out, however, that Bowen himself was never guilty "of such outrages." In response to the *Tribune*'s editorial, other newspapers immediately came to the defense of the police department.

Whether true or not, friction between the saloon element and the police department came to a head on the evening of October 13, 1873. Bowen had just returned from business in Springville when he was advised of trouble in front of the Stubbs & Dunkley Saloon near 400 West Center.

The trouble was Harrison Carter. At age twenty-four, Carter was described as "a devil-may-care" who sported a "swaggering style of walking." His

Provo City Marshal Albert Bowen was murdered while attempting to arrest an intoxicated man outside a city saloon. His killer became a prison trustee and later was killed while attempting to prevent a mass breakout from the Sugar House prison. (Provo Police Department)

forehead was dented in on one side from a previous blow by a pistol. The *Salt Lake Herald* referred to Carter as "a renegade and rough of the lowest order." On the day of the shooting, Carter had been bothering people all afternoon, announcing to everyone that he was going to "run the town" according to his own notions and that he would kill the first man who tried to touch him. At midday, Carter exchanged words with Sidney W. Worsely. Enraged by the argument, Carter went home and armed himself with a .36-caliber Colt Navy revolver. He returned to the saloon and began flashing the gun around.

Shortly after 6:00 p.m., Bowen arrived at the saloon, where he found a crowd. As Bowen approached, Carter took out the revolver and fired a shot into the ground between himself and the chief. He warned Bowen that no "damned policeman" would arrest him. When Bowen ignored the warning, Carter raised the pistol and shot the chief in the left side of the head. Spotting another officer in the crowd, Carter's brother Dominicus handed the killer a second pistol and said, "Here comes another damned policeman, shoot him."

Although more than a dozen men witnessed the shooting, Carter was successful in fleeing the scene. He was last spotted on a bridge north of Provo. Dominicus Carter was later arrested as an accessory to murder but eventually released for lack of evidence.

At first it was thought that the bullet, which struck Bowen just in front of his left ear, had only glanced off the chief's head. Alert and conversant despite his wound, Bowen was carried to a room in the home of Peter Stubbs. With limited medical knowledge of the brain, doctors could do little but wait to see how the wound developed.

Bowen's condition rapidly deteriorated. Surrounded by his wife, Catherine, and their many children, the chief struggled against death for three days. On

October 15, Dr. W.F. Anderson, a skilled surgeon, traveled from Salt Lake City and examined Bowen. Anderson announced that he was going to surgically explore Bowen's wound the following day to see if the bullet remained inside the lawman's head. However, at 11:00 a.m. on October 16, the thirteenth birthday of his eldest son, Bowen suddenly died.

Business in Provo came to a standstill as citizens buried Bowen in the city cemetery. A few days before the funeral of her husband, the Provo City Council gave Catherine Bowen a hundred dollars and adopted a resolution to wear a badge of crepe on their left sleeves out of respect. A committee was then formed to procure a carriage for councilmen to ride in during the funeral procession.

Carter managed to elude authorities for two months. He left the Provo area and traveled to Nevada, stopping briefly in Hamilton, Eureka, and Star Valley. On October 22, he made his way to a sheep ranch forty miles north of Elko, where he obtained work for his board. Elko Constable G.M. Banks learned of Carter's presence in the form of a telegram advising the lawman of a $500 reward for the killer's capture. On December 9, Banks went to the sheep ranch and arrested Carter without incident.

On January 9, 1874, Carter was arraigned before a Provo grand jury that quickly indicted him on a charge of first-degree murder. Ten months later, Carter was tried in First District Court and found guilty of second-degree murder by a Provo jury, which listened to evidence for four long days. Carter's defense was based on allegations that Bowen had a grudge against him and had threatened to kill him in the past. The jury deliberated just a few hours before returning a verdict of guilty. Carter was sentenced to ten years in the territorial prison. The press reported that the relatively light punishment "appeared to meet the approval of those acquainted with the circumstances of the killing."

In a strange ironic twist, Carter would yet pay with his life for the murder of Bowen. Transferred to the territorial prison on November 28, 1874, he soon proved himself a trustworthy prisoner, eventually earning the full confidence of the guards and the warden. Carter's behavior was such that he was afforded trustee status and periodic conjugal visits with his wife Nancy (Woolsey) in the guardhouse.

On June 23, 1876, Carter was assisting the prison cook when seven inmates staged a mass breakout. The prisoners overpowered the lone guard inside the prison and, after arming themselves, climbed out and captured the rest of the guards, who were then marched inside and locked up. Because of the prison's location outside the city proper, the break might have gone unnoticed for some time if Carter and another convict, F.J. Woodward, hadn't slipped away to alert authorities. While running from the prison, the two trustees were fired upon by the escaping convicts. A bullet struck Carter in the arm near the shoulder and entered his side. After dragging Carter to a nearby hiding place and binding up his wound, Woodward located a horse and rode to the police station in Salt Lake City, where he informed officers of the escape. All of the convicts were recaptured.

Carter was taken to St. Mark's Hospital in Salt Lake City, where doctors attempted to save his life. On June 25, the same day George Armstrong Custer and the Seventh Cavalry made their last stand at the Little Bighorn, Harrison Carter died. He was buried in a potter's field section of the Salt Lake City Cemetery. A headstone erected by the Carter family reads: "Sleep on my son, rest in peace. You left a wife and child, brothers and sisters and father and mother to weep for thee."

The tragedy of Bowen's murder had a final footnote. Five years following her husband's death, the Provo City Council reduced Catherine Bowen's taxes by $2.25.

Matthew B. Burgher

Utah Territorial Prison
March 16, 1876

A native of Michigan, Matthew B. Burgher arrived in Salt Lake City in the early summer of 1875. The Civil War veteran was unmarried, a gentile, and, by various accounts, a capable administrator. He was raised in Portage County, Ohio, and his family later relocated to a farm outside Hastings, Michigan. He was living in Michigan and working as a teacher when Fort Sumter was fired upon.

Burgher enlisted in the Union Army at Dowagiac, Michigan, on August 4, 1861, reporting his age as twenty-two, and his home of residence as Decatur. He mustered into Company M, 1st Michigan Cavalry, participating in the Battle of Bull Run, and thereafter spending considerable time with the scouts protecting the approaches to Washington, D.C. In January 1862, Confederate cavalry overwhelmed Burgher's patrol near Brentsville, Virginia. Only Burgher and his commanding officer, Captain George R. Maxwell, survived this engagement. Taken prisoner, the two men managed to escape the same day. On March 13, 1863, Burgher was discharged for wounds received in battle.

Not satisfied to sit out the remainder of the war, Burgher reenlisted, this time in Company C, 11th Michigan Cavalry. On August 1, 1863, he was commissioned as a second lieutenant. The unit saw a good deal of action in western Virginia as Union cavalry raided the Confederacy out of its bases in Kentucky. On October 2, 1864, Burgher was wounded again and was left on the field during a raid on the rebel salt works near Saltville, Virginia. Captured, he once again managed to escape and return to his unit. He spent the remainder of the war as aide-de-camp to Major General A.C. Gillem, and was discharged on August 10, 1865, at Pulaski, Tennessee.

For a time following the war, Burgher worked as a mail carrier in Pittsburgh, Pennsylvania, where he lived with his brother and was engaged to a local belle. Like many war veterans, he decided to go west and seek his fortune, eventually finding his way to Colorado.

By 1875, Burgher's former commander George Maxwell was U.S. marshal for the Territory of Utah and also was in charge of the territorial prison. A retired general, Maxwell managed to perform his duties as marshal despite the fact that he was missing a leg and some fingers and also had a crippled arm. Burgher went to Salt Lake City where, on July 1, 1875, he took over as the new prison warden.

An 1887 painting of the Utah Territorial Prison in Sugar House by Francis M. Treseder, now in possession of the Kaysville Company of the Daughters of Utah Pioneers. Warden Matthew B. Burgher (of whom no photo has been found) became the first corrections officer to die in the line of duty when he was killed during a prison escape from the Sugar House facility in 1873. (Utah State Historical Society)

Whether by virtue of his military background or because his predecessor was too lax, Burgher soon became a sore trial to the prisoners. A careful and strict man, he tightened the regimen at the prison, substantially reduced the cost of operation, and improved the facilities by forcing the prisoners to work. Six months later, a newspaper reported that Burgher's charges were becoming more manageable: "The prospects of a hard winter renders [the prisoners] well contented with free hash and lodgings."

Not everyone was happy, however. One of Burgher's charges was John D. Lee, of Mountain Meadows Massacre fame. Although Lee was on friendly terms with Burgher, he believed the warden was too hard on the prisoners. According to Lee, the prisoners were frequently cold and hungry. Burgher was also in the habit of chaining troublemakers to the walls of the prison, then cutting their rations until hunger and the weather convinced them of the merits of cooperation. By early spring, seven prisoners were so fed up with Burgher's methods that they felt they had little to lose in attempting to escape. The ringleaders of the group were convicted murderer James Caine, convicted robber Charles Williamson, and a horse thief by the name of Charles Patterson. The other four were W.T. Bell, J.H. Davis, W.D. Phelps, and a thief with the ironic name of the first Mormon prophet—Joseph Smith. The seven men bided their time until a snowy and cold afternoon in March.

At approximately 3:00 p.m. on March 14, 1876, Burgher and trustee Harry Gaines opened both the inner and outer doors of the prison to allow a work detail out to retrieve water and coal for the stove. With both doors open, the prisoners made their break. First through the door, Smith dropped his coal bucket and wrapped his arms around Burgher from behind, pinning the warden's arms. Patterson and Caine then charged through the door and bludgeoned Burgher with "slung shots," clubs fashioned by putting a fist-size rock in the toe of a woolen sock. In all, Burgher received nine blows to the head, fracturing his skull. Gaines, serving a term for stealing a horse in Bingham, tried to stop the assault. This prompted the remainder of the infuriated convicts to turn their attention to him. They chased him into the prison kitchen and pounded him senseless.

Armed with Burgher's pistol and another taken from the kitchen area, the prisoners quickly forced a female cook to show them out through the front door, where they scattered under fire from guards inside the prison. Reeling from his beating, Burgher ran upstairs to the guardroom, where he tried to bring a rifle to bear on the escaping prisoners. He collapsed before he could fire a shot.

With the guards trapped inside the prison, it was Gaines who prevented the day from becoming a complete disaster. His face horribly mangled from the beating, Gaines regained consciousness and went to the guardroom, where he armed himself with a Spencer rifle. Mounting a horse, he set out after his fellow prisoners. Within hours, he had recaptured Bell, Patterson, Caine, and Davis.

Burgher lapsed into a coma and was carried to his room, where doctors tried to determine the extent of his wounds. Serious doubt was held as to his recovery. Lee and the prison staff held watch over the warden, keeping ice bags on his head while he moaned in delirium. At about 3:00 a.m. on the sixteenth, Burgher died.

News of the escape soon had lawmen hot on the trail of the three remaining escapees. Phelps made his way to Santaquin and armed himself with a pistol at the home of the father of fellow escapee Smith. On the evening of March 17, Utah County Deputy Sheriff John D. Holladay spotted Phelps on a road near Santaquin and asked several men for help capturing him. When the men refused, Holladay went after Phelps alone. Rather than surrender as requested, Phelps fired a shot at Holladay, narrowly missing him. Holladay's aim was better. The mortally wounded Phelps died later that night on a train returning him to Salt Lake City.

Phelps and Burgher were buried on the same day. News accounts of the time claim that Burgher was buried in the Fort Douglas Cemetery under the direction of the Masons. However, fort cemetery historical records do not list him as buried there. On March 16, a telegram was received from Burgher's brother, John C. Burgher, a physician living in Pittsburgh, asking that Burgher be buried locally. However, no record exists of Burgher being buried in any of the Salt Lake Valley cemeteries, and local papers eventually retracted the statement that Burgher was buried under the direction of the Masons. Today the location of his grave is unknown. Possibly his body was temporarily interred before being exhumed and shipped back east to family members.

On March 19, Williamson and Smith were recaptured by a heavily armed posse near Slagtown, on the eastern shore of Rush Lake in Tooele County. Although Williamson was still carrying Burgher's pistol, and the posse pleaded almost tearfully with them to resist, the two men surrendered without a fight. The prisoners returned by train the following day. Word of their arrival leaked out and a crowd of about five hundred angry men met the train with every intention of lynching the terrified escapees. Only with considerable difficulty were officers able to get Williamson and Smith out of the depot and back to the prison.

Williamson told officers that the original escape plan called for Burgher to be overpowered and forced inside the prison without killing him. In April, the escapees were charged with murder in connection with the death of Burgher.

The indictment, a sure ticket to a firing squad, only increased their desire to escape. On June 23, Patterson, Caine, Williamson, and four other prisoners broke out of the territorial prison again. In the process, Caine murdered fellow inmate Harrison Carter as the latter ran to spread the alarm. Although several of the inmates were recaptured, nothing was heard again of Patterson or Caine. On July 8, the *Utah Evening Mail* reported that Williamson was last seen riding a stolen horse seventy-five miles northeast of Evanston, Wyoming.

Andrew H. Burt

Salt Lake City Police Department
August 25, 1883

A quarter of a century after the first murder of a Salt Lake police officer, City Marshal Andrew H. Burt was gunned down in the line of duty, prompting one of the darkest episodes in Utah history.

The incident began at a restaurant owned by F.H. Grice, located on the east side of Main Street next to the Old Salt Lake House between 100 and 200 South. During the lunch hour of August 25, 1883, Sam Harvey entered Grice's restaurant to inquire about a job. Little is known of Harvey other than that he was African-American and had garnered some fame as a boxer while serving in the U.S. Army. He arrived in Salt Lake from Wyoming in early August, and began working as a bootblack in front of Heinau's Barbershop at 234 South Main. According to those he associated with during this time, Harvey had a reputation for irrational behavior and was prone to violent confrontation. (Following Harvey's death, an elderly black man named A.S. Johnson told the coroner that he was Harvey's half-brother, and that Harvey's real identity was Joseph Samuels of Farmington, Louisiana.)

Grice offered Harvey work on a small farm located twelve miles outside the city for two dollars a day and transportation. Because of the distance, coupled with his own short fuse, Harvey flew into a rage and insulted Grice. When Grice ordered Harvey out of the restaurant, Harvey pulled a .44-caliber pistol and threatened him with it. Grice backed down and called police as soon as Harvey left.

Burt received Grice's call at the police station. The fifty-four-year-old devoted family man had been a Salt Lake City police officer for twenty-four years. Born October 20, 1828, in Scotland, Burt joined the Mormon Church in 1848 and immigrated to the United States, arriving in Utah in the fall of 1851. He joined the police department the following year and was named

The murder of Salt Lake City Marshal Andrew Burt in 1883 sparked one of the darkest episodes in Utah history. Burt's killer was lynched by a mob within minutes of the murder. (Salt Lake Police Museum)

chief of police in 1862. In 1876, he was elected to the position of city marshal. Burt rarely carried a gun, preferring instead to wade into any fracas with a heavy walking stick. In addition to police work, Burt was also a polygamist and LDS bishop of Salt Lake City's 21st Ward. Deeply religious, he nonetheless had a practical side. In a meeting of bishops at the Council House, he once encouraged fellow bishops to frequent local saloons if they wanted to know what the men in their wards were up to during the evenings.

At the time of Grice's call, city watermaster Charles H. Wilcken was visiting with Burt. Wilcken, who was also a special police officer, offered to accompany his friend. The two men eventually located Grice at the corner of Main and Tribune Avenue (200 South). While the officers scanned the busy streets for Harvey, Grice told them what had happened.

Harvey wasn't trying to hide. Something inside his head had obviously snapped. After leaving the restaurant, he proceeded to Thomas Carter's Hunting & Fishing Emporium, 137 South Main, where he paid twenty dollars for a .45-70 caliber Springfield rifle and two boxes of ammunition. Then he went looking for trouble. A few minutes later, Grice spotted Harvey coming up the street and pointed him out to the officers, saying, "That is the man, arrest him!"

The officers moved toward Harvey, intercepting him on the northeast corner of Main Street and 200 South. When Harvey saw Burt approaching, he raised the rifle and demanded, "Are you an officer?" Before Burt could answer, Harvey pulled the trigger. The bullet tore through Burt's right arm, passed completely through his chest, and into his left arm. Burt groaned and staggered into the door of the A.C. Smith & Co. drugstore a few feet away. Bleeding from five large wounds, he collapsed behind the prescription counter and died within a minute.

Fortunately for his own well-being, Wilcken was extraordinarily strong and quick. He grappled with Harvey immediately following the shot, seizing the assailant by the throat and tearing the rifle out of his grasp. While citizens scrambled for safety, the two men continued to fight on the sidewalk, Wilcken punching Harvey in the head while the latter tried to bring his pistol into play. Eventually, Harvey managed to shoot Wilcken through the left arm. Undaunted, Wilcken threw Harvey into a ditch and overpowered him. Harvey was struggling to get a second shot into Wilcken's chest when members of the crowd finally came to the officer's aid.

Salt Lake officers Thomas F. Thomas and William Salmon arrived on the scene and latched on to Harvey's wrists with iron "nippers," an early form of handcuffs employing a single iron clamp with a ratchet handle. While Salmon remained behind to check on Burt, Thomas dragged the cursing killer through a growing crowd to the city jail. Following close behind, individuals in the crowd started calling for a lynching. It was just talk at first, but when physician J.M. Benedict arrived and pronounced Burt dead, the crowd flew into a rage.

Pursued and jostled by the growing mob, Thomas managed to get Harvey into the marshal's office at city hall only by drawing his pistol and threatening the bolder members of the mob. Inside, Harvey was searched and relieved of a large number of pistol and rifle cartridges as well as $165.80 in cash, belying his earlier claim of being broke. At this point, Thomas and other officers were

Intersection of 200 South and Main where Salt Lake City Marshal Andrew Burt was murdered. (Utah State Historical Society)

still unaware that Burt was dead. When a member of the mob outside the office announced this fact loudly enough for those inside to hear, Harvey responded by jumping up with a curse. Thomas punched him between the eyes, knocking him to the floor. Others claimed that Thomas assaulted Harvey in a rage at the news of Burt's death.

By then, a reporter for the *Salt Lake Herald* estimated that the crowd outside the marshal's office had grown to two thousand angry citizens, shouting, "Hang the son-of-a-bitch!" Officer William Salmon opened the door and ordered the mob away at the point of a pistol. Instead, the mob surged toward the door, pulling Salmon aside and disarming him.

Witnesses disagreed later over what happened next. Some said officers tossed Harvey into the mob. Others said Harvey seized the opportunity of the open door and—perhaps underestimating the size and general humor of the crowd—bolted through it on his own. In either case, furious citizens of Salt Lake City were waiting for him.

The mob tore into Harvey, beating and stomping him into submission. A group of men tried to fashion a noose out of harness straps cut from teams of horses in front of city hall. When the noose proved too short, it was used to flog Harvey while a rope was sent for. When it arrived, Harvey was dragged to a stable shed west of the jail yard, where the rope was tossed over a beam. Several men then hoisted the still struggling Harvey into the air, one of them climbing onto a nearby carriage in order to kick Harvey's hands away from the noose strangling him. The crowd roared its approval. Twenty-five minutes after the murder of Burt, Harvey was dead. But the mob still wasn't through. Harvey's body was cut down and pulled through the alley out onto State Street, where it was tied to a horse and dragged. Furious at the behavior of his fellow citizens, Salt Lake City Mayor William Jennings confronted the mob and demanded that they disperse. Their rage vented, the crowd broke up.

That afternoon, a coroner's inquest concluded that Harvey had been killed by an infuriated mob whose names were unknown. Harvey's body was turned over to the city sexton for burial. Instead of burying him in the cemetery, workers dug a grave "near" it. Two months after the lynching, workers loading gravel in an area west of the cemetery accidentally unearthed Harvey's rotting corpse. It was hastily reinterred.

Harvey's lynching was the third in as many days in Utah. In addition to the Salt Lake City affair, a Chinese man was lynched in Ogden, and an alleged killer, who was white, was seized from the Park City jail and strung up. Virulently anti-Mormon at the time, the *Salt Lake Tribune* attempted to lay the blame for Harvey's death on the city's Mormon influence.

The *Salt Lake Daily Herald* responded to the allegations by pointing out that no Mormons were involved in the Park City lynching. "The lynching in Salt Lake was the result of a momentary outbreak of passion, a temporary aberration, or loss of reason and dethronement of judgement—not on the part of Mormons or Gentiles, but by both classes."

Services for Burt were held August 28 in the Salt Lake Tabernacle. His body was escorted to the Salt Lake City Cemetery by leaders of the LDS Church. While most of the city grieved his loss, at least one member of Burt's family claimed to have seen him after his death. Burt's eleven-year-old daughter Alice had been in Ogden for two weeks prior to his death, returning by train on the evening of the tragedy. Later that night, she astonished her family with the claim that she had seen her father. The *Deseret News* printed the following account:

> ... about half past eight o'clock [Alice] states that she saw her father in the yard of the City Hall. She immediately entered the house and told her mother that she had seen papa. After retiring to rest she refused to be comforted, and wept for several hours, when she states that she suddenly observed her father standing near. He looked at her and uttered a few kindly words, in his characteristic way when in life, and told her to go to sleep. She immediately became quiet and went to sleep. She states that her father was dressed in white and had no covering upon his head, that his face was perfectly natural.

Charles Wilcken recovered from his wound and continued to work until his death in 1915. In a strange twist of fate, Wilcken's son David became a prison guard and was badly wounded while capturing another police killer during a prison break in 1903.

Tensions over the lynching, divided primarily along Mormon and federal government lines, were kept at a fever pitch by the *Salt Lake Tribune*, which cried cover-up, official abuse, and racism. Eventually, federal prosecutors charged Thomas with assaulting Harvey and participating in the lynching. At the trial, which began May 13, 1885, witnesses for the prosecution testified that Thomas had savagely beaten Harvey with a police billy club before tossing the hapless prisoner into the arms of the mob. The witnesses further accused George Hilton and Salmon of being willing participants in the entire affair.

Witnesses for the defense, most notably doctors Jeter Clinton and J.M. Benedict, contradicted nearly all the allegations made against Thomas and Hilton, including the condition of Harvey's corpse and the locations and behavior of various officers during the action by the mob.

The jury believed the defense. On May 14, 1885, after deliberating for five hours, the jury acquitted Thomas.

James C. Burns

Sanpete County Sheriff's Office
September 26, 1894

A resident of Manti, James C. Burns was born somewhere in the eastern United States on September 18, 1849. Little is known of his early years. According to one source, Burns was quite young when his parents decided to answer Brigham Young's call to come to the Mormon Zion. Traveling with a California emigrant company, Burns's parents died on the plains, leaving him an orphan. Deposited with LDS Church authorities in Salt Lake City, young Burns was presented the following Sunday to the congregated Saints in the Bowery for the purposes of securing a set of foster parents. Ironically, as the story goes, Burns's grandmother was in the congregation, recognized him, and took him in.

Growing to adulthood in Utah, Burns later married and had several children. Two years prior to his death, he won the Sanpete County election for sheriff on the Democratic ticket. He was widely regarded as an effective but unforgiving lawman.

According to the *Salt Lake Herald*, Moen Kofford and Pete Mickel had reputations as sheep rustlers. Kofford was twenty-two years old and a member of a family that settled in Castle Valley. Mickel, whose real name according to one newspaper was James Peterson, was eighteen and from the Sanpete County area. They had been stealing sheep for more than four years in the mountains above Spring City, and reportedly had run off as many as seven hundred animals at one time. Although they had been arrested and tried once or twice, they had never been convicted.

A week prior to the killing, Kofford and Mickel were alleged to have rustled approximately four hundred sheep from the Moroni cooperative herds. Witnesses claimed the two young men drove the sheep to an isolated location where they cut off the marked ears and put the sheep in with their own stock. The owner of the sheep later found the ears buried in the ground and took them to a judge in Spring City. The judge asked Sheriff Burns to investigate.

On September 24, 1894, Burns rode into Spring City and spent the night there. While talking with a friend, Burns announced that he was going up to the "Kofford corrals" to arrest the two rustlers. Asked if he had a warrant, Burns is said to have patted the .45-caliber pistol on his side and replied, "This is all the warrant I need to take those boys."

The following morning, Burns and three men rode ten miles southeast of Spring City to Reeder Ridge, where they located Mickel and his brother Fred

Sanpete County Sheriff James C. Burns was shot to death while attempting to arrest sheep rustlers in the mountains above Spring City. (Sanpete County Sheriff's Office)

working in a sheep corral. Kofford was nowhere to be seen. The sheriff explained that he was there to arrest Kofford and Mickel. After some discussion, Fred asked Burns if he had a warrant. Again, Burns's response was to touch his pistol and repeat what he had said the night before. Fred told Burns that they would not go with him without a warrant. "You've taken us before without a warrant," Fred Mickel said, "and I told you we would never go with you again unless you brought a warrant of arrest, and we won't go."

In an apparent effort to avoid trouble, the Mickels invited the sheriff's party to spend the night. Hopefully, things would get straightened out in the morning. The following morning, Burns accompanied the Mickels to their corral, where he began separating the rustled sheep. No one was under arrest at this point, but the prospect weighed heavily on everyone's mind. Then Kofford rode in. He listened to what was going on and called the sheriff a liar. Kofford continued to insult the sheriff as the men separated the herds. Finally, Kofford said the lawmen weren't taking any more sheep.

Versions of the actual shooting vary widely. It is generally accepted that only Burns, Kofford, and Mickel were in the corral when the shooting started. Kofford was armed with a pistol, while Mickel had a rifle. Mickel and Kofford later claimed that Burns drew and started firing, forcing them to respond. More likely, Burns drew his gun to enforce an arrest and the two rustlers resisted. When the shooting stopped, Burns was dead and Mickel had a bullet in his side. One account claims that Mickel was wounded when a bullet fired by Kofford went through Burns and struck him. The story told by the outlaws themselves claims that a bullet from Burns struck the cylinder of Kofford's revolver, glanced off, and hit Mickel.

After the killing, Kofford stripped Burns of his weapons, and then he and Mickel threatened to kill the other three men who had accompanied the sheriff to the corrals, blaming them for the cause of the fight. The three were eventually released and allowed to walk back down the mountain.

When news of the murder reached Spring City, a large posse formed and immediately set out to recover Burns's body. Seven hours later they found the sheriff in the corral where he had fallen. The body was returned to Spring City strapped to a horse, then on to Mount Pleasant by wagon, where a coroner determined that Burns had been shot five times. Three of the bullets struck the sheriff in the chest, another in the right shoulder, and one in the right leg. At least two of the shots appeared to have been fired into Burns as he lay on the ground. A few days later, while lawmen scoured the hills for Kofford and Mickel, Burns was buried in the Mount Pleasant cemetery under the auspices of the Ancient Order of Workmen and the Independent Order of Odd Fellows, lodges of which Burns was an honorable member. The AOW later presented Burns's widow with a check for $2,000.

After the gunfight, Kofford and Mickel put some distance between themselves and the corral. They rode to Orangeville, where they stopped at the office of a Dr. Moore. While Kofford and his brother Abner bought supplies, Moore operated on Mickel. The bullet had passed through Mickel's wrist and lodged in his back near a kidney. Extracting the bullet, Moore first handed it to Mickel and then asked for it back, saying that Mickel wouldn't need it anymore. Mickel's response was that Sheriff Burns wouldn't need it anymore either. When Moore asked the men if they had killed Burns, Mickel answered, "Yes, we've killed him."

Threatening to return and kill Moore if he told lawmen of their visit, Kofford and Mickel rode away from Orangeville at about 9:00 p.m. Before they left, Kofford gave Moore a second warning to pass along to the expected posse. "Tell anyone that wants to follow us that the more comes the fewer returns," Kofford said. "We don't intend to be taken alive and suffer the fate of Enoch Davis." (Davis had been executed by firing squad on September 14, 1894, following a sensational trial for the murder of his wife.)

Moore apparently took Kofford's threat to heart, for he waited in his home until the following morning before venturing out to tell lawmen of the visit. By then, Kofford and Mickel had escaped into the San Rafael Swell, a natural stronghold of cliffs, canyons, and hidden caves.

On Saturday, September 29, the two were discovered camped in McCarty Canyon, a box canyon located about thirty miles southeast of Castle Dale. Officers quickly converged on the campsite and seized the killers' horses, food, medicine, and clothing. But Kofford and Mickel had seen the posse closing in and escaped by climbing into the rocks. The following morning the two were spotted high in the rocks and a long-range gunfight commenced. Unbeknownst to lawmen firing from below, Kofford was slightly wounded during the exchange by a bullet through his side.

During the gunfight, the rifles of two posse members malfunctioned. In addition, lawmen had failed to bring supplies necessary for a protracted siege. Sunday slipped away and it wasn't until Monday, March 1, that the posse felt reinforced enough to begin scaling the rocks after the killers. Again it was too late. Except for a few tracks and spent cartridge casings, Kofford and Mickel had vanished into the Swell.

For the next three months lawmen searched the San Rafael country, hampered by snowy weather and aid given to the outlaws by Kofford family members and friends. According to one posse member, it was difficult to get information from many people because of sympathies held for the Kofford family. Information passed to the killers enabled Kofford and Mickel to permanently elude posses. They were never caught.

On July 13, 1895, Abner Kofford was interviewed in Mount Pleasant by news reporters. He claimed that arrangements were being made for the surrender of his brother and Mickel, and that they were currently outside the jurisdiction of the United States. When asked if the two were hiding in Mexico, Kofford merely smiled. "I am not afraid to tell all I know concerning the tragedy and the boys at present, but no one will believe me," said Kofford, who fully expected to be charged with aiding his brother. "We have a hard name and public pressure is against us."

Despite Abner Kofford's assurances that "the boys" would soon surrender, Kofford and Mickel never availed themselves of their day in court. Over the years, rumors of sightings continued to appear in newspapers. The two killers were variously reported to be hiding in Canada or Mexico and many places in between. Rumors that persist to this day alternately claim that Mickel was killed in Arizona, that he bought a ranch in Texas, and that he even became a World War I Canadian Army hero.

The rewards for their capture eventually totalled $1,500 and were never recalled, a fact that probably kept Kofford and Mickel wanted posters hanging in police stations longer than normal. This led to several cases of mistaken identity, the most notable of which occurred in 1897 when the *Salt Lake Herald* announced the outlaws' capture in, of all places, Wilmington, Delaware. Officers there notified Utah authorities that they had picked up two men who matched photographs of Kofford and Mickel. When excited Utah officers arrived in Wilmington days later, however, they were disappointed to find that the two men were not the outlaws.

Wanted flier offering a reward for Pete Mickel and Moen Kofford, killers of Sheriff James Burns. Despite the large reward, neither was ever brought to justice. (Unknown source)

The death of their father and husband was not the last time a law enforcement tragedy would strike the Burns family. More than thirty years after his father's death, James Milton Burns was gunned down while serving as an officer with the Castle Gate Police Department.

Thomas A. Stagg

Echo City Police Department
July 30, 1895

While lawmen continued to hunt in vain for Kofford and Mickel, another pair of reckless young men set off on the outlaw trail. As usual, it started over something trivial—in this case, a few boxes of strawberries—but the repercussions would be devastating. The subsequent murders of Echo City Constable Thomas A. Stagg and former Evanston City Marshal Edward N. Dawes on July 30, 1895, precipitated one of the largest manhunts Utah had yet known.

In the summer of 1895, few people who knew him would have objected to Patrick Henry Coughlin being called a bad man. Born June 23, 1874, in Canton, Massachusetts, Coughlin came west with his parents and the construction of the Union Pacific Railroad. The family settled in Park City, where Coughlin's father died. Raised by his mother along with several brothers and sisters, "Patsy" quickly earned a reputation in Park City's Row district as a "tough kid." From his earliest childhood, he exhibited traits of extreme cruelty and

Echo Constable Thomas Stagg
(right) with unidentified man.
Although he knew Pat Coughlin
would try to kill him, the aging
lawman did not hesitate when
called upon to join a posse.
(Norma Mikkelsen)

hatred, frequently venting his anger on animals or smaller children. "Patsy, my boy," a Park City lawman reportedly said after one unpleasant episode, "you want to put on the brakes, or you'll find yourself in a tight box someday."

By the age of twenty-one, Coughlin had already served time behind bars for assorted offenses, most notably a short term in the territorial prison for the burglary of a saloon. Along with being the suspect in several robberies, he also had been tried and acquitted in 1893 for shooting and wounding a man over some perceived slight. Two years later, he seemed more than ready for that tight box.

Coughlin's best friend was twenty-year-old Fred George. Born into a staunch Mormon family in Salt Lake City's Eleventh Ward, George was raised by various relatives after his parents died. Rowdy and mischievous, George had served time in the state reformatory and was seen as a ringleader among the toughs of "the Park." George was also a crack shot with a rifle, frequently seen practicing near the sampling mill. Shortly before the murders, George worked in Park City driving a sprinkling cart to keep the dust down on the streets.

On Thursday, July 11, Coughlin, George, and another Row tough by the name of Frank Kennedy undertook the theft of six cases of strawberries from the wagon of Park City peddler S.A. Pace. Kennedy committed the actual

Patrick Coughlin following his arrest by Salt
Lake police officers for an unrelated charge on
November 27, 1892. (Salt Lake Police Museum)

theft, and the three then took the strawberries to the Row, where they quickly disposed of the goods. Officers soon arrested Kennedy, who implicated Coughlin and George. Kennedy told officers that the theft was actually the precursor to a larger robbery: the gang intended to rob one of the trains passing through the area. He posted twenty dollars bail and was released pending trial.

Fed up with the behavior of Coughlin and George, Summit County Sheriff John M. Harrington vowed to get the boys. Warrants were sworn out for Coughlin and George, who, catching wind of their new status, stole two horses and left town. They traveled down to Salt Lake City, where they stayed for a couple of weeks before becoming bored and deciding to return to Park City. Well armed now, Coughlin and George bragged that they intended to "ride into Park City one of these fine evenings and hold up some place of business."

Having learned of the return of the horse thieves, Harrington and temporary deputy Earl Williamson started after them on July 20. Going after Coughlin and George was not Williamson's idea of a good time. That morning he had actually ridden a short distance with Coughlin and George on their return to Park City. Later, as Williamson was in the act of chiding police officers for their inability to find the outlaws, Harrington deputized him on the spot and told him to lead the way with something other than his mouth.

At Wanship the small posse discovered that their quarry had stopped in the tiny hamlet long enough to purchase 200 rounds of ammunition and force a local blacksmith to shoe their horses. Borrowing an old rifle, Harrington and the reluctant Williamson followed the horse thieves south through Rockport and into Peoa before doubling back to Crandall Creek. The trail led Harrington up a wood road along the creek about four or five miles to a sheep wagon parked in some brush. Here the tiny posse found Coughlin and George waiting for them.

Riding up to the camp, Harrington spotted Coughlin inside the sheep wagon holding a Winchester at shoulder point. Dismounting and peering at Coughlin over the top of his saddle, the sheriff ordered Coughlin to drop the gun. Coughlin's reply was a bullet that struck Harrington's saddle horn, driving splinters of wood into the sheriff's face. Harrington managed to fire once in reply and then discovered to his horror that he could not eject the spent casing from the borrowed rifle. Fred George opened fire from the cover of some nearby brush, forcing the two lawmen to draw off.

Not knowing that Williamson had been pressed into police service against his better judgment, or perhaps because they were angry that he had led the sheriff to them, the outlaws marked him for special attention. Bullets smashed a bottle of "snake medicine" in Williamson's pocket, shot away the handle of his revolver, cut the buttons off his pants, and burned a flesh wound across his left wrist. Despite the heavy fire, however, neither Harrington nor Williamson was seriously wounded. With Harrington's rifle out of service and Williamson thoroughly demoralized by his short career as a deputy, the posse beat a hasty retreat. Their escape was the last bit of luck Utah police officers would have for more than a week.

The bushwhacking of Harrington transformed Coughlin and George from small-time thieves to first-class badmen. When Harrington reached a telegraph station, the wires sang with news of the gunfight. Posses from Rich, Wasatch, Utah, Summit, Cache, and Salt Lake Counties spread out over northeastern Utah searching for the horse thieves turned attempted killers.

Lawmen had reason to suspect that Coughlin and George were headed for Wyoming. An accomplice during their brief stay in Salt Lake City told officers that the two were headed east to start a gang. A.D. Bruce told officers that he had accompanied Coughlin and George on their return to Park City under the auspices of going to Wyoming to look for work. Fifteen miles into Emigration Canyon, however, Bruce became alarmed at his companions' brazen theft of provisions from a house. When he balked at going any farther with them, Coughlin and George took his rifle, robbed him of twelve dollars, shot his horse, and left him to trudge back to Salt Lake City on foot.

Four lawmen positioned themselves at Wahsatch, a small cluster of buildings located five miles from the Utah-Wyoming border, where they waited for the outlaws to pass through. The force consisted of Echo City Marshal Thomas A. Stagg, Uinta County (Wyoming) sheriff's deputies Robert Calverly and William Taylor, and a former Evanston marshal, Edward N. Dawes.

On the evening of July 29, a man named Allison who knew the outlaws rode into Wahsatch and told the four lawmen that he had seen Coughlin and George in the "Palmer cabin" on Duck Creek, three miles northeast of Wahsatch and about twelve miles from Evanston. Allison said the outlaws had been there for two nights and a day resting their horses. Allison refused to lead the officers back to the cabin and also refused to loan them his cartridge belt, facts which may have contributed to the later disaster.

While a great deal of personal information was reported in the newspapers regarding Coughlin and George, little was written about Stagg or Dawes. At age sixty-three, Stagg was a Utah pioneer, perhaps too old to be out chasing outlaws. Born February 19, 1833, Stagg had been a Summit County deputy sheriff before he took the job as constable of Echo City. Married and the father of a large family of grown children, the officer was held in high regard by Echo residents and the surrounding community. Despite his age, Stagg went directly to Wahsatch to search for the outlaws. He told the Wyoming deputies he met there that Coughlin would probably try to kill him rather than surrender because he had arrested him for shooting and wounding a man in April 1893.

Dawes also was married. The forty-three-year-old former Evanston city marshal was popular in Evanston, where the Civil War veteran commanded the Evanston post of the Grand Army of the Republic.

Although it was dark, the posse immediately set out for the Palmer cabin in a wagon, arriving at 1:30 a.m. on July 30. Unfamiliar with the area, the posse blundered past the cabin in the noisy wagon, no doubt alerting the outlaws inside. When they realized their mistake, the lawmen drove back and took up positions around the cabin, settling down to wait for daylight.

Calverly was unhappy with the positions taken by Dawes and Stagg. The two older officers were situated on opposite sides of the cabin less than 100 yards away from each other, Dawes in a prone position behind a post directly in front of a window and Stagg in a slight depression in the ground. Calverly told them to move to better cover, but the two refused to listen to the younger deputy.

Shortly after sunrise, Taylor tried to get a drink from a nearby spring. Coughlin came to the door of the cabin and drew a bead on him, but a shot from Dawes struck the side of the cabin and spoiled his aim. Coughlin jumped back into the cabin, slammed the door, and the fight was on. While George reloaded, Coughlin fired at officers from the window. Although the cabin received a furious volume of fire from the posse, it soon became apparent that Coughlin had the better position.

Stagg took a mortal wound almost immediately. A bullet struck him in the jaw and passed out through the back of his neck, severing the jugular. Coughlin later claimed that he never aimed at Stagg during the fight because the older

Right: Utah State Prisoner 772, Fred George, following his conviction for murder. A follower of the bolder Patrick Coughlin, he was wounded in the shootout at Palmer's cabin. He lived quietly following his release from prison. (Utah State Department of Corrections)

officer had known him since he was a kid. Coughlin insisted that Stagg was shot down by the posse in a cross-fire. Lawmen who responded to the scene found the ground surrounding Stagg's body torn up by bullets.

With Stagg out of the way, Coughlin crawled out a window and outflanked Dawes. He shot Dawes in the left side, the bullet passing through both lungs. Dawes fell in an exposed position. Coughlin then turned his fire on Calverly and Taylor. Taylor had his coat collar shot off and Calverly received a minor wound to his head. Coughlin was in the act of shooting at Taylor again when a shot from Calverly struck his rifle and knocked it out of his hands.

A ceasefire ensued during which Calverly and Taylor were shocked to discover that they were down to one cartridge apiece. Calverly was no coward. Five years before, he had traded shots with Butch Cassidy and won, landing the rustler in the penitentiary at Rawlins for two years. However, now bloodied and out of ammunition, he knew that discretion was definitely in order. The two remaining lawmen opted to pull back and go for help.

After the posse retreated, Coughlin and George approached Stagg and Dawes. Stagg was obviously dead. The outlaws stripped him of his guns and ammunition, leaving his personal effects untouched. Still alive, Dawes reached for his gun when the boys approached him. Coughlin covered him with a rifle and convinced him to surrender.

Later, at his trial, Coughlin claimed he gave Dawes water and moved him to a more comfortable position. Dawes was in great pain and allegedly told the men that he didn't blame them for shooting him and that he was sorry the posse fired on the cabin. "[He] said they wouldn't have done it if they had known only the two of us were in the cabin," Coughlin said. "They thought there was a nigger horse thief and another man in there, too." It should be pointed out that Coughlin repeatedly made contradictory statements during his subsequent trial and incarceration.

The officers were not the only ones injured in the fight at Palmer's cabin. George suffered an ugly flesh wound through both thighs. Coughlin dug pieces of lead out of the wounds with a pocketknife. Then the two outlaws rounded up their tired horses and left the wounded officer to die.

A second Evanston posse arrived on the scene a few hours later. After pouring more than a hundred rounds into the cabin on the off chance that the outlaws were still inside, they searched and found Dawes surrounded by cartridge casings. Stagg lay a short distance away. Some of the posse members took the bodies to an Evanston morgue while the rest went after Coughlin and George.

Instead of pressing on into Wyoming, the outlaws turned west back into Utah. Telegrams quickly alerted other lawmen to watch the canyons along the Wasatch Front. Despite heavy rains, officers followed the trail to Ogden, Kaysville, Farmington, and Salt Lake City. Meanwhile, wild newspaper reports had Coughlin and George headed at various times for Idaho, California, and even boarding an eastbound train for the World's Fair in Chicago.

On the evening of July 31, the two were spotted on the outskirts of Bountiful by a police patrol in command of Salt Lake City Police Captain John J.

The Palmer cabin the day after Echo Constable Thomas Stagg and Evanston, Wyoming, posse member Edward Dawes were murdered by Patrick Coughlin and Fred George. (Joseph E. Dunning, Jr.)

Donovan. Before officers had time to turn their wagon around, the two outlaws rode off into the dark toward City Creek Canyon. Quickly securing horses for his men, Donovan and his officers went in pursuit. The following day, they overtook the outlaws at the summit of the canyon and a sharp gunfight broke out. No one was injured during the fight and Coughlin and George managed to escape on foot into the mountains.

For a short time, Coughlin and George disappeared. Two days later, officers began receiving reports that the outlaws were lurking in the vicinity of Mill Creek, where they had asked people for food. Although officers scoured the area, they found no sign of the killers.

On the night of August 3, Coughlin and George stole two horses from in front of the U.P. Saloon in Murray and headed west toward California. Under cover of darkness, they passed around the northern end of the Oquirrh Mountains and into Tooele County. Tipped off by people who saw the two at various locations on the road to Grantsville, officers began sealing off the canyons and roads in the Stansbury Mountains.

On August 4, officers got their first break in the case. That evening, Ruel Barres came down from the Third Term Mine in South Willow Canyon and told officers that the outlaws had eaten dinner with him just a few hours before. "No use watching here anymore, boys," Barres said. "The desperadoes took supper with me tonight and are gone."

In fact, however, Coughlin and George had ridden only a short distance from Barres's cabin. Exhausted and believing themselves ahead of any posse, they flopped down in the brush and went to sleep.

Members of the guard returned to Grantsville, where a posse was raised by City Marshal J.P. Mecham. At daybreak on August 5, the posse converged on South Willow Canyon. About three miles below the mine, Mecham and posse member Richard Rydalch spotted a horse grazing near some brush. Believing that Coughlin and George were somewhere nearby, Mecham sent Rydalch back for the remainder of the posse while he climbed around and took up a position above the patch of brush.

Although he was alone, Mecham began yelling orders to a nonexistent posse, hoping to scare Coughlin and George into holing up deeper in the brush. It worked. While the outlaws took cover, Mecham's real posse arrived and sealed off all escape routes. As soon as it was light enough to see, the posse spotted Coughlin and began firing a few shots into the brush. Smashing the stock of his rifle on a rock and throwing the rest of his weapons into the creek, Coughlin surrendered. "Don't shoot, don't shoot," he shouted to the posse.

George required more convincing. After his partner surrendered, George made his way on foot farther into the canyon. He hid in some brush until

Coughlin began calling for him to surrender. An hour after Coughlin gave up, George emerged from the brush with his hands up. The two killers were placed in irons, taken back down the canyon, and turned over to Salt Lake City officers.

Coughlin's arrogance regarding the murders and the 300-mile crime spree was colossal. Mistaking the morbid curiosity of the reading public for adulation, he soon developed an inflated sense of his own importance. He bragged to anyone who would listen about shots he had made, women he had seduced, and police officers he had outsmarted. His claims regarding the crimes frequently had little to do with reality, although they filled newspapers for weeks following his capture. George was more reticent, invariably pointing news-hungry reporters in the direction of Coughlin.

On October 23, 1895, Coughlin and George were tried in Ogden on charges of first-degree murder. Reading the judicial wind better than Coughlin, George pleaded guilty and threw himself on the mercy of the court. He was subsequently found guilty and sentenced to life in prison. Coughlin pleaded self-defense, claiming that the officers had no right to shoot at him while attempting to capture him. The evidence was so overwhelmingly against him that the jury quickly found him guilty. Coughlin was sentenced to be executed. "Women and whiskey led me to it," Coughlin said in a moment of cavalier penitence, following his conviction.

It would take more than a year to execute Coughlin. In the interim, he was held in the state prison, where he reveled in the notoriety he received for being the condemned killer of two lawmen. His widowed mother made frequent visits to the prison, where Coughlin railed about being locked up and cursed her for the quality of lawyers she had hired for his defense. Gradually his arrogance wore thin and he began whining about the unfairness of his death sentence in comparison to George's life sentence. He frequently asked prison officials for morphine to soothe his nerves.

Coughlin's attorneys spent more than a year maneuvering to save his life. Appeal followed appeal. Eventually, even the Supreme Court of the United States refused to overturn his sentence and the Utah Board of Pardons refused to commute it.

Days before his execution, Coughlin was taken to Randolph and placed in a jail cell, where he was visited by his long-suffering mother and the family priest. As the date drew near, his arrogance and cruelty returned. He turned down a chicken dinner the day before his execution, saying, "What do I want with that stuff? I'd like to have a little Dawes and Stagg on toast, see?"

On December 15, 1896, a firing squad shot Coughlin to death in snow-covered Sage Hollow, about two miles north of Woodruff, Utah. The young killer's bravado remained with him until the end. While traveling to the scene of his execution from his jail cell in Randolph, Coughlin told Sheriff A.L. Dickson of Rich County, "You never killed a gamer man in your life than you will today." His last request was that no photographs be taken of his body.

The execution squad fired from slits cut in the side of a tent. One of the rifles used was the rifle with which Coughlin killed Dawes and Stagg. Robert Calverly, who narrowly escaped death at Palmer's cabin, was in charge of the firing squad. Coughlin's body was claimed by his mother and taken back to Park City for burial in the Glenwood Cemetery.

On December 20, 1902, after serving seven years of his life sentence, George was paroled from prison. He settled down, married, and lived quietly until his death of a heart ailment in 1936.

William A. Brown

Ogden City Police Department
April 30, 1899

On the night of April 29, 1899, Fred Hanson of Brigham City was carrying a bucket of milk home when two men stepped out of the bushes and stuck guns in his face. The men forced Hanson into a nearby field, where they tied him up, then robbed him of the milk, his shoes, and $1.90 in cash.

After the robbers left, Hanson worked his way free and reported the incident to Box Elder County Sheriff H.H. Cardon and Deputy Frank Thompson. Determining a direction of travel for the suspects, the two lawmen alerted Willard Constable George J. Wells. Then they went to the Hot Springs Hotel and waited for the robbers to pass by. At about 10:00 p.m., they spotted two men walking up the tracks. When the officers attempted to stop them for questioning, the men fled into nearby fields. A pursuit began that ended with an ineffective exchange of shots in the darkness.

Running low on ammunition, the officers withdrew and called for reinforcements from surrounding communities. One of those summoned would be the next Utah police officer murdered in the line of duty.

William Anderson Brown was born in Ogden, November 30, 1863, the son of Judge Francis A. Brown. Raised in Ogden, he married Hattie Lewis of Logan in 1885. On February 22, 1891, six years after they married, Brown joined the Ogden City Police Department. At the time of his murder, the couple lived at 2540 Orchard Avenue and had five children ranging in age from two to twelve.

Officer "Billy" Brown worked a foot beat and soon earned a reputation as

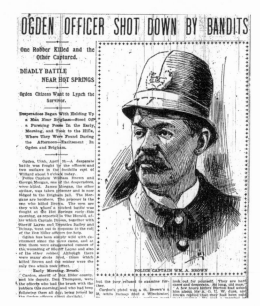

A *Salt Lake Tribune* headline reporting the death of Officer William Brown. Brown was promoted to police captain three weeks before his death in 1899. (*Salt Lake Tribune*)

an aggressive officer known and admired for his remarkable ability to recognize the criminal element at a glance. It was said that he rarely forgot the face of a wanted man. Brown spent a great deal of time in Ogden's train yards, accumulating a record of arrests unrivaled at the time in Ogden police ranks.

Because of his diligence and popularity, Brown was the natural choice in 1899 when the Ogden City Council created the position of police captain. On April 9, three weeks before his murder, Brown was promoted to the position with the full endorsement of Ogden Police Chief John E. Davenport and the popular support of the rest of the department. The promotion occurred while Brown was absent from the department, attending the funeral of his mother-in-law in Logan.

Brown was working the night shift at the police department in the early hours of April 30. He answered the telephone when Cardon called for reinforcements. Brown immediately got his superior out of bed and informed him of the request. Davenport replied that Ogden couldn't spare any officers for the posse and advised Brown to call Weber County Sheriff Charles Layne. Before hanging up, Brown asked permission to accompany the Weber County posse. In a move he would later regret, Davenport consented.

At 4:30 a.m. Brown left Ogden along with Layne and Weber County deputies Joseph Belnap and Joseph Bailey. Arriving at the Hot Springs stables, they were met by Cardon, Thompson, and Wells. The group immediately began scouring the country, and soon discovered that the bandits had slipped away during the night. The officers located some tracks and followed them east into the Wasatch Mountains.

The trail gave out around 9:00 a.m. and the officers stopped to rest. While going down to water the horses, Layne located the tracks again going east up the mountainside. The posse split up, with Brown, Belnap, and Cardon circling around to get ahead of the outlaws while the other officers continued on the trail. The three officers climbed the mountain until their horses could go no farther and then pressed ahead on foot. As they crossed a gully on the mountain just east of Willard, they saw the two robbers below. "We were coming west down the slope," Cardon said. "The fellows were hiding in the rocks and jumped up to run."

Shouting for them to surrender, the officers began closing in on them, with Brown in the lead. Although Cardon called for Brown to wait, the athletic police captain was constantly pressing ahead of the small posse, eager to make the capture. Brown was out in front when the two bandits, armed with long-barreled .45-caliber Colt revolvers, began to fire at the officers. The posse returned fire, killing one of the men instantly. A coroner's inquest later revealed that it was a bullet from Cardon's gun that killed the man.

When his companion fell, the second robber opted for escape and began running down the steep mountainside. "By hell, I'll get that fellow alive," Brown cried, running out ahead of the other officers again.

Belnap and Cardon shouted for Brown to wait, but he ignored them, plunging down the slope toward the suspect. Belnap told a reporter from the *Ogden Standard* what happened next. "Suddenly, when they were about forty yards apart, the robber turned and fired at Billy. Billy was running on the side of the hill and was off his balance, but he fired at the robber. Both had missed. Then the robber turned and whipped his revolver to an aim and fired again, this time striking Billy and he fell face downward on the rocks."

The heavy bullet struck Brown on the right side, cutting through a thick notebook and passing through his heart before exiting his body. Brown made a brief attempt to get back up before collapsing a final time.

When Cardon and Belnap returned fire, Brown's killer took cover behind a large rock. He shouted that the posse had killed his brother. Cardon and Belnap's response was an offer to kill him as well unless he was of a mind to surrender. Mulling this over while the posse kept up a steady fire at the rock, the killer finally put up his hands and surrendered.

The killer identified himself as James Morgan and the dead man as Robert Morgan. He readily admitted his guilt in the robbery, even pointing out the fact that he was wearing Hanson's shoes and socks. But he claimed that he shot Brown only because he was afraid that Brown was about to shoot him, an admission he would later recant. Morgan gave his age as nineteen, claiming that he and his brother were from Chicago and that the Brigham City robbery was their first criminal undertaking.

The truth was considerably different. A photograph recovered from the body of the dead robber bore an inscription, "to my dear wife Lena," and a stamp from a photography studio in Alameda, California. After contacting the photographer and an Alameda newspaper, officers had a better view of Morgan's true identity in a matter of days. Morgan was nineteen and the dead man was indeed his older brother, but everything else he said was a lie. Morgan was really Abraham Majors, an accomplished criminal recently paroled from Folsom Prison in California. According to a San Francisco newspaper, Majors had terrorized Oakland in 1896 as "the boy burglar," looting stores and homes at will until his arrest and subsequent imprisonment. The dead man was his older brother Archie, also a hardened criminal. The two were reportedly the sons of Lloyd Majors, a man hanged for murder in Los Gatos several years before.

Majors later said that he and his brother were trying to get to Salt Lake City to look for work after failing to reach the Yukon gold fields from Seattle. The woman in the photograph—"Lena"—turned out to be Lena Stone Majors. In 1896, she was an inmate at the Florence Crittenton Rescue house, an Ogden home for wayward girls. The following year, she joined the Salvation Army and left for California. Several months later she wrote friends to say that she had married a man named [Archie] Majors. The couple moved to Seattle, where Majors eventually deserted her.

While Abe Majors was kept under heavy guard in Brigham City, a large crowd gathered in Ogden at the intersection of Washington Avenue and 24th Street, blocking traffic. There was brief, enthusiastic talk of a lynching. But when Brown's body arrived at Larkin's undertaking establishment the crowd grew somber and dispersed without incident.

Funeral services for Brown were held May 3 in the Ogden LDS Tabernacle. Apostle Joseph F. Smith was scheduled to be the principal speaker but was unavoidably detained in Salt Lake City. Instead, city and local church officials eulogized Brown, calling him a brave and true man who had laid down his life for his people. Following the services, Brown's body was escorted to the Ogden City Cemetery by an honor guard of police officers, firefighters, and the city's baseball team, of which Brown had once been the star pitcher. Archie Majors's body was dumped into a potter's grave in Brigham City.

On May 2, Abraham Majors was arraigned in Brigham City, charged with first-degree murder, and ordered held without bail. Although officers confronted

Abraham Majors, following his conviction for the murder of an Ogden police officer. He was released from prison in 1919 after his death sentence was commuted to life in prison, making him eligible for parole. (Utah State Department of Corrections)

him with a photograph of himself from California, Majors continued to insist that he was Morgan.

On May 9, Majors was tried in First District Court. Attorneys for the defense claimed that it was actually Archie Majors who shot Brown before being killed by Cardon. The jury didn't agree. Four days later it found Majors guilty of murder and sentenced him to be shot on July 7.

Because of his youth, Majors quickly developed a sympathetic following, particularly among women belonging to the Christian Science Church. The women campaigned to have his sentenced commuted to life in prison, thus beginning a two-year legal battle. First, came an appeal to the Utah Supreme Court. On June 4, 1900, the high court upheld Majors's conviction, and again ordered him shot. An appeal to the Utah Board of Pardons for a commutation of his sentence was also denied. Later that year, Majors was granted a second trial that ended in yet another conviction. The Utah Supreme Court stepped in and overturned that verdict, ordering a third trial that was held in Logan on September 7, 1901. That trial lasted four weeks and ended with Majors's third conviction, this time of second-degree murder. He was sentenced to spend the rest of his natural life in prison.

Questioned later, jury members told news reporters that Majors's attorneys were successful in creating doubt as to who actually killed Brown. A few jurors even wondered if it wasn't possible that Brown had been accidentally shot by fellow officers. After eight hours of deliberation, the doubt caused jurors to drop first-degree murder charges in favor of second-degree.

In prison, Majors was anything but a model inmate. Records there show that he was frequently in trouble for assault and abusive behavior. On October

9, 1903, Majors and six other inmates staged a mass breakout of the state prison in Sugar House. Armed with two pistols smuggled into the prison, the inmates briefly overpowered several guards and made a dash for the wall. Two of the prisoners managed to escape and remained at large for several days before being recaptured. However, Majors was not one of them. Holding a gun to the head of a guard, he made it to the top of the prison wall, where the guard suddenly fought back. Majors was shot in the arm by another guard and then suffered a back injury when his hostage pushed him off the wall. The hostage guard was David Wilcken, son of Charles Wilcken, wounded in 1883 while capturing the killer of Salt Lake Marshal Andrew Burt. After pushing Majors off the wall, Wilcken was seriously wounded in the leg by guards firing at the prisoners.

Time eventually mellowed Majors. During the latter years of his sentence, his name appeared less frequently in the prison's punishment book. In 1915, his mother secured the services of a lawyer who was able to convince the state Board of Pardons that Majors no longer represented a danger to society. On January 22, 1918, he was paroled from prison. On the day of his parole an ecstatic Majors told a newspaper reporter, "I shall make all the members of the board, my mother and all my dear friends glad that I have a chance to prove that I am a man by living as a man should."

On January 18, 1919, Majors's sentence was commuted and he went immediately to Milford, where he worked in a mine. His attempt to go straight lasted less than a year. A note dated December 1920 in his Utah prison record states that he was back in Folsom Prison, serving a five-year sentence for a burglary committed in Los Angeles. Majors died of generalized arteriosclerosis in Los Angeles on November 6, 1957.

William Strong

Provo City Police Department
June 27, 1899

In the spring of 1899, Provo City was being overrun. Riding freight cars or walking, hundreds of jobless men beat their way through the city every week. Tramps, hobos, or "knights of the dust," the men were seldom tolerated in small communities, where their presence invariably led to an increase in crime.

Most of the tramps kept traveling when they reached Provo, moved along by the promise of work elsewhere or the insistence of local police officers hired to protect businesses and homes. But despite Provo officers' best efforts in 1899, the number of tramp-related crimes continued to grow. By June, the town's hobo problem was so bad that Mayor S.S. Jones and City Marshal Newell Knight decided to hire a number of temporary police officers. The job of these "special officers" was to make Provo unattractive to the hobos.

Among those hired was fifty-nine-year-old William Strong, a former city marshal now retired. Routing vagrants was nothing new to Strong; in fact, it was something of a specialty. He had served the community for more than thirty years as city marshal, police officer, and deputy sheriff. Born in Kendall, Westmoreland, England, Strong came to Provo in 1855. He was married and the father of four children, the youngest a twelve-year-old daughter. Perhaps because his family lived within a block of the depot, Strong developed a special interest in keeping the hobo population mobile. Seven years before his death, a newspaper published an account of a fight between Strong and several hobos:

> Officer Strong last evening had an encounter with one of the footpads who have been holding high carnival for some time in Provo. Three of them had just served out a term for stealing hams and resumed their old tricks by getting on a toot and rolling a man in the mud with the intention of fleecing him. Strong attempted their arrest but received a blow with brass knuckles full in the nose from one of them, the others escaping. The cop pushed the fight and put in a few telling blows but was confronted with a razor in the hand of the hobo, which made the fight a dangerous one. A ringing biff behind the ear brought the fellow to grass, however, and then the officer administered to him a neat pummeling. The tramp was bound over to await the action of the grand jury for resisting an officer with a deadly weapon, while the other two ham thieves, who were also arrested, were sent to the bastile for ten days.

On the night of June 26, Strong put on his badge one more time and walked from his home at 190 East 500 South to the railyard. There he stood guard, keeping an eye on the freights passing through town. Although the mayor had initially offered Strong the assistance of another police officer, Strong had refused, preferring to wait for a partner until his son-in-law John Cummings returned from a short trip. Strong assured the mayor that "there was no danger."

Shortly after midnight, a westbound freight passed through Provo. When it stopped for a few minutes, a number of hobos slipped off and hid in the bushes. Strong spotted the tramps and began routing them out. Two of the hobos were Frank Morris and Frank Connors, armed and on the run from a burglary committed in Scofield the week before. While little is known of Morris, Connors was an ex-convict who had already served time in Deer Lodge, Montana, for burglary and forgery.

Called out of retirement to protect Provo from an influx of transients, Officer William Strong was murdered in 1899 by a hobo he was escorting to jail. (Provo Police Department)

Almost immediately, Strong discovered Morris hiding his belongings in some bushes near the depot. Strong arrested the man and began escorting him to the city jail at 100 South and University Avenue. Morris cooperated with the officer for a short distance but then broke and ran, jumping through a set of stationary rail cars with Strong in pursuit. Morris managed to get away, but Strong found Connors hiding near some boxcars and arrested him instead. Strong ordered Connors to bring his pack and accompany him to the city jail. Unbeknownst to Strong, the pack contained loot from the Scofield burglary and a .38-caliber pistol.

The two men walked north along J Street (University Avenue). When they reached 400 South, less than two blocks from Strong's home, Connors pulled the pistol from his pack and struck the officer behind the right ear with it. The blow knocked Strong down. Dazed, the officer attempted to draw his own pistol. Connors leaned down, pressed the muzzle of the gun against the officer's chest and shot him through the heart, killing him instantly.

Provo Officer Frank J. Tucker was standing guard in front of the First National Bank at Center and University Avenue, four blocks north of the scene. Hearing the shot, he jumped on his bicycle and raced to where he discovered Strong's body lying in the street.

Fire bells and whistles pulled Provo out of a sound sleep. Hundreds of armed men quickly sealed every road, trail, and railroad track leading out of town. Others patrolled the fields and riverbanks. Within an hour, Utah County Sheriff George A. Storrs had sent the following telegram throughout Utah: "Policeman Strong murdered. Arrest and hold all transients. Notify us."

More than fifty hobos were rounded up in the Provo area alone, all summarily thrown in jail. When word came that the man seen running from the murder scene had a dark complexion, attention temporarily focused on African-Americans. A black hobo was spotted eating in a Lehi restaurant. He was immediately set upon and pursued through town by officers firing at him as they ran. The man was eventually caught and cleared of any connection with the murder.

One of those arrested in the tramp sweep was Morris. Connors's partner in crime was picked up while walking south on the railroad tracks near Springville and returned to Provo, where he immediately started talking. Morris told officers that after eluding Strong he saw the officer run into the area where Connors was hiding. He confessed to the burglary in Scofield and implicated Connors in that as well.

Despite massive efforts to locate him, Connors remained at large until the evening of June 27. Shortly before dark, George Cook, a farmer living about a mile west of Provo, went out to his cow barn to do chores and discovered Connors hiding inside. Cook suspected that Connors was Strong's killer and tried to arrest him by threatening him with a club, but he changed his mind when Connors pulled a pistol.

The incident served to alert guards in the area. Shortly after 11:00 p.m., three guards stationed at the intersection of Center Street and the railroad tracks west of town observed Connors creeping along the edge of the road. Samuel Richards, F.W. Smart, and Amos Holdaway trained their rifles on Connors and the hunt for Strong's killer came to an end.

When he was arrested, Connors tossed a small bundle into the bushes. Recovered the following morning, the bundle contained a recently fired .38-caliber pistol with two empty chambers. Connors first claimed that the gun wasn't his but later said he had fired the pistol at a rat. He denied any involvement in Strong's murder, insisting that he had arrived in Provo from Salt Lake City just minutes before being arrested.

Initially, there was little on which to hold Connors. However, in a legal maneuver designed to keep him in custody while authorities finished gathering evidence against him, Connors was charged with assaulting Cook. He pled guilty and received ninety days in jail. He also admitted his guilt in the Scofield burglary.

While Connors sat in jail, Provo buried its fallen officer. Funeral services for Strong were held June 29 in the Provo LDS Tabernacle. Church apostle John H. Smith first eulogized Strong and then commended Provo for the admirable restraint the community showed in not lynching Connors. Strong's body was conveyed to the Provo city cemetery by an honor guard comprised

Frank Connors was on the run from a Scofield burglary when William Strong arrested him for vagrancy. Unbeknownst to Strong, Connors had a pistol in his bedroll. (Utah State Department of Corrections)

of his comrades from the Blackhawk War, fought in the 1860s against territorial Native Americans. He was buried a short distance from former Provo chief of police Albert Bowen, murdered a quarter of a century before.

On July 8, prosecutors formally charged Connors with first-degree murder. Connors pled not guilty before Justice S.K. King. The case against Connors was almost entirely circumstantial. In addition to the pistol, officers found that his shoes matched some tracks left in the mud near the murder scene. Witnesses also tenuously identified Connors as the man they saw being escorted to the jail by Strong just minutes before the murder. Most damning was the deposition given by Morris that tied several elements of the case to Connors. Prosecutors believed that Morris's testimony would seal Connors's fate in court. But on August 6 Morris escaped, using a hacksaw to cut through an iron bar in a window. He was not recaptured.

Connors's trial began on September 26. Strong's widow, forty-five-year-old Celestia, and one of his married daughters attended the trial dressed in mourning. The two women sobbed through the description of the murder and when Strong's bloody, gunpowder-burned vest was displayed.

The trial lasted a week. On October 1, after deliberating for nearly twenty-four hours, the jury returned a verdict of guilty. But rather than a recommendation of death, the jury advocated that Connors be sentenced to life in prison. The recommendation surprised even Connors, who admitted to newsmen that he fully expected to be hanged. On October 9, Connors was sentenced to life at hard labor and transferred to the state prison, where he soon earned a reputation as one of that institution's most vicious inmates.

In 1902, the Utah Supreme Court overturned a conviction in a murder case similar to Connors's. Sensing that judicial winds would soon blow in their direction, Utah County officials took Connors to Price, where he pled guilty to the Scofield burglary and received an additional ten-year sentence. Within a few months, the Utah Supreme Court had overturned Connors's murder conviction and ordered him released at the end of the burglary sentence.

Meanwhile, Connors was proving himself to be something less than a model prisoner. His name appears frequently in the prison's punishment book. On October 9, 1903, he helped orchestrate a mass breakout attempt in which several guards were taken hostage with pistols smuggled into the prison. Prior to charging the outside wall, Connors decided that he needed some traveling money and robbed several of the guards at gunpoint. One of the items he took was a large gold watch. Moments later, as he was trying to scale the wall under heavy gunfire, the watch prevented his death when it stopped a bullet from a guard's rifle. Shoved off the wall by one of the hostage guards, Connors suffered a broken kneecap.

In 1911, Utah County retried Connors for the murder of Strong. However, the passage of time had weakened the case against him. Important witnesses either were dead or could not be located. What physical evidence remained had too greatly deteriorated to be of value. On May 11, after deliberating for eight hours, a Provo jury acquitted Connors. However, because of his participation in the 1903 escape attempt, Connors would have to serve the remaining eighteen months of his ten-year sentence for the Scofield burglary. Prior to returning to prison, Connors announced to reporters his intent to forsake all further criminal enterprises and become a chicken farmer upon release.

On October 14, 1912, the prison gates swung open and Frank Connors walked out a free man. He was met by Salt Lake City Police Chief B.F. Grant, who drove him around the city in an automobile. Eventually, the two men ended up on the roof of the Hotel Utah, where Connors got a good look at the changes that had occurred in Salt Lake City during his thirteen-year incarceration. "This is rather unusual treatment for a chief of police to give an ex-convict, isn't it?" Connors asked. "That may be," answered the chief, "but now that you are a free man, I am more interested in seeing you prove that you are able to stay straight than I am in watching out to see if you will commit some new crime."

Connors swore that he wouldn't commit crimes and vowed to report to Grant whenever he found himself in Salt Lake. Finishing their tour, Grant took Connors to the train station. The ex-con bought a ticket to Ogden, where he had arranged for the purchase of a wagon and team of horses with money earned from making harnesses while in prison. Whether Connors was able to keep his promise to Grant is not known.

Tucker, the officer who found Strong's body, was the next Provo police officer killed in the line of duty. On June 16, 1904, he was accidentally shot to death while preparing to go on patrol. As he was standing up from a chair, Tucker's automatic pistol fell out of his back pocket and discharged when it hit the floor. The bullet struck him in the heart, killing him almost instantly.

Chapter 2

1900–1925

As Utah modernized, so did its law-enforcement efforts. The murder of Grand County Sheriff Jesse Tyler—close on the heels of the May 26, 1900, Scofield mine disaster—marked the last time an officer would lose his life chasing rustlers with a horse-mounted posse. Horseless carriages, motorcycles, and trolleys became the preferred modes of transportation for those who pursued lawbreakers.

Although often considered a backwater state, Utah was on the cutting edge of public safety in one important respect. In 1912 Salt Lake City Patrolman Lester F. Wire invented the traffic light, an idea that soon spread across the country.

Despite the modernization of Utah law enforcement, the increasing number of officers, and even public attitudes about improving on the frontier mentality, the first quarter of the twentieth century was the most dangerous time for Utah police officers. This was true although Utah had relatively few problems with bootleggers and other illegal alcohol operations. This may have encouraged the majority of the state to vote for the repeal of Prohibition, Utah becoming the thirty-sixth (and deciding) state to ratify the proposed Twenty-first Amendment in 1933. Also, gangland violence common in eastern cities was rare in Utah, and organized crime was almost unheard of. Utah suffered only two law-enforcement deaths attributable to Prohibition, and one of those was accidental (that of Salt Lake City Detective Carl J. Carlson in 1929).

The primary threat to police officers during this period came largely from the dispossessed. On any given day between 1899 and 1925, a steady stream of unemployed men poured through the railroad yards and hobo camps of the Wasatch Mountains. California in particular tried to solve its unemployment problem during the late 1890s by putting jobless men on trains heading east, many of them eventually arriving at canyon rail choke points in Ogden and Salt Lake City.

51

Patrolling the yards and camps was brutally dangerous. Clashes with desperate men were common and sometimes fatal. More than half the officers who fell during this time were murdered in connection with the iron highway.

As the modernization of Utah continued, the first traffic-related death of a police officer occurred. On April 7, 1920, Ogden Patrolman Albert Smalley died five months after being struck by a car while driving his motorcycle. Traffic-related accidents would eventually account for nearly a quarter of all Utah officers killed in the line of duty.

Jesse Tyler

Grand County Sheriff's Department
May 26, 1900

At midday on May 26, 1900, Uintah County Sheriff William Preece and a posse were hunting rustlers in the Roan Cliffs, twenty miles north of Thompson Springs. Preece's band was working in conjunction with a smaller posse led by Grand County Sheriff Jesse Tyler. In order to cover more ground, the two groups had split up several hours before.

Shortly after noon, Preece spotted a rider coming hard toward his posse. When the rider drew up, Preece recognized the man as Tyler's deputy, Herbert Day. The news was bad: Tyler and posse member Sam Jenkins were dead, gunned down after stumbling into a band of outlaws three miles away on the west fork of Hill Creek.

A renowned lawman and tracker, Tyler was born thirty-six years before in Fillmore. Following the death of his parents while he was still young, Tyler was taken in and raised by John King. Tyler spent much of his early life in the stock business. In 1893, he moved to Grand County, an area he first visited in 1879 while driving a herd of cattle to La Sal. After the move, Tyler drove the stage between Thompson Springs and Moab, eventually going into business as a freighter on the same route.

In 1898 Tyler ran for sheriff of Grand County as a Democrat. He won the election by just three votes, defeating the incumbent, D.B. Wilson, only after a hotly contested recount. Tyler was aloof and a quiet bachelor, traits that came in handy for a sheriff whose county included the notorious Robber's Roost. A scrupulous personal integrity had earned him the nickname of "Honest Jack." Tyler also proved himself a tenacious tracker of outlaws, a skill that earned him the enmity of rustlers who considered the canyons and mountains of Grand Country their personal fiefdom. Tyler's fearlessness was such that some believed he became careless with his life, often making solitary treks into the Roost that lasted for weeks.

Word of Tyler's murder badly rattled Preece. Although Day wanted to start back to the scene immediately, Preece decided that he did not have enough men to take on a determined band of outlaws. He led the posse back toward Thompson Springs, and any chance of catching up with the killers soon evaporated.

The events leading up to Tyler's death actually began the month before, when the sheriff and a posse went into the Book Cliffs looking for rustlers. Although any rustler or outlaw would do, the man Tyler really wanted to find was Tom Dilly, charged with assault and rustling stock from the Webster City Cattle Company. The assault charge stemmed from a pistol-whipping Dilly had meted out to a cowboy named Sam Jenkins while the two men were working for the Webster outfit.

Where the Green River and Rattlesnake Canyon intersect, the posse came upon a man who at least from a distance looked like Dilly. Alternate versions of the story claim the man was building a raft to cross the creek or working a cow brand over with a running iron. One thing both versions agree upon is that the man ran when he spotted the posse, prompting a short gunfight that ended when someone in the posse fatally wounded him. Instead of Dilly, however, the corpse the posse gathered around belonged to "Flat Nose" George Curry, a former leader of the Hole-in-the-Wall Gang and a known associate of Dilly.

In Thrapp's *Encyclopedia of Frontier Biography*, Flat Nose's real name is listed as George Sutherland. Several people claimed to have killed Curry, perhaps prompted by the fact that the Union Pacific railroad had a standing warrant of $3,000 for his arrest or demise. One account claims that Doc King, foreman of the Webster outfit, hit Curry with a lucky shot from a distance of several hundred yards. A newspaper alternately claimed that Tyler fired the fatal shot. Finally, Uintah County Sheriff William Preece also laid claim to the killing. A story circulated that Curry was shot in the back while fleeing, but a photo of him clearly shows a bullet hole in his forehead.

Tyler didn't care that the dead outlaw was not Dilly. In his mind, whether behind bars or underground, one less outlaw was good for Grand County. But the death of this particular outlaw, while a boon for local stockmen, reportedly set in motion a series of events that resulted in Tyler's own death. When Curry's Wild Bunch colleague Harvey "Kid Curry" Logan read about the killing in a newspaper, he vowed to kill Tyler in revenge. Flat Nose had taken Logan under his wing in earlier days, teaching the Kid how to handle livestock and shoot. The name Kid Curry was reportedly bestowed on Logan because of this mentoring.

Logan was in Moab when he learned about the killing. He headed for Thompson Springs and then on into the Book Cliffs, eventually locating Dilly driving cattle on a plateau near the head of Florence Creek. Logan asked Dilly about Flat Nose and was told that the posse had shot the outlaw in the back. Knowing that Tyler was still after Dilly, Logan decided to tag along with the rustler with the idea that sooner or later the sheriff would turn up. Information

Known as "Honest Jack," Grand County Sheriff Jesse Tyler was murdered in 1900, allegedly by Wild Bunch member Harvey Logan. (Grand County Historical Society)

regarding Dilly's participation in Tyler's murder is sketchy. One account claims that Dilly was not present at the killing, while others say he was and that he played an active part.

On the night of May 25, Dilly, Logan, and another man reportedly made camp in a bunch of willows on the bank of the west fork of Hill Creek. The following morning was cold, with patches of mist hanging over the creek bottoms. Wrapped in their blankets, the outlaws had built a fire and settled down with their coffee when two men approached the camp on foot.

The two men were Tyler and Jenkins. Mistaking the men in camp for Indians or honest cowpunchers, Tyler decided to question them concerning the whereabouts of Dilly. Jenkins went with him while the other half of the posse, Day and a young man named Mert Wade, waited about fifty yards away.

"Hello, boys," Tyler called as he came within a few yards of the camp.

When the men looked up, both Tyler and Jenkins recognized their mistake. Turning around, they walked quickly toward their horses and the rifles on the saddles. Jenkins managed a single word of warning to Day and Wade, calling the name "Dilly" as the outlaws threw back their blankets. Day watched in horror as Tyler and Jenkins fell under a barrage of pistol shots. One source claims that Logan killed both men by firing from under his blanket.

As soon as Tyler and Jenkins were down, the outlaws turned their attention on Day and Wade. Bullets cut the air all around them. Since Wade was only a boy and the odds were decidedly against Day, the deputy wisely opted for retreat. As soon as they were out of range, Day sent Wade to Thompson Springs to spread the word while he rode to alert Preece.

The following morning, a large posse led by Richard Westwood and Day left Thompson Springs and reached the bodies of Tyler and Jenkins at about 10:00 a.m. Tyler had been shot twice through the right side, both bullets exiting over his left hip. Jenkins was shot a total of six times in the back, several of the bullets coming after he was already down. This was believed to be the work of Dilly. A coroner's examination found that the large-caliber bullets were notched to expand on impact, causing exit wounds as large as a man's fist and inflicting almost instant death.

After the murders, the outlaws stripped Tyler and Jenkins of their weapons and valuables, abandoned a string of horses, and rode hard for Wyoming. The trail was easy to follow at first, heading north through what is now the Uinta-Ouray Reservation, and passing close enough to ranches so that the outlaws could easily obtain fresh horses.

As news of the killings spread, posses from Uintah, Carbon, Salt Lake, and Emery Counties joined the pursuit, swarming through the Roost in an effort to box the killers in. No one knew for certain exactly who the killers were, although most suspected Dilly. Several other outlaws became suspects, including Butch Cassidy, bandits from Arizona, and even Moen Kofford, who had killed Sanpete County Sheriff James C. Burns near Spring City six years before. It wasn't until later that attention centered on Logan and a band of outlaws who were believed to have murdered lawmen in Arizona.

On May 29, Moab citizens turned out for Tyler's funeral. Services were held in the county courthouse, which was crowded to the point of suffocation. Following the services, a large number of people followed the funeral procession two miles to the city cemetery. Earlier that morning, a metal coffin containing Jenkins's body left Thompson Springs on a train bound for Ogden, where he was born and his family still lived.

For thirty-two days, Westwood's posse trailed Logan north, crossing the White River east of Ouray, then the Yampa River near the Utah-Colorado border. From there, the trail led through Powder Springs, Colorado, to Baggs, Wyoming. Finally, near Rawlins, the trail gave out. Horses and men nearing collapse from exhaustion, there was no use going any farther. It was possible that Logan had slipped over into Brown's Park, where Cassidy and other members of the Wild Bunch were reported to be lurking. Any attempt by a posse to storm Brown's Park would be suicide.

During his absence, Westwood was appointed to fill the remainder of Tyler's term. Known as "Dangerous Dick" from his earlier exploits as a lawman, Westwood was the logical choice. Between the years of 1916 and 1925, he served one term as sheriff and four terms as deputy sheriff. Later, in December 1927, Westwood again stepped forward to fill the term of Sheriff Joe Johnson, killed during a riding accident. On September 5, 1929, Westwood was shot to death during a jailbreak in Moab.

But Westwood outlived Logan. From 1900 until the summer of 1903, Logan participated in several Wild Bunch robberies, including the Tipton, Wyoming, train robbery. He drifted through Texas and into Tennessee, where he shot and wounded two Knoxville police officers before being captured. Escaping from jail, Logan returned to Colorado, where in June 1904 he and two others robbed a train near Parachute. Two days later, suffering from a bullet wound inflicted by a pursuing posse, Logan shot himself in the head near Glenwood Springs.

Whether or not this was actually Logan has been hotly debated through the years by researchers. Although the body was identified by people familiar with Logan, reported sightings of the bandit continued for years afterward, including several in South America. Like the stories of other Wild Bunch members, the facts have been so obscured by years of romance and storytelling that today the truth is difficult to distinguish from legend.

What eventually happened to Dilly is unknown. One account claims that it was he, not Cassidy, who died with Harry "Sundance Kid" Longabaugh in Bolivia. Another holds that Dilly skipped the country with money swindled in a stock sale and lived out his days comfortably in England.

One arrest was made in connection with Tyler's murder. On August 22, 1901, Todd Carver (a.k.a. T.C. Hilliard) was charged in Seventh Judicial District Court with the sheriff's murder. Exactly what evidence the state had against Carver is not known. He was ordered released for lack of evidence on December 26, 1901.

Charles S. Ford
Salt Lake City Police Department
December 14, 1907

In the early morning hours of December 14, 1907, the doors of St. Mark's Hospital burst open. Salt Lake City police officers carried one of their wounded comrades into the emergency room. Although mortally wounded, Officer Charles Ford managed to tell what had happened to him.

I was patrolling my beat, and knew nothing of the hold up at the Albany saloon. I reached the northeast corner of Fifth West [now 600 West] and Second South streets about the time the robbers were leaving the saloon, after the hold up. I did not see them as they ran out. The first

Salt Lake City Patrolman Charles S. Ford was mortally wounded while walking his beat just five days after being sworn in as an officer. (Salt Lake Police Museum)

I knew of the presence of the two robbers was when one of them shouted for me to hold up my hands. I turned my head and saw two men in the street near where I stood. One was a little in advance of the other.

Almost at the same instant the other man fired his revolver. His bullet struck me in the breast. It dazed me, and although I was able to discharge two shots in return, I was not able to stop them.

Surgeons examined Ford. The bullet had traveled through his chest, piercing a lung and exiting under his left shoulder blade. The bullet was later found trapped in his clothing. Although in great pain, Ford was conversant with his wife when she arrived at the hospital two hours later. However, little hope was held for his recovery. Doctors administered an opiate and Ford slipped in and out of consciousness until his death at approximately 1:30 p.m. He was the third Salt Lake City police officer murdered in the line of duty.

Ford was born March 25, 1856, in Syracuse, New York (although also reported as Sudbury, Vermont, by the *Salt Lake Herald* on December 16, 1907), and came to Salt Lake City as a teenager. On April 19, 1892, Ford was appointed to the Salt Lake City Police Department, where he worked for just six months before quitting to become a contractor. At the time of his death Ford lived with his wife and a grown daughter at 531 South 200 East. An active member of the local musicians' union, Ford also served as a drum major in local political party bands.

On December 9, 1907, after a sixteen-year absence, Ford returned to police work. His assignment was a night foot beat in the area of 600 West 200 South.

On the night of his murder, the fifty-one-year-old officer was working his third shift since being sworn in.

Ironically, December 9 was also an important day for Joseph Sullivan. After serving five years for an Ogden armed robbery, the twenty-eight-year-old Washington state native was released from the Utah State Prison, where he was widely regarded as one of the worst inmates. Prison officials weren't the only ones tired of his antics. Three days before his release, Sullivan's wife, the former Minnie Pierce of Green River, had obtained a divorce from him, a matter that did not improve Sullivan's frame of mind. When he left the prison in Sugar House, Sullivan went straight downtown and bought a pistol for three dollars. Then he went looking for trouble.

According to Salt Lake police daily arrest records, Sullivan was hauled in within hours of the gun purchase, picked up by officers working the Commercial Street (now Regent Street) beat, an area of opium dens, brothels, and saloons. They confiscated the pistol that had somehow become spattered with blood during its brief ownership. Sullivan refused to talk about the bloody gun and was held until the evening of December 12. When no evidence of a crime turned up, he was released and told to get out of town for being an "undesirable citizen." What officers didn't know is that Sullivan had used the gun to beat an intoxicated robbery victim behind a Commercial Street saloon— and that he had no intention of leaving town broke.

Shortly after 2:30 a.m. on the morning of December 14, two masked gunmen burst into the bar of the Albany Hotel, located on the southeast corner of 200 South and 600 West, and ordered the four patrons inside to throw up their hands. Everyone complied with the exception of an elderly deaf man unaware that anything was amiss. When he failed to respond, one of the robbers pistol-whipped him. Taking forty-five dollars from the cash drawer, the robbers fled.

Outside, a light snow limited visibility as Ford walked his beat. When he reached the intersection of 200 South 600 West he observed two men standing outside the Albany saloon. The two men realized that he was a police officer and rushed toward him, the smaller of the two shouting for Ford to raise his hands. Almost immediately the taller suspect fired, striking Ford in the chest. Ford was able to return fire, but his shots went wild and his assailants disappeared into the night.

Two plainclothes officers, Emil Johnson and Fred Clough, were within a hundred feet of Ford when the shots were fired. They gave chase but lost sight of the suspects in the darkness and falling snow. Ford was taken to the emergency hospital at the police station and then to St. Mark's, where he died that afternoon. By then, detectives already had a good idea who the robbers were.

James Owens was arrested the night of Ford's murder and confessed to being the lookout during the robbery that ended in the officer's death. (Utah Department of Corrections)

An hour after the shooting officers arrested James Owens about a mile from the scene. Owens was covered with mud and out of breath. Questioned by detectives, he broke down and admitted helping Sullivan and a man named Joe Garcia (also known as Joseph Cordova) plan the robbery. Owens claimed that he was on lookout outside the saloon when the crime occurred. Acting on the information Owens gave them, police raided a Main Street apartment rented to "Tip" Belcher, where they arrested Belcher and two more suspects in connection with the robbery and murder. None of them had an active hand in the robbery and were released. However, Owens was charged with robbery.

Officers began combing Salt Lake City for the two killers. Garcia, of Mexican and Chinese descent, was from Colorado, where he had served time in prison at Canon City for burglary. While there, he once escaped by holding the wife of the warden on his lap to prevent guards from shooting as he drove out of the prison yard. Recaptured a short time later, he finished his sentence. A known "porch climber," or burglar, Garcia came to Utah several weeks prior to the Albany robbery. He roomed with Belcher and was suspected by police of committing several local burglaries, typically entering the homes of his victims by climbing atop porches and entering through unlocked windows.

Ford was buried on December 17, in the Mount Olivet Cemetery. Funeral services were conducted in the clubhouse of the Fraternal Order of Elks, after which the body was escorted to its final resting place by members of the police department, the Knights of Pythias, and the Woodmen of the World.

For days officers searched alleys, flophouses, and the railyards but found no sign of Garcia and Sullivan. Weeks went by and hope of ever capturing Ford's killers began to dwindle. Then on January 5, 1908, word was received that Sullivan had been arrested in Portland, Oregon, when a sharp-eyed officer noticed him acting suspicious. Further checking proved that Sullivan matched a wanted flyer from Utah. Salt Lake City detectives went immediately to Portland and brought Sullivan back to Utah on January 17.

Hanging on to Sullivan was almost as hard as catching him in the first place. Salt Lake City jailers discovered that within hours of being locked up, Sullivan had manufactured a thirty-foot rope out of the blankets in his cell. Three days later, a jailer was alerted to another breakout attempt when iron filings filtered down onto his head from an upstairs window. A check of Sullivan's cell revealed the bars in the window partially sawn through. Fed up, jailers took Sullivan to the prison in Sugar House, where he was placed in solitary confinement and monitored around the clock.

On March 22, Sullivan pled not guilty to murder and robbery charges. His trial began May 16 and quickly became known for the squabbling among jurors and the grandstanding behavior of defense attorneys J.H. Bailey, Jr., and F.E. Vickery. When Sullivan took the stand on May 19, he denied any knowledge of the crimes and tried to shift the blame to Garcia and Owen. Sullivan claimed that he had left Salt Lake City hours before the crimes by jumping a train.

Although many people believed that the constant bickering among the jurors would make it impossible for them to reach a verdict, the jury convicted Sullivan of first-degree murder after thirty-six hours of deliberation, recommending a sentence of life imprisonment. Sullivan's only response to the verdict was a slight smile. Bailey and Vickery filed an appeal on April 1, the same day that Sullivan was sentenced to spend the rest of his life behind bars.

Ten days later, Governor John C. Cutler offered a $500 reward for the capture of Garcia. An informant whose identity was kept secret by police came forward and offered to lead officers to Garcia in return for the reward. The informant told officers that Garcia was running a burglary ring in Seattle, Washington. The city bought a train ticket and sent the informant to meet with Garcia. A few days later the informant wired Utah authorities with the information that he had contacted Garcia and was willing to betray him.

On May 6, the still unidentified informant (who many believed was "Tip" Belcher, who allegedly hated Garcia because of the latter's attempt to seduce his wife) led Garcia into a trap set by a combined force of Utah and Seattle police officers at the intersection of Pike Street and First Avenue in Seattle. The two men were nonchalantly walking toward a park when officers closed in and called for Garcia's surrender. Garcia immediately drew two pistols from his coat pockets. Fortunately for the officers, Garcia's draw was slowed

A burglar and known "porch climber," Joe Garcia (a.k.a. Joseph H. Cordova) made good his escape from Salt Lake City only to die in a shootout with Seattle police. (Colorado State Archives)

when the hammer of a revolver became caught in his coat. Garcia still managed to fire one shot before a hail of police bullets cut him down.

Garcia died a week later, but not before confessing to the Albany saloon robbery and the murder of Ford. "Sullivan and I had just held up the saloon there and were making our getaway," Garcia told a newspaper reporter. "The copper was coming down the street on the opposite side. I knew he didn't know anything about the stickup of the saloon, but I knew that he would know about it in a short time. If he was out of the way, I figured that we would have that much more chance to make a getaway. I just went across the street and croaked him."

Officers refused to believe the deathbed confession, suspecting that it was a ploy to get Sullivan off. According to them, too many witnesses insisted that the taller robber shot Ford. When no one claimed it, Garcia's body was turned over to the medical department at the University of Washington.

Sullivan's appeals went nowhere. Authorities refused to take into account Garcia's confession, believing that he was willing to take credit for the murder because he was dying anyway. The conviction stuck, and Sullivan was left facing the remainder of his life behind bars.

Utah Department of Correction files indicate that Sullivan initially returned to his old habits of causing trouble while incarcerated. But he eventually became a model prisoner and, in 1917, something remarkable happened while Sullivan was assigned to a work camp in Spanish Fork Canyon. Following the escape of two dangerous prisoners, Sullivan participated in the search for them, eventually becoming separated from the guards. Instead of escaping, Sullivan kept in touch with prison officials for days, notifying them of his whereabouts

Convicted of Ford's murder, Joseph Sullivan would lead a somewhat paradoxical existence in prison before his death in California. (Utah Department of Corrections)

by telegram as he continued tracking the two escapees. Receiving a tip that the men had gone to Kansas, Sullivan apparently followed them there until he lost the trail. He then voluntarily returned to Utah and prison.

Sullivan's behavior apparently impressed the Board of Pardons, as did the fact that his health was failing. In early 1918 his sentence was terminated. Sullivan went to California, from where he wrote to Warden George A. Storrs saying that he intended to go to sea as soon as he recovered his health. It was not to be. In May, Sullivan died of tuberculosis in a Fresno hospital.

Seymore L. Clark
Weber County Sheriff's Office
November 27, 1908

The murder of Weber County Chief Deputy Seymore L. Clark on a cold November night in 1908 became one of the most baffling cases in northern Utah history. Despite months of investigation, witness reports, and even a confession, Clark's killer was never brought to justice. (Clark's given name is also spelled "Seymour" in some records.)

Events leading up to Clark's death began at approximately 9:00 p.m. on November 27 when Timothy Kendall of Uintah, a hamlet located a few miles southeast of Ogden, telephoned the sheriff's office to report a trespasser in his barn. Kendall had discovered a tramp sleeping in a pile of hay. When he ordered the man off his property, the man refused to budge.

The tramp was John Flatella, an Italian immigrant who spoke no English. Recently arrived in America, Flatella had attempted to reach family members in Nevada by alternately walking and riding freights. By the time he reached Utah, he was sick and hungry and in no condition to continue his journey. He collapsed in Kendall's barn, unaware that his already abysmal situation was about to get worse.

Clark and Deputy John Murphy received the call at the sheriff's office in Ogden. Securing a double-seated rig from a livery, they set off for Uintah at 9:30 p.m., arriving approximately two hours later. They arrested Flatella for trespassing. Loading him into the buggy, they started back to Ogden.

The county road through Uintah paralleled the Union Pacific railroad tracks for a distance. The deputies had traveled a few hundred yards from the Kendall place when they noticed a man picking up something from the ground near a line of stationary freight cars. The officers stopped the buggy and called to the man, surmising that he was "rustling coal," a tolerated but illegal practice of picking up coal fallen from passing rail cars. "What are you doing there?" Clark called, unable to see the man clearly in the dark.

Perhaps believing that the officers were only meddlesome passersby, the man responded with a curse. Clark stopped the buggy a few feet away and jumped down. When the man took a defensive stance, Murphy tried to calm him down. "Don't get excited," Murphy called out. "We're officers of the law."

Murphy's words cleared things up for the unidentified man. He raised his hand and began firing. Eight bullets from a .32-caliber automatic hit Clark, Murphy, and Flatella. Clark was hit four times, once each in the right arm, right wrist, chest, and abdomen. Two bullets struck Flatella in the left arm, while Murphy was shot in the hand, a wound that caused him to fall from the buggy. Frightened by the sound of the shots, the horses raced off down the road. Flatella managed to stay in the buggy until it struck a dip, whereupon he was thrown high into the air, landing heavily on the road.

The suspect ran north along the tracks and disappeared into the darkness. Murphy fired two shots at the man but missed. He crawled to Clark and lifted the mortally wounded deputy in his arms. "John, I am dying," Clark gasped.

While Flatella alternately moaned and screeched in the distance, Murphy held Clark for the few moments that it took him to die. Once, Murphy thought he saw a figure moving furtively toward him along the boxcars. Fearing that the killer was returning, he readied himself for a fight, but the figure moved off.

Alerted by the sound of the shots, Uintah residents converged on the scene. Clark's body was carried to the depot, while groups of men fanned out in search of the suspect. They discovered the reason for the shooting. Instead of rustling coal when surprised by the deputies, the killer had instead been looting a boxcar. Five cases of new shoes were stacked near the road, obviously waiting for someone in a wagon to pick them up. The contents of a sixth case, broken open by the fall from the car, lay scattered about.

Within an hour, deputies, railroad detectives, and special officers from Salt Lake City, Ogden, and Morgan arrived. Weber County Sheriff Barlow B. Wilson telephoned the state prison in Salt Lake City, requesting that prison officials send bloodhounds to the scene, but was told that the prison's dogs were too old to follow a scent.

One of Wilson's search parties located and began following the suspect's tracks in the snow. They first led toward Kendall's barn, then back to the railroad tracks, where searchers followed them to the Riverdale crossing approximately three miles south of Ogden. Here searchers lost the tracks because a section crew had begun tearing up old ties early in the morning, obliterating further traces of the fugitive's flight.

Several witnesses came forward, claiming to have seen the man running from the scene. They described him as a young white male, wearing a cap and a double-breasted coat of dark material. Although several men answering this description were arrested and hauled to the sheriff's office, none proved to be the killer.

For days officers combed the area in and around Uintah, convinced that the crates of shoes stacked beside the road meant that someone near the town was an accomplice of the killer. So intense was the focus on Uintah that its citizens began to complain about officers treating the entire town as if it were suspect.

On December 1, Clark was laid to rest in the Ogden City Cemetery following funeral services in the LDS Second Ward meetinghouse. So many people attended the services that hundreds were forced to listen to eulogies while standing outside in the cold. A former state fish and game officer before joining the sheriff's department, Clark was born May 12, 1871, in Ogden, where he lived his entire life. He married Margarett Dallimore on November 7, 1907. The couple had no children.

Two days following Clark's burial, Weber County and the state of Utah offered a combined reward of $1,200 for the capture of the killer. Police efforts were bogging down and it was hoped that the money would convince someone in the bandit gang to turn the others in. It didn't work.

As weeks dragged into months and still no arrests were made, serious doubts began to arise that Clark's killer would ever be caught. But just when most were ready to give up, the police got a tip from a woman in Salt Lake City.

Three weeks following a dismal Christmas, Mrs. Herbert Preston was being

Herbert Preston confessed to his wife and detectives that he was part of the gang that murdered Weber County Deputy Seymore Clark. (Salt Lake Police Museum)

evicted from the shabby Salt Lake City apartment she occupied with her three children. Her husband, a known "hop fiend," had disappeared into Salt Lake's opium dens two weeks before, leaving her without support. Desperate, she turned to the LDS Church for assistance. The man sent by the church to assist was also a Salt Lake County deputy. After the deputy gave her ten dollars to cover the rent, Mrs. Preston broke down and told her benefactor that she thought her husband was involved in the murder of Clark.

According to Mrs. Preston, her husband had returned home on the morning of November 28, out of breath and in an agitated state. When his behavior indicated that he was hiding out in the apartment, Mrs. Preston asked him if he had killed the deputy. "No, but I was a party to it, although I did not shoot," Herbert Preston allegedly told her. "At the time I was unarmed, but [Frank] Burns, my companion, killed Clark."

Preston claimed that following the burglary a third man by the name of Shine was supposed to have loaded the boxes into a wagon and brought them to Salt Lake City for disposal. The arrival of the officers spoiled everything, and Preston fled when Burns began shooting at them. Two days later, Preston met up with Burns and asked him why he killed Clark. "I had to 'cop' the officer in order to get away," Burns told him.

After admitting this to his wife, Preston promptly vanished again. When news of his possible participation in the murder became known, officers began scouring Salt Lake's underworld, eventually locating Preston in an opium den, where he was arrested on February 5. Following his arrest, Preston supposedly repeated to Weber County deputies what he had told his wife. Wilson was ecstatic. Now that his deputies knew whom to look for, it wouldn't be long, the sheriff told reporters, before both Burns and Shine were also brought to justice.

Doubts concerning Preston's "confession" surfaced the following day. Salt Lake officers who arrested Preston called his confession the ramblings of a "hop head" and insisted that he could not be trusted with the truth even if he knew what it was. With the exception of Burns and Shine, everything that Preston told his wife about the murder had previously appeared in the newspapers. To make matters worse, by the time he had dried out in jail, Preston agreed with the officers and promptly recanted his confession. Still, Weber County detectives adamantly insisted that they had their man.

Although everyone was willing to admit that Preston had not pulled the trigger, he still represented the best lead officers had in tracking down the real killer, and they weren't about to let him go until he got his mind straight about what happened. Consequently, Preston sat in jail without bail for weeks, during which time he resisted attempts by detectives to get him to retract the retraction of his confession.

On April 6, Preston was arraigned in court and formally charged with burglarizing the boxcar the night Clark was murdered. He pleaded not guilty. Unable to post the required $500 bond, he was sent back to the Weber County jail to await trial. But without his confession, Weber County investigators had nothing to pin on Preston. When they failed to substantiate the charges against him with any hard evidence a month later, a judge ordered Preston released from jail.

Whether Preston was telling the truth regarding his involvement in Clark's murder can only be guessed at. Despite a plausible confession that included elements of the crime not widely known, he insisted that his confession was the fabricated result of a drug habit and the badgering of police officials. Furthermore, no trace of Burns or Shine was ever found.

Margarett never remarried. She died in Ogden on December 25, 1948, and is buried beside her husband.

While some killers of other police officers were able to elude capture through the years, their identities in every case eventually became known to the men pursuing them. Some were never caught; others were able to beat the charges in court. Without Preston, however, Weber County officers could not proceed with their investigation. They simply had no other suspects or leads. Although detectives continued to investigate his death for years, it was never determined who actually killed Clark. Today, his death remains the only unsolved murder of a Utah police officer.

John Murphy recovered from his wound, but it would not be his last brush with death as an officer. Ten years later, while working for the Ogden Police

Department, Murphy was shot in the face by a man he caught robbing a grocery store at Jefferson and 24th Street. Badly scarred, he recovered and later returned to work.

John H. Johnston
Salt Lake City Police Department
July 8, 1911

Following his arrest for the murder of Salt Lake City Police Sergeant John Henry Johnston, Elmer Dewey claimed that the killing was all a big mistake. The person he really wanted to murder was his loving wife, Minnie.

Well after midnight on July 5, 1911, Elmer and Minnie Dewey debated the matter of her being shot long and loud in their room at the Albert Hotel, 119 South on West Temple Street. Elmer, a cigar store clerk and sometimes informant for the Pinkerton Detective Agency, was drunk and armed with a pistol. Cursing at the top of his lungs, he accused Minnie of stepping out on him with "race track men."

The argument persisted until a guest in the room below them, Paris Campbell of Boulder, Colorado, finally had enough. Campbell knew Dewey, having previously had a few drinks with him in the hotel bar. Annoyed and concerned, Campbell went to the door of the Deweys' room and knocked. "I asked him to please keep quiet, as he was disturbing the other guests." Campbell later told a newspaper reporter. "I heard his wife say: 'Please don't point that gun at me.' I kept on knocking, and Dewey yelled that he would shoot me if I entered the room."

Fearful for Minnie's well-being, Campbell took a chance and stepped inside the room. He was able to convince Dewey to put a Colt .32-20 revolver down on a nearby bureau, but, as Minnie Dewey moved toward the gun, Dewey snatched it back up. At that moment, summoned by a telephone call, the police entered the room, led by Sergeant Johnston. The brawny sergeant faced Dewey, stepping in front of Campbell as Officer Dennis Sullivan and Special Officer Frank Riley waited in the doorway. "What's the matter here?" Johnston asked, moving toward Dewey.

Dewey backed away from the police sergeant until he came up against a wall. As Johnston moved closer, Dewey fired, striking the officer in the center of the stomach. Mortally wounded, Johnston was able to grab Dewey by the shoulders and pull him to the floor. "He stepped in front of me just as Dewey shot, or I would have been hit by the bullet myself," Campbell said later.

Marked for death by the owners of Plum Alley opium dens, Sergeant John Henry Johnston was killed instead during a common domestic quarrel in a Salt Lake City hotel. (Salt Lake Police Museum)

At the sound of the shot, Riley and Sullivan charged through the door and tore the revolver out of Dewey's hand. As Dewey pleaded with the officers to leave him alone, he was manhandled out to a waiting patrol wagon and taken to the police station. Minnie Dewey was taken into custody as a material witness.

Although Dewey had never been in trouble before, the police were acquainted with him. A native of Durango, Colorado, Dewey had come to Salt Lake City six years before and found work in a cigar store on 200 South. Several months prior to the shooting, Dewey affiliated himself with the Pinkerton Detective Agency. He liked to brag that he was a detective, but, in fact, he was an informant, associating with criminals in order to get information that he then turned over to his employers. Minnie Dewey, an aspiring actress and singer, was from Brigham City. The couple became well known for their neurotic behavior and the frequent disturbances they caused when one or both had been drinking.

News of the shooting spread swiftly through the police ranks. Originally from New York, John H. Johnston came to Salt Lake City from Leadville, Colorado, where he worked as a miner. After trying his hand at mining in Utah, Johnston opted for a change in professions and became a member of the police department in 1899. He was promoted to sergeant in 1907, just days before the murder of Officer Charles Ford. Johnston was an imaginative and aggressive police officer, who at one time actually commandeered a railway engine to chase down a group of thugs responsible for a series of street-car holdups. He was also previously "marked" for death because of his law enforcement activity in the opium dens of Salt Lake's notorious Plum Alley.

An informant for the Pinkerton Detective Agency, Elmer Dewey wanted to shoot his wife for stepping out on him with "race track men." Dewey served less than eight years for the murder of Sergeant Johnston. (Utah Department of Corrections)

When not on duty, the forty-two-year-old father of two lived with his wife, Tishia, at 1172 Emerson Avenue.

Given the surgical practices of the day, stomach wounds were nearly always fatal. Consequently, little hope was held for Johnston's recovery. He was rushed first to the police emergency hospital, where Father F. Corcoran of St. Mary's administered the last rites of the Catholic Church. Afterward, the sergeant was taken to St. Mark's, arriving nearly dead from the loss of blood. At St. Mark's, surgeons performed an operation and discovered ten separate holes in Johnston's intestines. There was nothing they could do but sew him back up and let nature take its course. Remarkably, Johnston began to rally the day after the shooting. Although doctors warned them not to be overly optimistic, Johnston's family began hoping that his rugged constitution would pull him through. Prayers at his bedside increased.

Doctors weren't the only ones concerned about Johnston's chances of survival. The angry muttering of his officers made Salt Lake City Police Chief S.M. Barlow nervous about what might happen to Dewey in the city jail if Johnston were to die. Shortly after midnight on July 6, detectives slipped Dewey out of his cell and whisked him to the state prison for safekeeping. Following her release from custody, Minnie Dewey visited her husband at the prison, where they prayed together for Johnston's recovery. Minnie told news reporters that Johnston could prove that her husband hadn't intended to commit murder.

"Johnston knows it was all an accident," Mrs. Dewey said time after time. "The policeman jumped at Elmer and tried to take the revolver away from him. They grappled and fell to the floor. The revolver was not discharged until after they were on the floor, and then by accident."

Minnie Christensen Dewey swore she would stand by her husband but later divorced him for being a convicted felon. Her histrionics were in evidence during both of Dewey's trials. (*Salt Lake Herald*)

Although Dewey claimed that he could not remember shooting Johnston, he gave a lengthy interview to a newspaper reporter in which he admitted that he intended to shoot his wife. Dewey's recollections of the events, which he would later recant during his trials, were clear to the point of the actual pulling of the trigger. "I was crazy drunk," Dewey said. "I don't remember what Johnston said to me. I knew him. I have seen him lots of times and never had any trouble with him in my life. I had it in my brain to kill my wife and myself, too. I know I had the gun cocked in my hand."

By the evening of July 7, Johnston was fighting for his life. Infection had set in and the family priest was called to the hospital. Shortly before dawn on July 8, Johnston rallied one last time. He raised his hands and looked at them. "Well, doctor," he said. "I have pretty good color and I'm going to get well." He died ten hours later.

Johnston was buried in Salt Lake's Mount Calvary Cemetery on July 11. Fifty police officers led by Sergeant Nephi Pierce escorted the body from the mortuary to St. Mary's Catholic Church. After the services, mounted officers led the procession to the cemetery as a band played the "Dead March." Pierce and one of the mounted officers, David Crowther, would later be murdered in the line of duty.

On July 12, a visibly dazed Dewey was arraigned in court on a charge of first-degree murder. His attorney, C. Stanley Price, said that his client's current mental stupor was the result of his having been pounded on the head with a metal object for ten minutes by the arresting officers. Price said that officers then placed Dewey in the patrol wagon and beat him all the way to police headquarters. Neither claim was supported by photographs of Dewey taken within a day or two of his arrest. The facts notwithstanding, Price asked that the charges against Dewey be dropped. The judge thought differently, and Dewey was ordered to stand trial on a charge of first-degree murder.

The trial, which began December 8, became a stage primarily for the histrionics of Minnie Dewey and Dewey's mother, Margaret Mueller. Dressed in black, Johnston's widow attended the trial with her younger daughter. News reporters closely monitored the reactions of all three women as much as they did the trial itself. Mrs. Johnston sat through much of the trial with her daughter on her lap. She rarely spoke or showed emotion. Conversely, the behavior of Mrs. Dewey and Mrs. Mueller included frequent and loud gasps, prolonged bouts of weeping, and soulful looks directed at Elmer Dewey.

Dewey pleaded temporary insanity. Witnesses described his behavior before the event as intoxicated and anguished, brought on by the infidelities of his wife. Minnie Dewey took the stand and, while not admitting to any adulterous behavior per se, said that her husband's current plight was the result of her having "many friends."

Witnesses to the shooting, in particular Riley and a *Salt Lake Tribune* newsman who had accompanied the officers to the scene, testified that when the gun was pulled from Dewey's hand, it was cocked and ready to fire; a clear indication, said the prosecution, that the shooting was not an accident and that Dewey intended to fire a second time.

On December 15, after deliberating for fourteen hours, the jury returned a verdict of guilty. However, they recommended a life sentence rather than execution. Upon hearing the verdict, Dewey's mother promptly fainted. Minnie Dewey became hysterical, throwing herself to the floor and thrashing her way under a table. Court deputies finally dragged her into the hall.

Dewey was sentenced to life in prison while appeals were filed with higher courts. In 1913, the Utah Supreme Court ordered a new trial, citing errors in the way his insanity plea was handled by the lower court.

On October 27, 1913, Dewey entered into a plea agreement with prosecutors. Rather than go through the rigors of another trial, he would plead guilty to second-degree murder. Prosecutors agreed to the charge primarily because the passage of time had substantially reduced their case against Dewey. Witnesses staying at the Albert Hotel on the night of the murder had since scattered and would be almost impossible to locate. Also, Special Officer Riley, one of the prosecution's star witnesses, had since died.

Minnie, who claimed to have received offers from a New York acting company, made another dramatic appearance to support her husband. When Judge Frederick C. Loofbuorow sentenced Dewey to fourteen years, Minnie vowed to reporters that she would stand by Elmer no matter how long it took for him to become a free man. Her promise lasted less than a year. Seven months later, Minnie filed for divorce, charging Dewey with non-support. When a judge pointed out that her husband was in prison and therefore had a legitimate explanation for said lack of support, Minnie amended her complaint, citing Dewey with being a convicted felon. There was no arguing with that, and the divorce was granted on May 22, 1914.

Three years later, Dewey, a model prisoner by then, was paroled despite a petition of protest signed by eighty-five members of the police department, including four officers who would eventually die in the line of duty. Following his parole, Dewey remained in Salt Lake for a short time, working as a bookkeeper. In September 1918, Dewey applied for a pardon that would allow him to leave the state of Utah, claiming that because of the war against Germany, he was urgently needed to work in a Seattle shipyard. The pardon was granted. The war ended two months later. In 1933, the *Salt Lake Tribune* reported that Dewey was living in Texas.

Tishia Johnston remained in Salt Lake, where she finished raising her children. She died in 1944 and was laid to rest beside her husband.

Francis Allan Colclough

Midvale Police Department
August 7, 1912

Several days before he was shot and killed during the attempted robbery of a saloon, Midvale Night Marshal Frank A. Colclough, 55, had a series of dreams about his death. Colclough confided to friends that in the dreams he was confronted by the vague forms of two armed thugs outlined against a saloon bar. Unable to shake the premonitions, Colclough swore that if the dreams ever materialized into reality he would do his duty or die in the attempt.

Midvale Night Marshal Frank Colclough wearing the uniform of a Midvale volunteer fireman. The fiery Scotsman had a premonition that he would shoot it out with the robbers of a Midvale saloon. (Colclough family)

Although Colclough's dream came true a few days later, the dream was perhaps born more of injured pride than a vision of the future. Colclough, a proud man, had recently suffered a personal affront in the form of a saloon robbery on his beat. On July 29, Colclough narrowly missed capturing two men who held up the Vincent Saloon when he walked through the front door just as the robbers fled out the back. Colclough gave chase, but the robbers got away. In the days following the robbery, he told friends and co-workers that he thought the robbers would strike again, and that he would be ready for them when they did.

Colclough was the kind of man who took such things personally. Born February 27, 1857, in Paisley, Scotland, he married Annie Murrin in 1879 in Glasgow. In 1884, the couple immigrated to Utah, settling in Salt Lake City, where Colclough worked for the Utah Light & Railway Company. In 1906, he moved his wife and their four children to Midvale and soon established himself as a machinist and a prominent figure in town. A man of considerable talent and energies, Colclough was a member of the fraternal order of Woodmen of the World as well as a charter member of the Midvale Volunteer Fire Department.

On January 1, 1912, Colclough was appointed the night marshal of Midvale. His duties included patrolling the town's business district and ensuring that the saloons closed on time. The Bingham Highway passed directly into the town, bringing a constant flow of rough trade from the mines. It was the night marshal's job to make sure that this traffic did not adversely affect the town after dark. In that respect, Colclough was more than capable. If any of Midvale's residents doubted the night marshal's other abilities, none questioned his devotion to duty or his courage.

On August 7, Colclough not only was laboring under the self-imposed humiliation of the Vincent Saloon robbery but was grief-stricken as well. Earlier that morning the four-month-old child of his daughter Margaret Le Page passed away. Colclough asked Midvale Marshal R.W. Stokes for permission to leave his post early in order to get some sleep before the funeral the following day. Stokes agreed, telling Colclough to go home as soon as the saloons were shut up for the night.

Colclough was still on duty at 9:30 p.m., making his final rounds. He stopped in at the Vienna Saloon to visit with his friend, bartender Paul Scherich. The two men talked about the Vincent robbery. Coclough stepped behind the bar to demonstrate how he expected to deal with the two robbers if they struck again. "If I had been there, I would have got one of those fellows anyway, or died in the attempt," Colclough said.

At that moment the door of the saloon burst open and two men with handkerchiefs tied over their faces and pistols drawn entered. The *Deseret Evening News* published the following account:

> "Throw up your hands," ordered the taller of the two men. The marshal instinctively reached for his revolver, hesitated, then raised his hands. Scherich quickly raised his hands, as did customers in the back of the saloon.
>
> "Now, where's this night marshal? We're going to kill him," cried one of the robbers.
>
> "I'm the town marshal," bravely replied Marshal Colclough, and quick as a flash, he drew his revolver and fired. At the same instant the robber fired. The shots were almost as one, and the officer and the larger of the two robbers sank to the floor together.

A pitched battle followed. Approximately twenty shots were fired in the small room as Colclough and others shot it out with the robbers. Scherich snatched a revolver from under the bar and blazed away at the other bandit, who began backing toward the door. A customer seized an old rifle from the wall and fired it in the general direction of the robbers. The heavy slug ripped through the wall and shattered the legs of William and James Kastrinskis, two brothers walking toward the saloon for a drink.

When the smoke cleared, Colclough was dead, while the larger of the two robbers lay mortally wounded. Colclough had been struck by three .38-caliber bullets, one through the center of his chest, one toward the back of his head, and the last through his left wrist. The dying robber had been hit four times by both Colclough and Scherich, the most serious wound above his right eye penetrating to the back of his head. The second robber escaped, apparently unscathed.

Salt Lake County Deputy Sheriff Ira Beckstead arrived while smoke from the battle was still thick. He found the wounded robber humming a tune and crawling around on the floor. Beckstead pulled the suspect to his feet and stripped off his mask, revealing a white male in his late twenties. The bleeding bandit offered no resistance as the deputy marched him a quarter of a mile to the city jail.

Despite the seriousness of his wounds, the captured robber was conversant. He refused to answer Beckstead's questions about the identity of his companion, whom he claimed to have met just that day; instead, he began singing "Silver Threads Among the Gold." A doctor treated the other wounds to his wrist, leg, and knee, but there was little to be done about the hole in his head.

"This was my first trick," the robber muttered. A few minutes later, the man lapsed into unconsciousness. He was moved to St. Mark's Hospital the

Jack Callahan, whom many thought to be the mastermind behind the saloon holdups. He was never convicted of the robbery and subsequent gun battle. (Utah Department of Corrections)

following day, where he died of a blood clot in his brain on August 10. On August 9, Midvale and Governor William Spry offered a combined reward of $1,000 for the capture of his unidentified partner.

While his killer was being escorted to jail, several men carried Colclough's body to an undertaker. Less than an hour later, his wife and daughter Agnes returned from Salt Lake City, where they had spent the day in preparation for the funeral of their granddaughter and niece. Unaware of the new tragedy, the two women returned to Midvale on the same streetcar carrying newspaper reporters rushing to cover the story of the battle. When the women reached Midvale and were informed of Colclough's death, they collapsed with grief.

Within a day of the murder, officers established the identity of the dead robber as Charles A. Gammett. Although never certain where Gammett originally came from, authorities were able to prove that he had worked in Alta during the early summer before coming to work in the Highland Boy Mine at Bingham. Evidence gathered in Bingham made him the prime suspect in the July 1 robbery of the Yampa Saloon as well as the murder of a man in an isolated part of that canyon. Witnesses said he also matched the general description of one of the two men who robbed the Vincent Saloon and eluded Colclough.

Funeral services for Colclough were held August 11 at the Woodmen of the World Hall in Salt Lake City. LDS bishop and Midvale Mayor Joseph B. Wright, who came to America with Colclough aboard the same ship, spoke warmly of the dead officer. "I had been associated with Marshal Colclough many times ... and I always found him to be a friend and as honest, straightforward and reliable as any man of my acquaintance," said Wright.

Colclough's body was escorted to the Salt Lake City Cemetery by a platoon of Salt Lake City police officers, Midvale fire department members, and a drill team from the Woodmen of the World.

On August 14, newspapers announced that authorities had identified Gammett's companion as thirty-year-old Jack Callahan. A search of Gammett's quarters by police revealed that the two men roomed together while working at the Highland Boy. Officers also discovered that Callahan had fled to Montana following the bloodbath in the Vienna Saloon. Wanted circulars were sent to Butte, where police arrested Callahan on August 18 as he prepared to board a train for Missoula.

Salt Lake County Sheriff Joseph C. Sharp immediately dispatched Deputy Otto Witbeck to Butte. There, Callahan admitted being Gammett's roommate but denied participating in the robbery and said that he would fight extradition to Utah. Within hours, however, Callahan changed his mind. An ongoing investigation by Butte officers had connected him with two armed robberies that occurred there in March, including one resulting in the murder of a bartender and the wounding of a police officer. Talk in Butte centered on a nocturnal lengthening of Callahan's neck, making him more than eager to waive extradition proceedings.

On August 20, Witbeck returned to Utah with Callahan. That same day, Callahan was taken to the Midvale jail, where seven witnesses identified him as Gammett's partner. The following day, he pleaded not guilty when arraigned on a charge of first-degree murder before Justice J.A. Williams.

Callahan would not stand trial, however. Charges against him were dismissed at a preliminary hearing in October, when authorities were unable to provide sufficient evidence directly linking him to the crime. By then officers had arrested another man.

Jack Murphy was arrested September 7 while working in the Snake Creek tunnel nine miles north of Heber City. He was arrested largely on the strength of some ongoing correspondence with Callahan in Butte. Brought to Midvale, Murphy was eventually identified as J.A. Hill. According to witnesses, he and Callahan had been seen together with Gammett the day before Colclough was murdered. Hill was charged with first-degree murder. The trial, which began March 25, 1913, produced a guilty verdict ten days later. Unfortunately, the prosecution's evidence was entirely circumstantial, and Hill's attorneys immediately appealed. On January 14, 1914, the Utah Supreme Court reversed the conviction. Hill was not retried.

Tragedy was not finished with the Colclough family. Following the death of her father, Agnes Colclough became engaged to William "Billie" Nelson, a local boilermaker's helper. Nelson, just twenty-one, had an interest in law enforcement and was hired by Midvale as a temporary augmentation to the city's police force during the Christmas holiday, a position he had briefly held two years before. On December 25, 1912, just hours into his first shift, Nelson was shot to death by a group of men he and the regular night marshal were attempting to detain for firing pistols into the air. While the men were being questioned, one in the group crept up behind Nelson and fired a shot into the back of his head. The killers scattered and were never caught.

Thomas F. Griffiths
Salt Lake City Police Department
June 25, 1913

Shortly before 10:30 a.m. on the morning of June 25, 1913, Peter Masi lurched out of the Shamrock Saloon, 219 West 200 South, bleeding from a razor cut on his right shoulder. He had just lost an argument with another man over who was going to pay for a round of drinks. Within a few minutes, Masi located Salt Lake City Patrolman Thomas Griffiths, 47, walking his beat. The short, congenial officer whom everyone liked was in exceptionally good humor. Griffiths's youngest daughter, Winnie, had celebrated her first birthday the previous day by having her photograph taken.

Masi told Griffiths that an Italian immigrant named Giovanni Anselmo had cut him after Anselmo lost a roll of dice and refused to pay for drinks. The news surprised Griffiths, who knew the suspect. The twenty-three-year-old Anselmo lived quietly with his father and was not known as a troublemaker. The younger Anselmo, who worked as a tailor, had come to Utah three years before from the Calabria region of Italy.

Griffiths was an immigrant himself. Born in South Wales on November 12, 1865, Griffiths came to Utah while still a young man. He married Lydia Beynon, the sister of a Salt Lake City patrolman. The couple eventually had six children and lived at 1056 Pierpont Avenue.

Griffiths started his police career late in life. On June 12, 1907, at the age of forty-one, he was appointed to the police department. He patrolled an area of Salt Lake City known as Greek Town. He was highly regarded by Greek Town's ethnic population as an easygoing man who knew everyone and rarely resorted to arrests as a means of settling disputes.

Griffiths tried to calm the injured Masi, who claimed that Anselmo was crazy. "Oh, don't worry, Pete," Griffiths said. "He won't do anything bad, I guess." Griffiths and Masi returned to the saloon. There they learned that

Anselmo had gone next door to the Milwaukee Cafe. In fact, Anselmo had bought a gun before going to the cafe. Griffiths located Anselmo in the cafe and told him that he was under arrest and would have to come down to the station. Anselmo complied, stumbling along beside the officer. The two men, with Masi trailing along, walked across 200 South to a call box on the northeast corner of 200 West. Griffiths opened the box, intending to ring for a car to take Anselmo to the station. As he was placing the call, Anselmo broke and ran. Griffiths immediately gave chase. Although Anselmo was younger, Griffiths was an accomplished track and field man.

Anselmo ran across the street and through a lot behind the Sweet Candy Company at 224 South 200 West. Griffiths caught him there and the two scuffled briefly before Anselmo threw the officer against a pole. As Griffiths tried to recover, Anselmo pulled a pistol and fired three shots.

One of the first two shots struck Griffiths under his right shoulder blade, exiting through his chest. The second inflicted a superficial wound in his left shoulder. Griffiths sank to his knees. People watching in horror from the surrounding windows testified later that Anselmo steadied his aim and then deliberately shot Griffiths in the forehead.

Salt Lake City fireman J.B. Kilpatrick was riding a streetcar past the location of the murder when he heard the shots and spotted Anselmo running away. Jumping off the streetcar, Kilpatrick and another man ran to aid Griffiths. Loading the wounded officer into an automobile, they rushed him to the emergency hospital at the police station where Griffiths breathed his last just as they carried him inside.

Word of the killing spread rapidly. Within minutes, a crowd of several hundred citizens gathered outside police headquarters. Griffiths's murder was the second killing of a law enforcement nature in two weeks. On June 10, C.G. VanDenAkker, a night watchman, was murdered by a burglary suspect at 1177 East South Temple. Fed up by the growing lawlessness, the crowd demanded to be included in the search for Anselmo. Uniformed officers and detectives raced to the scene and began combing the alleys and bars for Anselmo. Mayor Samuel C. Park went to police headquarters and offered a reward of $500 for the killer's capture. Park's automobile was pressed into service to take policemen to various points in an effort to close off and search the city.

Ford P. Driggs, a former police officer and co-worker of Griffiths, heard about the murder just as he was in the process of selling his old police revolver at a nearby pawn shop. Snatching the gun away from the merchant, Driggs shouted, "the deal's off!" and ran out. He spent the entire day in Greek Town searching for the killer.

Officer Thomas F. "Little Tommy" Griffiths was well known for his beautiful singing voice and patient manner. (Salt Lake Police Museum)

A car was sent to Griffiths's home, where his wife received news of the shooting. Brought to the station, Mrs. Griffiths fainted as soon as she saw her husband's body. Placed under a physician's care, she was taken back to the family home.

Officers arrested several men matching Anselmo's description, but none proved to be the killer. Police brought Frank Anselmo to the station for questioning. Distraught by the news of Griffiths's death, Frank Anselmo could not or would not provide information as to his son's whereabouts. But officers believed that he was hiding something. They had followed him during the day and observed him going to the homes of friends and then to the offices of a steamship company. They were certain that the elder Anselmo was attempting to raise funds to send his son back to Italy.

For ten hours the police department turned Salt Lake City upside down looking for Anselmo. Vagrants who even remotely matched the description were hauled in for questioning. Bars and brothels were raided—all for naught. Just when officers began to believe that he had successfully escaped their dragnet, they got a tip from someone who knew where Anselmo was hiding.

At 9:15 p.m., a woman living at 5 Love's Court (550 South 450 West) telephoned police headquarters with the news that she had seen her neighbors Mike and Mary Anselmo hiding a young man in a shed behind their apartment. Minutes earlier, Alice Cook had witnessed a search of the Anselmo residence by police officers looking for the killer. As the officers were going in the front door, Cook said she saw Mary Anselmo escort a young man out the back door and to the shed.

Officers returned to Love's Court and began surrounding the shed. As the officers closed in on him in the dark, Anselmo burst out of the shed and ran down a narrow lane.

As he began to draw a pistol from inside his coat, police opened fire. Patrolman J.P. Emery fired twice, grazing the killer's chest. Motorcycle patrolman W.H. Hendrickson then shot Anselmo in the left buttock, punching a hole through his wallet and knocking him down. The killer was still waving the gun and trying to get back on his feet as officers surrounded him. Several officers took deliberate aim, but Captain Emil V. Johnson ordered them not to fire. Instead, they jumped on Anselmo, kicking the pistol out of his hand and dragging him to a car for transportation to police headquarters. Along the way, Anselmo wept and said he hadn't intended to kill Griffiths. "I no mean to killa him," he sobbed. "I drunk this morning. I mean to shoot other Italian."

When the car arrived at the station, it was immediately surrounded by a group of grim police officers. "Little Tommy" had been their friend and the officers wanted a few minutes alone with his killer. Events of the day might have turned worse if not for Johnson, who leapt in and sternly faced his men. "Remember, boys, you are sworn officers of the law, and the law must be upheld at any cost," Johnson said. "You have captured your man, and it is your duty to see that the law takes its course."

Johnson's men backed down. Their hands were soon full keeping a crowd of more than one thousand people from becoming unruly as news of the capture spread.

Anselmo was taken into the emergency hospital where a doctor examined his wound and determined that the bullet had lodged in his groin. Deciding that the bullet wouldn't be worth the trouble to remove, Anselmo was bandaged and tossed into a cell. For the next few days, he refused to talk or eat.

Salt Lake City tried to do right by the Griffiths family. Benefits were held for Griffiths's widow and children, the money going toward paying off the mortgage on the family home. Greek Town, where Griffiths had walked a beat for so many years, also collected money for the family's relief. The city donated a burial plot and agreed to carry Griffiths on the police payroll for an additional two months.

On June 29, Griffiths was laid to rest in the Salt Lake City Cemetery under the direction of the Mount Moriah Masonic Lodge. At the graveside, the Sons and Daughters of Wales Society sang an ancient Welsh hymn known to have been a favorite of the dead officer.

A week later, still suffering from his wound, Anselmo was brought before Justice Harry S. Harper for a preliminary hearing. Ironically, Anselmo, who spoke little English, had to rely on the man he initially assaulted to interpret for him. Anselmo complained about the medical attention he was receiving and insisted that he hadn't intended to shoot Griffiths but instead was trying to kill Masi, who he claimed had beaten him during an argument. He then asked for a lawyer.

Anselmo eventually pleaded not guilty by reason of insanity. On December 15, his trial got under way before Third District Judge Frederick C. Loofbourow. The prosecution was slightly hampered in the beginning. Masi, terrified that vengeful Anselmo friends and family members would kill him if he testified, left town shortly after the preliminary hearing and was not seen again. However, four other people testified that they saw Anselmo kill Griffiths.

Two days after the trial began, tragedy struck the Griffiths family again when little Winnie died. The cause of death was officially determined as gastritis, but family members believed that drugs prescribed to calm Lydia's nerves were passed on to Winnie by nursing. She was buried near her father. The death of her youngest daughter so unhinged Lydia Griffiths that she had to be closely monitored by a physician.

Attorney W.H. King attempted to show that the Anselmo family suffered from "psychic epilepsy," a condition brought on by stress like that Giovanni Anselmo suffered during his fight with Masi and subsequent arrest by Griffiths. King produced fifteen depositions taken from Anselmo friends and relatives living in Italy, testifying that the epilepsy was common among Anselmos and in some cases rendered moronic those afflicted.

The jury didn't agree. On January 1, 1914, after deliberating nearly twenty hours—primarily over whether to show mercy—the jurors returned a "guilty as charged" verdict. Two weeks later, Anselmo was sentenced to death.

A two-year appeal process began. Anselmo's case eventually came to the attention of the Utah Supreme Court, which overturned his conviction based on the admission of hearsay evidence in the first trial. A new trial was ordered. On January 22, 1916, just days before the new trial was to begin, Anselmo abruptly pleaded guilty to a charge of second-degree murder. King believed that his client's good behavior while a prisoner during the last two years would reflect favorably on him before the parole board.

Anselmo was sentenced to life at hard labor. For the next three years, he worked on the state road crew while filing petitions for parole. Beyond a continual insistence that he didn't belong in prison, Anselmo caused little trouble.

On November 22, 1919, while working at a state road camp above Castle Gate, Anselmo received word that his petition for parole had been denied by the state Board of Pardons. Fearing that the news would prompt Anselmo to make a break from the work gang, Warden George A. Storrs ordered him returned to the state prison in Salt Lake City, where a closer watch could be

Giovanni Anselmo, following his arrest for the murder of Griffiths. The Italian immigrant carried a bullet in his buttocks received while attempting to flee from arresting officers. Prison could not hold Anselmo. Following the parole board's denial of a commutation of his sentence, he escaped and reportedly fled to Italy. (Utah State Department of Corrections)

kept on him. It was too late. Shortly after breakfast on the following day, a guard sent to fetch Anselmo from his tent discovered it empty.

Camp officials believed that Anselmo either jumped into the waiting automobile of a friend or was driven out of the camp district by a stranger. Although the search lasted for months, Anselmo was never recaptured. Authorities believed that he hid out briefly in the mountains before eventually making his way back to Italy.

After the death of her husband, Lydia Griffiths was given a job cleaning the police department, a position she held for five years. She eventually remarried. She died in 1953 and was buried next to "Little Tommy" and Winnie in the Salt Lake City Cemetery.

John W. "Billy" Grant
Bingham Police Department

Nephi S. Jensen
Otto Witbeck
Salt Lake County Sheriff's Office
November 21, 1913

Utah law enforcement suffered its worst tragedy in 1913, when a Bingham Canyon miner killed six men and held the entire state of Utah at bay for more than a month before vanishing into the blackness of a mine. Three of the murdered men were police officers, and their deaths rocked Utah law enforcement to its foundation.

It began with the killing of one Latino by another, a murder that in normal times would have barely warranted mention in local newspapers. There was nothing unusual about bloodshed during Utah's mining boom, particularly among ethnic groups inhabiting the rough-and-tumble town of Bingham. The mines attracted large populations of Serbs, Croats, Greeks, and Italians, many of whom brought their Old World blood feuds to Utah.

But if there was one group universally disliked by all the others, it was the Mexicans. In 1912, area mining companies broke a long and bitter strike called by the Western Federation of Miners when they imported more than 150 Mexican laborers. The Hispanics who remained in the area following the strike occupied the lowest rung on Bingham's troubled social ladder. Violence between the various groups, but especially violence directed at the Mexican community, was common.

Shortly after midnight on November 21, 1918, Salt Lake County Deputy Julius Sorenson was called to the front of the McKensie Boardinghouse in Sap Gap, an unincorporated area of the county near Bingham. The fifty-eight-year-old lawman and Spanish-American War veteran found the body of Juan Valdez sprawled in the muddy road, shot through the heart. Standing nearby was Thomas Carrillo, bleeding from facial lacerations.

Carillo told Sorenson that "Ralph" (actually Rafael) Lopez had pistol-whipped him, then shot Valdez when the latter attempted to intervene with a knife. Sorenson promptly arrested Carrillo and hauled him off to jail as a material witness. It wasn't that the deputy did not believe Carrillo, but rather that he knew Lopez. He also had a more than passing familiarity with the transient nature of the mining population. If Lopez didn't find Carrillo later and kill him, it was entirely possible that Carrillo would have second thoughts about testifying against Lopez and take off for parts unknown. Sorenson wanted to make sure that his case was strong, and that meant that any witnesses had to stick around.

Sorenson had arrested Lopez on two prior occasions. The first occurred in July when Lopez stabbed another man during a saloon brawl. Based largely on the testimony of Carillo, Lopez served two weeks in the county jail. After his release, Lopez again ran afoul of Sorenson when he reportedly used a rifle to bludgeon two Greek miners attempting to accost two young girls on the road between Bingham and the Highland Boy Mine. Although he claimed that Sorenson had it in for him, and that he was merely protecting the girls, Lopez again served a short term in jail.

When Lopez confronted Carrillo and Valdez in front of the boardinghouse, it is possible that he did not intend to kill anyone. He tried to push a fight with Carrillo and ended up striking him with a pistol. But when Valdez pulled a knife, Lopez promptly shot him. Knowing that Sorenson would be after him, and that time in prison for this crime would not be a short stretch, Lopez went into the boardinghouse and got his rifle. He then set off through the falling snow into the mountains above the mining camp.

There are many versions of who exactly Rafael Lopez was. James Thomas Powell of Lehi, who worked with Lopez for two years in the Mercur Canyon mines, gave one account to the *Salt Lake Tribune* on November 29, 1913. According to Powell, Rafael Lopez was more Anglo than Hispanic. The twenty-seven-year-old son of a Spanish father and an English mother, Lopez was born in Colorado. Before coming to Utah, he spent considerable time in Colorado as well as in Mexico and Wyoming. In Wyoming, Lopez reportedly owned a small ranch before he was sent to prison at Rawlins for two years on a manslaughter charge. He arrived in Utah in 1910, worked in Mercur Canyon, and became friends with Powell. (It should be noted that Lopez was also believed by some to be a native of Texas. Furthermore, the Wyoming State Archives has no record of Lopez serving time in that state.)

After knocking around the mining camps of Utah and Nevada, Lopez and Powell eventually parted company and Powell returned to his home in Lehi. Lopez arrived in Bingham sometime in February 1913, where he found few jobs available for Hispanics. Although an American citizen and by his own estimation a "white man," Lopez encountered an enormous amount of animosity from the Slavic community and city officials. Lacking employment opportunities, Lopez went into business for himself. He found a partner, and the two men explored old mines, searching for promising silver leads to lease from the larger mining companies.

Although Lopez was a violent man when pushed, it was said that he got along well with most people. His partner and other miners remembered him as friendly and a hard worker. He was respected enough in his business dealings to acquire a sizeable line of credit with the Miners Mercantile Company at Highland Boy. Lopez was also considered something of a ladies' man, alternately courting a woman who lived in the local boardinghouse and a prostitute in Bingham's red-light district. Following the death of Valdez, stories circulated that the killing was actually the result of a feud Lopez had with Valdez over the affections of a Bingham prostitute.

None of that mattered to Sorenson, who now had a dangerous murderer to catch. Lopez was smart and strong. Catching him would not be easy. After scouting around the boardinghouse and discovering Lopez's tracks leading into the mountain, Sorenson saw that he would need help. He telephoned Chief

Deputy Otto Witbeck and told him what had happened. The two lawmen agreed that Lopez would strike over the mountains toward Tooele. Because the killer was on foot and it was snowing, Sorenson and Witbeck concluded that running him down would not be too much trouble. However, capturing him might be.

Neither deputy was a novice at tracking the worst kind of men. At forty, Witbeck had been a lawman for years. Born and raised in Levan, he spent his boyhood helping his family tend sheep herds between Scipio and the San Rafael Swell. Later, he lived in Silver City and worked the tough Tintic mining district as a Juab County deputy. After a couple of years as a fireman for Salt Lake City, Witbeck joined the Salt Lake County Sheriff's Department in time for the vicious mining strike of 1912. His wife, Marie, and the couple's two teenage children lived at 2405 Walnut Avenue, Salt Lake City. Before leaving to track Lopez, Witbeck called Marie and told her that he would be home in time for Thanksgiving.

Sorenson also was married and was the father of nine children. Despite his age, the Danish-born immigrant was hard as nails. His fondness for guns, the outdoors, and horses made him perfectly suited to go after Lopez.

Even with their experience, the lawmen had a tough time locating Lopez. He had several hours head start on them and was taking a circular route. By 9:00 a.m. Sorenson and Witbeck realized that Lopez was not heading for Tooele but instead seemed to be turning south toward Utah Lake. They stopped at the United States Mine and used the telephone to call for assistance from Salt Lake County Deputy Nephi S. Jensen and Bingham Marshal Billy Grant.

Over the phone, the lawmen hatched a plan to catch Lopez between them. Witbeck and Sorenson would continue tracking the killer while Grant and Jensen went to Lark in an effort to head him off. They failed to take into consideration Lopez's stamina. The killer moved so fast that he was out of the mountains and into Utah County before the trap could be sprung. Frustrated, the lawmen joined forces in Lark and continued on the trail.

By dusk, with the lawmen closing in on him, Lopez came upon the cabin of Edward and Rose Jones, located west of Utah Lake and four miles north of Pelican Point. Exhausted and hungry, Lopez stopped at the cabin and asked Mrs. Jones for something to eat. He was wolfing his food when he spotted the four lawmen riding toward the cabin in the distance. Snatching up his rifle, he slipped out the door and ran into a greasewood thicket, where he concealed himself in an irrigation ditch and watched as the lawmen closed in.

A quarter of a mile from the cabin the four officers stopped to plan their approach. They had seen a man enter the cabin and had a good idea that it was Lopez. They decided that Grant and Jensen would stay back and keep watch while Witbeck and Sorenson approached the cabin.

Bingham City Police Chief John "Billy" Grant died in an ambush near Utah Lake while searching for Rafael Lopez. (Salt Lake County Sheriff's Office)

Lopez watched as two of the horsemen went to the cabin and talked to Mrs. Jones. The other two men began ambling their horses in his direction. He waited until they closed to within a hundred yards. From the cover of the irrigation ditch, Lopez opened fire, shooting Grant and Jensen from their horses. Grant was killed instantly. Jensen was hit in the lower back, the bullet lodging in his groin. The shots attracted the attention of Witbeck and Sorenson, who began riding toward the riderless horses, scanning the field for Grant and Jensen. A third shot drove Witbeck out of the saddle. Sorenson's life was spared when his horse reared, dumping him to the ground. One account claims that the killer's rifle snapped on a defective cartridge as he tried to shoot Sorenson.

Witbeck shouted that he was hit, pointing in the direction that the shots had come from. Sorenson began firing at the brush but Lopez was already moving away. Sorenson crawled to Witbeck, who was in agony. Cupping snow in his hand, Sorenson melted it, letting the water trickle into Witbeck's mouth. Witbeck gave Sorenson messages for his family before lapsing into unconsciousness. Sorenson then jumped up and ran back to the cabin.

Rose Jones was already on the telephone. As soon as she heard gunfire, she began calling for help. She turned the phone over to Sorenson when the lawman burst in with tears in his eyes. Within minutes, police officers, a doctor, and some citizens were converging on the Jones ranch.

Witbeck died before Sorenson could get help to move him. Sorenson and Harold L. Jones, a brother-in-law of Mrs. Jones, searched for the two missing officers. They found Grant dead and Jensen still alive. They carried Jensen to the cabin, where Mrs. Jones attempted to stanch his bleeding. Jensen lived for about three hours, expiring twenty minutes before the arrival of a doctor. "I don't care for myself, but I wish I could live for my wife and children," Jensen said just before he died.

Mortally wounded, Salt Lake County Sheriff's Deputy Nephi Stannard Jensen wanted only to live for his family. (Salt Lake County Sheriff's Office)

The killing of the three officers dramatically changed the public view of Lopez. While most Bingham residents didn't care that Lopez had killed another Mexican, the murder of three police officers—particularly Grant, who was widely admired—was another matter. Citizens began clamoring to join the manhunt. Within an hour, posses from Salt Lake City, Bingham, Lehi, and Provo arrived and fanned out looking for Lopez's tracks. Salt Lake County Sheriff Andrew Smith, Jr., accompanied his deputies to the scene, telling them to bring all the firepower they could find and to be prepared for a long chase. By midnight, more than fifty lawmen had gathered with about 150 citizen volunteers.

Because Lopez had killed four Salt Lake County men, Utah County Sheriff Henry East deferred management of the search to Smith. Shortly after midnight, Lopez's tracks were located in the snow leading away from the scene. Deputies followed them south along the edge of the lake and then west into the rough terrain of the Lake Mountains.

Although newspapers announced that Lopez's capture was imminent, the killer soon proved that alone, on foot, and suffering from frostbite, he was still capable of outsmarting hundreds of men on his trail. His tracks led posses to the south end of the Lake Mountains, where they turned west as if heading into Cedar Valley. Instead, he doubled back and crossed Soldiers Pass, slogging north along the western side of the Lake Mountains. On the afternoon of November 22, near Long Canyon, Lopez climbed atop a horseshoe-shaped ledge, piled up some rocks for protection from bullets, and rested.

A posse had been getting closer to Lopez all morning. From the condition of the tracks in the snow, lawmen could tell that Lopez was tiring and that he

Salt Lake County Sheriff's Deputy Otto Witbeck
in a Salt Lake City Fire Department uniform.
Witbeck died instantly in the ambush that also
claimed Grant and Jensen. (Salt Lake County
Sheriff's Office)

wasn't too far ahead of them. The posse, consisting of Salt Lake County
Deputies C.L. Schettler, R.L. Eddington, and Michael Earl, as well as an
eighteen-year-old guide from Lehi, Elton Cooley, approached Lopez's position
on foot. They drew fire almost immediately. While the deputies took cover,
Lopez taunted them from his ledge.

"Is Sorenson down there?"

"Yes, he's here," replied Eddington.

"Send him up, I'd like to get a clear shot at him."

Sorenson was agreeable. He led a group of seven men, including tracker
Douglas Hulsey, to the other side of the ledge, where they began firing from a
distance of about two hundred yards. Several hundred shots were fired by the
posse, and answered by about twenty from Lopez.

The lawmen were so confident that they had Lopez boxed in that they
decided not to storm his position. Instead, they opted to let him spend the
night on the freezing ledge and arrest him in the morning after he had been
weakened by the cold. Four deputies were assigned to watch the ledge while
the remainder of the force, hungry and exhausted, scattered to Fairfield and
Mosida for shelter and something to eat.

During the night, the temperature dropped until the guard force was
shivering. Astoundingly, they decided to leave their post for the Mosida hotel
several miles away. Lopez was gone when they returned on the morning of
November 23. When the posse swarmed over his ledge, all they found were
some scraps of food and spent cartridge casings.

Deputies soon picked up Lopez's trail. By now he was limping and his
footprints had blood in them. But any confidence the lawmen might have

gained from the evidence of his weakened condition soon evaporated as Lopez led them through the roughest part of the mountains and then, in a move that amazed everyone with its audacity, back past the Jones ranch, where the killings had occurred. Hiding in the fog around Utah Lake, Lopez continued north, using sheep herds and roads to obscure his tracks. It was thought that he might attempt to cross Utah Lake in a boat, and considerable effort was wasted combing the shore and posting guards.

On the morning of November 24, lawmen admitted that they didn't have the slightest idea of Lopez's whereabouts. His tracks had become lost in the tracks of those following him. Worse, a break in the storms allowed the sun to melt the snow that had made tracking him easy in the first place. Worn out and confused, lawmen began making mistakes. They tracked each other or raced to the sound of shots only to find volunteer posse members shooting off their guns out of boredom. For the next two days, Smith had posses working the hills while guards posted at strategic points along roads and railroad tracks kept watch.

In reality, only one posse was on Lopez's trail. Led by volunteer Douglas Hulsey, the twelve-man posse had picked up a faint trail five miles north of the Jones ranch and followed it northwest. It led them across the divide at the top of Butterfield Canyon and down into the Highland Boy Mine at the head of Carr Fork. When Hulsey reported that he had trailed Lopez back to Bingham, everyone laughed at him. But he was right. Outnumbered and almost dead from exhaustion, Lopez had returned to the ground he knew best: the mines.

Late on the night of November 26, Mike Stefano, a miner living with his family just twenty-five yards from the entrance of the Minnie Mine, was awakened by a tapping on his window. When he got up to investigate, Lopez pointed a pistol at him through the window and ordered him to come outside. Later, Stefano told reporters that Lopez was in agony from frozen feet swollen to twice their normal size. The men visited for several hours. Before he left, Lopez took some food and blankets and traded his .30-06 rifle for Stefano's .30-30 Winchester. Because Lopez could barely walk, Stefano helped him carry his provisions to the entrance of the Minnie Mine. "I know you are my friend," Lopez told Stefano, "and I don't think you will tell the officers. If you do, I will come out of the mine and kill you and all of your family."

Stefano kept the secret until the afternoon of November 27, when he told his foreman. Within hours, word reached Hulsey, who found the tracks in the snow leading from Stefano's cabin to the mine. Hulsey sent a message to Smith, who was conducting the search in Juab County. Guards were immediately posted around the works and fires lighted near the portals of the Minnie Mine. Thus began the longest siege in Utah history.

From November 28 to January 3, 1914, lawmen tried every conceivable way to capture or kill Lopez in the Utah-Apex mine system. Search parties combed the labyrinth but returned empty-handed. Bulkheads were built across the portals and smoke pumped into the mines. It failed to force Lopez out.

On November 29, men working in the mine were accosted at various points by Lopez, who asked for information or robbed them of their candles and tobacco. That afternoon, a man with a rifle took a shot at a deputy inside the mine. By 2:00 p.m., lawmen thought they had Lopez pinpointed and decided to use smudge pots to smoke him out. Crude oil, hay, and sulfur were brought in. Douglas Hulsey, a Serbian miner named Thomas Manderich, Dr. David Ray, and Bingham resident Frank Thompson were dragging and pushing the combustibles to a strategic point when Lopez ambushed them.

A barrage of shots killed Hulsey and Manderich and sent Ray and Thompson running for cover. For thirty minutes lawmen were pinned down, listening to the wounded men groan while Lopez sent bullets richocheting along the shafts. Eventually, they shot out the electric lights and retreated under the cover of darkness. On the following day, rescuers returned to the mine and brought out the bodies.

For five days, lawmen poured smoke into the mines. Miners laughed at the attempts to smoke Lopez out, saying that there were enough air pockets to keep him alive. "When I see rats running from the tunnels," a miner said laughingly, "then I'll believe there is enough smoke in the mine to kill the Mexican."

On December 5, the fires went out and the bulkheads were torn down, allowing air to circulate back into the mine. Searchers combed the mine throughout the day and found nothing more than a few spent cartridges near the murder scene. At one point, deputies thought they had Lopez cornered in a narrow pocket. Dynamite was brought in, but the subsequent blast produced no body.

On December 8, Greek miner William Karos claimed he was working in the Andy Tunnel when a visibly weakened but still defiant Lopez stopped him and took his tobacco and candles. Despite Lopez's threat to kill him if he told anyone, Karos spread the word as soon as he exited the mine.

On December 9, Governor William Spry offered a $1,000 reward to anyone who could bring in Lopez "dead or alive." The notice merely served to attract the worst kind of manhunters to Bingham, further compounding the problems local law enforcement was already having with crowd control.

The last credible sighting of the killer occurred late in the afternoon of December 12 as shift boss Sam Rogers was walking down the Andy Tunnel. Lopez suddenly appeared at Rogers's side and began talking. The outlaw was

Rafael Lopez killed five Utah law enforcement officers before escaping from the Highland Boy Mine. Texas Ranger Frank Hamer would later claim to have killed Lopez in a battle near the Mexican border. (University of Utah)

filthy and gaunt but firm in his refusal to surrender. He said he was aware that the mine would be his grave. After cursing Stefano and Corrello for their treachery, Lopez vanished. The following day, Rogers claimed Lopez appeared again at the same spot. This time, Lopez told Rogers to stay out of the mine. The encounter so unnerved Rogers that he promptly quit his job, leaving Bingham without stopping to draw his pay. A warrant for Rogers's arrest as a material witness was issued by Salt Lake County but never served.

If Rogers wasn't helping Lopez, it was apparent that other miners were. Searchers occasionally found packages of sandwiches and other supplies left in prominent locations by miners. Some Utahns, particularly those Bingham miners who were no great admirers of the sheriff's department, openly admired the way the killer was keeping hundreds of lawmen at bay.

On December 17, Smith claimed that he would have Lopez out of the mine, dead or alive, by Christmas. It was a desperate and hollow boast. The day came and went with no sign of Lopez. Hope that they would ever catch Lopez began to slip away from Smith. Subsequent searches of the miles of tunnels proved that there were places the smoke never reached. Worse was the revelation that stretches of tunnels originally thought to be dead ends actually led to old works and hidden exits.

The last search of the mine was conducted between December 26 and January 2, and produced nothing more than a few ragged blankets, empty bottles, and footprints. Lopez was never seen again in Utah. The following day, Smith withdrew his deputies and announced an end to the siege.

Theories as to how Lopez got out of the mine are legion. One says he simply walked out with a shift change, disguised as just another miner. Another says he slipped out through some old works and walked down the west side of the Oquirrh Mountains.

On February 9, 1914, the *Deseret Evening News* reported that approximately one month earlier a brakeman for the Bingham & Garfield Railroad found a rifle and an empty pistol belt under a trestle across Cottonwood Gulch. Mike Stefano's description of the rifle taken from his home by Lopez matched the found rifle.

The manhunt cost Salt Lake County nearly $30,000 and ruined Sheriff Andrew Smith's law enforcement career. When he came up for reelection in November 1914, the Republican party didn't even bother to renominate him. There were too many candidates eagerly waiting for the political opportunity to tear Smith apart over the Bingham disaster. Smith left law enforcement and devoted the remainder of his life to carpentry and church work. He died in 1941.

Four months after the Lopez debacle, Deputy Julius Sorenson was wounded when he attempted to stop a dispute between Serb and Croat miners. After a miner was shot and killed while resisting arrest by another officer, the mob turned on Sorenson. He was disarmed and stabbed. The old lawman recovered but his wife refused to let him resume his deputy duties. Instead, he became a fireman and later sold household goods around the Salt Lake Valley. He died in 1944.

The widows of Jensen, Witbeck, and Grant received some financial compensation for the deaths of their husbands. Donations were solicited and tickets to a benefit dance were sold, but the money collected didn't go very far. Each of the women did the best she could to raise her children. Marie Witbeck never remarried. She took in washing and boarders, while her two teenage children worked to help make ends meet. Like Marie, Catherine Grant never remarried. With the financial help of her seven children and the Methodist Church, she managed to hang on to her home in Bingham. Cora Jensen relied on the close-knit Jensen family for support. She died in 1946. Martha Manderich received support from her extended family until she remarried and moved with her new husband to Wyoming. Hulsey, a bachelor, was buried in Texas.

All that remained of Lopez were rumors and legend. Miners later whispered among themselves that his ghost haunted the Utah-Apex digs. A poem attributed to E.G. Locke spelled out law enforcement's frustration for the killer who got away and left a nation wondering what happened.

With baited breath a nation, all anxious for the news,
In spirit traveled with them in search for Mex or clues.

They scrambled up the ladders, through cross-cut and through winze;
They fell down shafts, boulders made bruises on their shins;
They found some ancient blankets, some candles and some twine—
But found no Mex at Bingham, at Bingham in the Mine.

For nearly a century, the fate of Lopez remained a mystery. Speculation was all that lawmen and historians had to go on until the killer's trail was picked up once again by Salt Lake County Sheriff's Deputy Randy Lish. In 1998, while reading *Manhunter*, a fictionalized account of the life of Texas Ranger Frank Hamer written by Gene Shelton, Lish came across an account of Hamer killing a border bandit named Ralph "Red" Lopez, who was also wanted in Utah for the murder of several police officers. "It seemed a little more than just coincidence to me," Lish reported. "So I started doing some checking."

Lish obtained permssion from Salt Lake County Sheriff Aaron Kennard to pursue the investigation in his off-duty hours. He obtained a copy of Hamer's biography, *I'm Frank Hamer*, and in it was a brief description of a battle between a group of Texas Rangers led by Hamer and a gang led by Lopez. The gang operated out of Mexico and claimed responsibility for the 1914 massacre of nineteen Americans aboard a train traveling near the Rio Grande. The depredations committed by the gang continued for eight more years, until Hamer was sent to put a stop to them. Hamer, whose reputation in the Texas Rangers even today approaches that of deity, is best known for his later exploits in tracking and killing the infamous murderers Bonnie Parker and Clyde Barrow in Louisiana in 1934.

The incident with Lopez reportedly occurred in October or November 1921, when an informant from Brownsville agreed to lead Lopez and his gang into a Ranger ambush near Quemado, Texas, thirty-six miles southeast of Del Rio. Prior to the battle, the unidentified informant guided Hamer and his men to a dry irrigation ditch near the Rio Grande and told them to wait, that he would soon lure the bandit gang to them. After the informant left, Hamer became suspicious and moved his men away from positions known to the informant. When twenty heavily armed bandits arrived just before dark, it was obvious that they expected the rangers to be where the informant had left them. As they prepared to shoot into the rangers' former positions, Hamer and his men opened fire. Eleven bandits died in the lopsided battle, and Hamer was slightly wounded. Lopez was found by Hamer shot through the heart, the bullet drilling a hole through a gold pocket watch he wore in the chest pocket of his bib overalls. The ruined watch later hung in a Laredo customs house, where it served for years as a reminder of what happened to bandits on the Rio Grande.

There is no evidence that Utah ever paid the reward it offered for Lopez, but Hamer and his men collected a reward from the railroad in Texas. When Lish interviewed Hamer's son in 2002, Frank Hamer, Jr., said Lopez's identity and Utah connection was common knowledge among rangers and bandits on the border. Nor was the claim a matter of the elder Hamer bragging about his exploits. Known for his reluctance to talk about his exploits, Hamer quietly divided the reward money with his men and the matter was closed. His son heard the story from other rangers in the ambush and eventually convinced his father to tell him about it.

"There was never any doubt to anyone in Texas that this was the same Lopez from Utah," Lish said. "The chronology, the physical description, everything points to it being Rafael Lopez. I couldn't find anything that proved that it wasn't."

Lish submitted his case to Salt Lake County District Attorney David C. Yocom, and on January 24, 2003, Yocom signed a memorandum formally closing the investigation into the murders of Grant, Jensen, Witbeck, Hulsey, and Manderich.

Alexander J. Robertson
Eureka Police Department
December 5, 1915

Eureka Night Marshal Alex Robertson lost his life while trying to do a favor for a friend. The murder occurred on the front steps of the Eureka City Courthouse when William Elmer Horton, a twenty-six-year-old unemployed miner, inexplicably shot Robertson in the back of the head.

Ten days before the murder, Horton lost his job at the Chief Consolidated Mine because a Eureka storekeeper had garnisheed his paycheck. The loss of income hit the father of four small children hard. Despondent, Horton began drinking heavily. By December 5, witnesses said he was ready to collapse. Instead, however, Horton borrowed a pistol from his brother Marlin. Later that night, Horton showed up at the Oxford Cafe, where Marlin worked. He started flashing the pistol around and making threats against supervisors at the Chief Consolidated. When he finally fired a shot into the air, Marlin decided something had to be done. He sent twelve-year-old Bryan Parker to fetch the night marshal.

The forty-year-old night marshal was the secretary of the local Eagles lodge and wanted to attend a lodge meeting the following morning. Previous arrangements had been made for Officer Daniel Martin to relieve Robertson at 8:00 p.m. so that he could get some sleep. At approximately 7:45 p.m., Parker located Robertson and delivered the message.

A man of "unusually quiet disposition" and a resident of Eureka for approximately fifteen years, Robertson had been the town's night marshal for the past two. The youngest of eleven children, he was born April 16, 1874, in Spanish Fork to Scottish immigrants William and Eliza Carter Robertson. A bachelor, Robertson lived alone on upper Main Street in Eureka. His term as night marshal was to expire at the end of the month.

Robertson's attitude of fairness and consideration toward the feelings of others enabled him to get to know most of the town's residents on a friendly basis. In particular, Robertson knew and got along well with the Hortons. He was a close friend of George, William's eldest brother. Robertson probably reasoned that convincing William to "sleep it off" in jail overnight would therefore take only a few minutes. After he encountered George Horton on the street, the two went to the Oxford but found that William had already left. The marshal and George Horton split up and began looking for him.

Within minutes, Robertson located Horton at the Gatley Brothers' Saloon. After talking to his friend and calming him down, Robertson told Horton that he needed to see him "over at the office." He led Horton over to the courthouse. Rather than embarrass him in front of others in the saloon, Robertson did not handcuff Horton or even search him for the pistol. The two walked side by side to the courthouse and up the steps.

When they arrived at the door, Robertson stepped ahead of Horton to unlock it but in doing so dropped the keys. As the marshal bent over to pick them up, Horton whipped out the pistol and fired three shots. The first shot probably hit Robertson in the back of his head and exited out his mouth. The second or third struck him in the right shoulder and lodged inside his torso. At least one of the shots missed and struck the door jamb. Robertson fell dead in the doorway.

Half a dozen people witnessed the murder, including George Horton, following close behind. George saw his brother draw the gun as Robertson stepped forward to unlock the door. George later testified before a coroner's jury that he thought his brother was going to toss the gun away in order to avoid a charge for carrying a concealed weapon. Instead, he watched helplessly as Robertson was murdered.

Immediately after firing the shots, William Horton ran toward the old Keystone Mine dump, with his brother and witness David Mills hot on his heels. Cornered at the dump, Horton turned and attempted to shoot his brother, but the hammer snapped on a defective cartridge. George Horton and Mills

Eureka Night Marshal Alexander Robertson was gunned down on the steps of city hall by a prisoner he neglected to search. (*Salt Lake Herald*)

wrestled the killer to the ground, tore the pistol out of his hand, and dragged him back to the courthouse, where they turned him over to Juab County Sheriff Angus MacDonald.

The senseless killing stunned Eureka. No one could conceive of a reason why anyone would want to shoot the easygoing night marshal. After he sobered up, Horton himself didn't have an explanation for what had happened. Two days later, Horton told Salt Lake City reporters that he still didn't know why he committed the crime. "I haven't the slightest idea why I killed him," said Horton. "I had been drinking on the night that this terrible thing happened and what is all the more horrible to me is that I am accused of a crime which I have absolutely no recollection of committing. It was when I came to my senses in jail in Eureka when I understood for the first time that I was accused of having killed the night marshal. I never had anything against him."

On December 7, Horton was taken to Nephi. Ten days later, a preliminary hearing resulted in his binding over for trial on a charge of first-degree murder. Immediately after the hearing, officers secretly whisked Horton to the state prison in Salt Lake City. The move was probably a wise one. The county jail in Nephi had a bad reputation for escapes. Moreover, some Eureka residents were talking about holding a court of their own.

Funeral services for Robertson were held the evening of December 8. Most of Eureka filled the LDS chapel and spilled out onto the lawn as officials eulogized the fallen officer. The following day, dozens of residents escorted the body to Spanish Fork, where a second service was held in the LDS tabernacle there before burial in the city cemetery. Members of the Eureka Eagles Lodge served as pallbearers.

Elmer Horton killed his brother's best friend after being arrested. His term in prison was the shortest on record for the killing of a Utah police officer. (Utah State Department of Corrections)

On June 6, 1916, Horton pled guilty to a charge of second-degree murder in Nephi's district court. He was sentenced to twenty years to life at hard labor but would serve a mere fraction of the time.

In February 1920, Horton filed an application for parole with the Utah Board of Pardons. Accompanying his application was a petition signed by more than one hundred Eureka residents asking the board to grant Horton his parole.

Horton was released from prison on March 27, 1920, after serving just five years. His sentence remains the shortest ever served for the murder of a Utah police officer. He died in California on June 15, 1943.

Rudolf E. Mellenthin

National Forest Service
August 23, 1918

One thing Rudolf Mellenthin did not want to be in the summer of 1918 was a forest ranger. More than anything, the German native wanted to be in the U.S. Army and shooting at other Germans. Despite being rejected by the army, however, the ranger would yet lose his life in the service of his country.

Born February 4, 1884, in Germany, Mellenthin immigrated to the United States with his family. They located in the west, where Mellenthin fell in love with the cowboy lifestyle. In 1909, he applied for a position as a "forest guard" on the La Sal National Forest. The testing process for applicants was grueling.

In addition to a six-hour written test, Mellenthin had to demonstrate his skills in marksmanship, mapping, surveying, packing horses, and keeping a journal. On August 1, he was hired. Three years later, Mellenthin married Blanche Adele Christensen in Moab. The couple bought a home in town and eventually had three sons.

Guarding the forest was confusing in the early days of the service. Not only were the ranger ranks thin, protecting government land was not exactly an admired occupation, particularly by local ranchers and stockmen who had come to regard the La Sal Mountains as their own personal grazing range. The job was especially hard for Mellenthin. Although he spoke English well, it was with a distinctive German accent. Coupled with an intense, almost fanatical devotion to the law and forest regulations, Mellenthin's autocratic demeanor and flashy style of dress soon earned him the nickname "Kaiser" from annoyed local land users.

The irritating nickname and his German heritage troubled Mellenthin. In the spring of 1918, while savage fighting raged in Europe, the thirty-four-year-old forest ranger wrote to his sister, expressing a desire to join the cavalry and serve his adopted country:

> It isn't that I have any great desire to kill off a few of my playmates or that I am thirsting for any possible glory but it seems to me it is the most advisable thing I can do at the present.
>
> First of all you realize that after this war is over and for a long time to come every German in the country will be hated more than they are hated right today. Now I've got three kids that have a long life before them and shall I let them grow up and be despised and called all sorts of names until they finally wish their father had been like the other kids daddies? There is nothing I want my boys to have as much as a good clean name and by serving the country now I can give them something that they will be proud of.

No one could accuse Mellenthin of being afraid to do his job or play his part in the war effort. When he failed to get into the army, the tenacious immigrant turned his attention to war work and became known for his enthusiasm in the Liberty Bond and war stamp savings drives. If he could not fight in the trenches of France to make an honorable name for his children, he would do what he could for America on the home front.

While Mellenthin struggled to prove his loyalty to his adopted country, several hundred miles to the east, another man, nineteen-year-old Ramon Archuletta, was proving just the opposite. In September 1917, shortly after he married Eliza Martinez in Chama, New Mexico, Archuletta was inducted into

U.S. National Forest Ranger Rudolph Mellenthin
failed to get into the U.S. Army during World
War I and ironically was killed by an army
deserter. (Mellenthin family)

the U.S. Army. Taken to Kansas City for training, he promptly deserted and returned to New Mexico. Archuletta hid out near Chama for a week before being captured. He escaped again, this time heading to the Navajo Reservation, where he found work as a sheepherder. In February 1918 he sent a letter to his father-in-law, fifty-one-year-old Ignacio Martinez, who was working near Moab, asking for work. On July 15, 1918, Archuletta came to Moab, where he met his father-in-law for the first time. The two men traveled to a sheep camp on Pine Bluff, a few miles north of La Sal, and settled down to work.

Within a few days of Achuletta's arrival, Mellenthin became aware of the deserter's presence in the mountains. He talked the matter over with San Juan County Sheriff Frank Barnes, who informed Mellenthin that he had arrested Archuletta a few days before but had turned him loose when Martinez convinced him that Archuletta was the wrong man. Angry at being deceived, Barnes deputized Mellenthin, adding local police powers to the ranger's federal authority.

On August 23, Mellenthin learned that Martinez, Archuletta, and Francisco Maestas were constructing a sheep dipping plant on Pine Bluff. Along with friends James Moore and Tomas Vigil, Mellenthin went to investigate. Locating the dipping plant was no problem for Mellenthin. He had lived and worked in the La Sal Mountains for more than a decade and knew them well. What he did not know was just how desperate Archuletta was to avoid being returned to the army. Prior to their arrival at the camp, Mellenthin told his two companions to be ready, and that if Martinez and Archuletta offered any resistance they were to ride for help.

Mellenthin confronted the three men at their camp. Archuletta was squatting in the opening of a tent, holding a rifle. Martinez was a dozen feet off to the side, also holding a rifle. With a hand on his holstered pistol, Mellenthin placed Archuletta under arrest and told him that he would have to go to jail. After some discussion, Martinez sent Maestas to get a horse for Archuletta to ride.

Archuletta had different ideas. When Mellenthin ordered him to hand his rifle to Martinez, the deserter instead raised it and began firing. Vigil later testified that the distance between the two men was about five feet. Mellenthin was hit twice in the abdomen and again in the hip after he fell. Mortally wounded, he still managed to draw his pistol and shoot Archuletta through the knee and hand.

Vigil and Moore said that Martinez also began firing at Mellenthin. As soon as the shooting started, the ranger's companions took off running. Vigil claimed the suspects fired at them, one of the bullets striking the ground between his feet as he ran. The two men did not stop until they reached the ranger station, where they telephoned La Sal and reported the incident.

A heavily armed posse left La Sal almost immediately and reached the sheep camp within a couple of hours. They found Mellenthin unconscious but alive. He died a few minutes later. Archuletta was easy to locate. The posse

La Sal National Forest Service Rangers Sterling Colton (left) and Rudolph Mellenthin, accompanied by Blanche Mellenthin, preparing to leave for forest service detail in San Juan County, 1913. (Manti–La Sal National Forest Service)

Ramon Achuletta nearly lost his leg in the shootout with Mellenthin. (Utah State Department of Corrections)

followed his blood trail and located him a short distance away, hiding in some brush. Although armed with a rifle and Mellenthin's pistol, the killer surrendered without a fight. Martinez was also arrested without incident. He placed the blame for the ranger's murder squarely on the shoulders of his son-in-law.

Despite Martinez's denial that he had participated in the murder, a tobacco can in Mellenthin's shirt pocket had a hole in it that fit the .30-30 rifle Martinez carried, whereas Archuletta's rifle fired a .25-30 cartridge. Investigators also noticed that at least one of the bullets that killed the ranger came from the direction where Martinez had been standing when the gunfight started. Based on this evidence and the testimony of Vigil and Moore, Martinez was charged with first-degree murder together with Archuletta.

However, before Archuletta could be tried, authorities had to make sure that he stayed alive. His leg was so mangled by Mellenthin's bullet that he was taken to a hospital in Fruita, Colorado, where doctors briefly considered amputation.

Mellenthin was buried in Moab, where he had lived with his family. The entire town turned out to lay the "Kaiser" to rest. Many noted the irony of his death, pointing out that no soldier on the battlefield had ever served his country better.

On September 12, a preliminary hearing for Martinez was held at Monticello. It lasted four days and concluded with Martinez being ordered to stand trial for murder. Martinez was taken to Salt Lake City and locked up in the state prison for safekeeping. As soon as his condition allowed, Archuletta joined him.

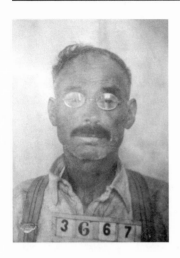

Ignacio Martinez, Archuletta's father-in-law and accomplice. (Utah State Department of Corrections)

Because of the widespread sentiment against the killers, attorneys for Martinez and Archuletta convinced authorities that their clients would not be able to get a fair trial in San Juan County. A change of venue was therefore granted, and the trial, which began May 31, was moved to Manti.

Martinez was tried first. The proceedings lasted for twelve days. Archuletta took the stand in defense of his father-in-law, claiming that Martinez did not participate in the gunfight. Archuletta admitted killing Mellenthin, but claimed he did so in self-defense when the ranger shot him in the hand without warning or provocation. The jury deliberated for nine hours and, on June 11, found Martinez guilty of second-degree murder. He was sentenced to fifteen years at hard labor. No trial was necessary for Archuletta. He pleaded guilty to second-degree murder and was immediately sentenced to life in prison.

Through the appeals process, the Utah Supreme Court overturned Martinez's conviction, citing a lack of evidence. He then was ordered to stand trial again. Unable to furnish additional proof of his guilt, San Juan County officials had no other recourse but to turn him loose in September 1920.

Archuletta served six years of a life sentence. On September 28, 1925, in a move that outraged the residents of Grand and San Juan Counties, Archuletta was paroled.

World War I ended eighty days after Mellenthin gave his life for his country. Although he never made it to the fields of France, his country still appreciated his sacrifice. Twenty miles southeast of Moab, in the Manti–La Sal National Forest, Mount Mellenthin today bears the name of a man who wanted only to leave his children a good name.

Green B. Hamby
Salt Lake City Police Department
February 8, 1921

Shortly after 4:00 a.m. on February 8, 1921, the night clerk of Salt Lake City's Delphi Hotel at 233 South State telephoned the police department to report a possible burglary. During his rounds, the clerk had discovered a skylight broken in the men's common lavatory. Detective C.W. Rosenkrantz and Patrolman Morris M. Riley were sent to investigate.

A brief examination revealed that the Delphi's skylight had been broken out in an attempt to gain access to the roof of the neighboring J.C. Penney Store. In a corner of the lavatory the officers found a package containing dynamite caps and blasting power. Believing that the burglars were already in the store or hiding nearby, Rosenkrantz sent Riley to the lobby to telephone for reinforcements. Then the detective began reconnoitering the dark halls. Almost immediately he encountered a seedy-looking character on the first floor. When Rosenkrantz asked where he was coming from, the man tried to charm him. "I've been in the room around the corner," the man said. "You can see if you want."

Rosenkrantz, a member of the Salt Lake police force for only a year, ordered the man to lead the way back to the room. A veteran officer might have been more suspicious. What Rosenkrantz did not know was that the suspect, thirty-six-year-old Walter "Dopey" Smith, was one of four armed burglars.

As Rosenkrantz followed Smith around a corner, a second man, Thomas "Blackie" Burns, shoved a pistol into the detective's ribs and ordered him to raise his hands. The detective briefly considered a grab for the pistol, but then Smith produced a pistol of his own. A third man, Oscar Blaney, came out of Room 14. Together the three men shoved Rosenkrantz inside. Holding a gun to the detective's head, Burns forced Rosenkrantz face down onto a bed and took his service revolver. After beating the detective unconscious, Burns tied him with strips torn from the bedding.

Rosenkrantz had stumbled into a gang of thieves that had been operating in Salt Lake City for several weeks. Their crime spree began in Fellows, California, where they blew the safe in the local railroad depot office and got away with cash and traveler's checks amounting to $1,300. After pulling additional jobs in Bakersfield, Dunsmir, and Medford, Oregon, the gang came to Salt Lake City, where they checked in to the Nord Hotel, 59 1/2 East 200 South. By then the gang consisted of Burns (a.k.a. Tom Gleason),

Detective Green B. Hamby was gunned down in a notorious Salt Lake hotel by the leader of a burglary ring. (Salt Lake Police Museum)

approximately thirty years old and leader by right of his ability to intimidate the others; the none-too-bright Smith, who hailed from Texas; twenty-five-year-old Blaney, a World War I army veteran and native of California; and twenty-three-year-old Henry "Shorty" Evans from Iowa.

Burns brought his gang to Salt Lake City because he knew the area. The previous March he and a cohort had burglarized the Salduro Chemical Company in Tooele County, making off with fifty gallons of alcohol. Burns's partner in that crime was later caught and sent to prison, but Burns didn't intend such a fate for himself. Prior to skipping Utah, he wrote a letter to Tooele County Sheriff D.M. Adamson, threatening to kill the officer if he came after him.

In Salt Lake City, Burns and his gang lived at the Nord Hotel off the proceeds of the stolen traveler's checks and other petty crimes. They tried to blow the safe at the Consolidated Oil Company but were scared off by a night watchman. They also robbed two women in the yard of a home near 700 East and South Temple.

At approximately 2:30 on the morning of February 8, Burns and company were in his room drinking whiskey when Smith suggested that they blow the safe in the J.C. Penney store. The gang went to the Delphi, where they rented a room. Smith and Burns broke out the skylight but found the drop to the store roof too high for their liking. While Blaney waited in the room and Evans acted as a lookout, Burns and Smith went in search of something to lower themselves to the roof. They stumbled into Rosenkrantz instead.

After slugging the detective, Burns went to the front desk and brought the clerk to the room. Ordering Blaney to stand watch over the two men, he went back to the lavatory with the intent of finishing the job. By then, however, the reinforcements Riley had called for were arriving on the scene. Fortunately for Rosenkrantz, commanding the reinforcements was Sergeant Nephi Pierce. A veteran of numerous street fights, Pierce cordoned off the Delphi with reserves scraped together from downtown foot beats. He then went inside alone to investigate.

Walking through the hall, Pierce heard loud talk coming from a room near the front of the hotel. He knocked on the door and demanded entrance. When the occupants refused, Pierce kicked the door in and grappled immediately with Burns, who broke away and fired a shot that struck the door jamb near the sergeant's head. Fleeing into an adjoining room, Burns jumped out a window and escaped over the rooftops. Pierce considered chasing Burns but decided that he needed to locate Rosenkrantz first.

Concerned for the missing officer, Pierce and Riley conducted a room-to-room search of the Delphi. Blaney surrendered as soon as they knocked on the door of Room 14. Bleeding from a gashed head, Rosenkrantz was dazed but alive. He joined the search in company with Officer Brigham Honey. The two arrested Smith when they found him hiding in a bed, pretending to be asleep. Evans was taken into custody as he tried to slip through the ring of officers outside.

Within minutes, the three frightened suspects arrived at police headquarters, where, absent the courage normally supplied by Burns, detectives were unable to get them to shut up. All made lengthy confessions, and within the hour officers knew everything, including the location of their hideout at the Nord.

Chief of Police Joseph E. Burbidge immediately organized a raid on the notorious flophouse. Rosenkrantz, his head wrapped in bandages, wanted to go along, but Burbidge sent him home. At approximately 10:30 a.m., officers surrounded the Nord. Fearing a liquor raid, one of the Nord residents flung a bottle of whiskey from an upstairs window where Patrolman Arthur Merrick arrived at his post just in time to catch it.

Once the Nord was sealed off, Burbidge and three other officers, Chief of Detectives Riley Beckstead and Detectives Green Hamby and Clifford Patten, began searching the rooms for Burns. While Beckstead and Patten questioned the clerk on the first floor, Burbidge and Hamby went to the second floor and knocked on Room 7, the room registered to Burns. When no one answered, the two men entered.

"We searched that room and while I was going over several details, Hamby went to the next room and knocked on the door," Burbidge said later. "He called to me that there was someone in the room, but that they would not open the door. I added my voice to the command to open, that we were officers. When we did not get a reply, we put our weight against the door."

Oscar Blaney, one of the
burglary ring members. (Utah
Department of Corrections)

Walt "Dopey" Smith, another
burglary suspect. (Utah
Department of Corrections)

Burns was hiding in the room. As the door swung open, he shot Hamby in the face. A second shot grazed Burbidge's chest. Spinning away from the door, Burbidge shouted for help and tried to bring his own revolver into play. Burns jumped into the hallway and was preparing to shoot Burbidge again when a shot fired by Patten from the stairway struck him in the left side, staggering him. Before Burns could recover, Burbidge shot him in the chest. Burns dragged himself back into a room and collapsed. Taken to the police emergency hospital, he died an hour later.

There was nothing the officers could do for Hamby. The forty-nine-year-old Missouri native died instantly when the bullet struck him in the right eye and exited the back of his head. A five-year veteran of the local police force, Hamby had previously worked as chief of detectives for the Boise (Idaho) Police Department. In Salt Lake City, Hamby worked the Greek Town area and rapidly became known for his investigative prowess, a fact that led to his appointment as a detective in 1920. Hamby lived at 267 Devon Court with his wife, Louise, and three children. His twenty-two-year-old son William, also a Salt Lake police officer, had participated in the early morning raid on the Delphi.

Hamby's death precipitated one of the most concerted efforts by city officials in memory to clean up Salt Lake City. Immediately following the murder, all residents at the Nord Hotel were thrown into jail until they were able to prove that they had no connection with Burns. The arrests escalated as officers swept through the city's underworld. Most of those hauled in were given twenty-four hours to get out of town, a warning few failed to heed given the present mood of the police. Almost as rapidly, the Salt Lake City Council voted an eleven o'clock closing time for all billiard halls and saloons. The license of the Nord Hotel, deemed a disorderly house by the city council, was revoked, and owner C.H. Grady was jailed.

If official reactions were excessive, they weren't necessarily effective in curtailing assaults on officers. Within three years, four more Salt Lake City police officers would be shot to death in clashes with criminals. Among the dead would be Pierce and Honey. Nor were all of the repercussions official or even legal. When Burns's body was removed to the police morgue, several off-duty police officers entered after dark and sliced a swatch of flesh from his body. The tanned skin still adorns the trigger guard of an old service revolver in the Salt Lake Police Museum.

On February 11, Salt Lake City buried Hamby. Long before the services began at O'Donnell & Company, the mortuary chapel was filled to overflowing, forcing thousands of mourners to stand in the street. A procession of uniformed officers and firefighters several blocks long escorted Hamby's body to the city cemetery.

On February 10, Blaney, Evans, and Smith pleaded guilty in Third District Court to assault and robbery charges stemming from the incident with Rosenkrantz. Sentenced to prison, they were paroled in 1925. Meanwhile, Burns's unclaimed body was turned over to the medical department of the University of Utah for study, and it was later buried in a potter's field at the city cemetery.

A memorial fund established by the *Salt Lake Tribune* raised more than $2,000 for Hamby's widow and children. The family also received insurance monies. Although Louise Hamby eventually remarried, she was buried next to Green Hamby following her death in 1951.

Charles Manzel

Ogden Police Department
May 8, 1921

As he left the Ogden Police Station on the night of May 8, 1921, Patrolman Charles Manzel's last words to Desk Sergeant William Lowder were, "Once a policeman, always a policeman." The words were prophetic. A few hours later, Manzel would become a police officer for eternity.

Leaving the station, Manzel went to his foot beat in the area of Twenty-fifth Street and Grant Avenue. He no doubt felt some excitement. That night was his first shift since returning to the department following a three-year absence. In 1918, after serving eight years as an Ogden City police officer, Manzel left the department to accept a job with J.G. Read and Brothers, who manufactured harness for the war effort.

There was, however, a grimmer side to Manzel's return. The officer whose beat Manzel now patrolled was serving a prison sentence for burglarizing the very businesses he was sworn to protect. In the early hours of May 1, Officer Frederick A. Bacherd was arrested by co-workers who caught the former Idaho farmer slithering out of a window in the James & Russell grocery store. Bacherd had been on the force for about a year, the last three months of which he had become the prime suspect in a string of burglaries on his beat, crimes that coincided with nights he called in sick. While investigators grilled Bacherd in jail, an officer called his home. When the officer inquired as to his whereabouts, Mrs. Bacherd claimed that her husband was sick in bed. Bacherd wasn't ill, but his sixty-four-year-old mother-in-law Ella West Hall was, and news of his predicament apparently didn't make her feel any better. She suddenly died several hours later. Bacherd eventually confessed to eight burglaries and was sent to prison on May 4. He served five months before being paroled.

Bacherd's departure created an opening on the force that Manzel gratefully accepted. With the war long over, work at the harness factory had slowed considerably and it was becoming tough to make ends meet. The forty-five-year-old Spanish-American War veteran lived with his wife Marzette (Storer) and three children at 1741 River Drive. Born February 5, 1876, in Fremont, Nebraska, Manzel came to Utah as a young man. He lived for a time in Echo. Following their marriage in that town, the Manzels moved to Ogden in 1905.

Although his beat was a few blocks from the state's busiest rail yard, a haven for hobos, the majority of Manzel's first shift was spent without incident. Then, just before he was to go off duty, Manzel discovered a burglary at the N.O. Ogden clothing store at 236 Twenty-fifth Street. Peering in, Manzel could see that the store had been ransacked, boxes and merchandise strewn about the floor.

As Manzel checked the premises, he spotted a man leaving the back door of the Carlyle rooming house located next to the store. The man carried a new suitcase and wore a spotless new suit coat. When the man moved furtively toward the store, Manzel stopped him. The man's suitcase proved to be empty and his shoes brand new. It was enough for Manzel. He arrested the suspect, a Mexican national who claimed to have a room in the Carlyle. Manzel escorted his prisoner to a call box, where he telephoned the station for assistance.

Returning to the Ogden Police Department after a three-year absence during World War I, Patrolman Charles Manzel was shot to death on his first night of duty. (Ogden Police Department)

Sergeant A.H. Stephens and Detective W.A. Jones responded to the call. Leaving the station, they found Manzel and his prisoner waiting in the dark alley behind the store and the Carlyle rooming house. Manzel requested that Stephens and Jones watch the store while he accompanied the prisoner into the Carlyle to search his room for plunder. The officers agreed. Stephens waited in the alley while Jones watched the front of the store.

Because the rear door of the rooming house was locked, Manzel took his prisoner around to the front. Somewhere from the time he left Stephens and the time he entered the rooming house, Manzel apparently encountered a second suspect. In the upstairs hallway, Manzel rang the night bell to summon Frank and May Manda, proprietors of the Carlyle.

When Mrs. Manda came out of her bedroom rubbing her eyes, she found Manzel and two men in the upstairs hallway leading to an elevated back door. Mrs. Manda later testified that she recognized the suspects as two men who had rented a room the night before. She directed Manzel to their room. After looking in the room and finding items from the store, Manzel led his suspects down the hallway to the back door.

Manzel allowed the suspects to stand behind him while he unbolted the rear door to let Stephens in. At the moment Manzel unlatched the door, one of the suspects raised a .32-caliber pistol and shot him in the back of the head.

The officer never knew what hit him. The bullet punched through his skull behind the right ear, lodging just under the skin above his left eye.

The instant the shot was fired, the suspects wheeled and ran back up the hall, knocking Mrs. Manda to the floor and dropping the empty suitcase. As the two men pounded down the stairs, Frank Manda called for them to stop. Their response was a second bullet that struck the wall inches from Manda's head. Because of the dim light in the hall, the Mandas were unable to tell officers exactly who fired the shots, a fact that became pivotal during the trial.

When Stephens heard the shot inside the Carlyle, he ran up the back steps and forced open the door. Leaping over Manzel, the sergeant pursued the suspects out onto Twenty-fifth Street, where he last saw them rounding the corner south on Lincoln Street. The suspects had such a lead on Stephens that he soon lost sight of them in the dark. Jones, watching the front of the store, never got close enough to take part in the chase.

News of Manzel's death spread rapidly. The Salt Lake City police department posted guards on all roads leading into the city from the north, while Weber County deputies began searching the foothills and rural roads. More than fifty volunteers joined the search from the Ogden Fire Department, Spanish-American War veterans, and the Moose Lodge of which Manzel had been a member.

Four hours after the shooting, at approximately 7:30 a.m., Detective Joseph McLean saw a man emerge from the bushes near where the railroad tracks crossed Seventeenth Street. The man lurked in the bushes until a police patrol passed by before stepping out onto the street. When McClean stopped him, the man claimed he had just arrived in Ogden after walking all night along the railroad tracks from Salt Lake City. Because the man fit the general description of the killer, McClean placed him under arrest. A search of his pockets turned up a small key and a bar of soap wrapped in an Ogden laundry ticket dated May 2. McLean also noticed that the man's suit coat and shoes were brand new. In particular, the shoes did not look like they had spent the night being walked in on a railroad bed.

McLean put the suspect in the car of *Ogden Standard-Examiner* reporter Floyd Timmerman, who was assisting in the search. Timmerman took his prisoner to the police station, where the suspect soon proved himself to be a determined if unimaginative liar. The suspect, who spoke English clearly, claimed to be a twenty-eight-year-old Mexican immigrant. He told detectives that his name was Francisco Hernandez but later changed his mind and alternately claimed to be Francisco San Luiz, Francisco San Diez, Francisco Ernande, Francisco Sanchez, and Esequil Palma. Hernandez, for that's who the suspect eventually proved to be, also claimed that he spent the night of the murder sleeping in a boxcar. He had no explanation as to why his clothing looked fresh. When detectives pressed him about this and other inconsistencies in his alibi, Hernandez suddenly forgot how to speak English.

On the afternoon of May 9, Mrs. Manda identified Hernandez as one of the two men she saw with Manzel at the time of the murder. She said Hernandez had registered at the Carlyle under the name "Pedro." She did not know the name of the other man, or if Hernandez was the one who actually fired the fatal shot. Other witnesses claimed they saw Hernandez and the other suspect fleeing from the scene. Andrew Garcia, a railroad section hand, told detectives that Hernandez and another man came to his room several hours after the murder and told him that they had "kicked in" a store and were trying to escape the police.

In addition to the witnesses, there was direct evidence linking Hernandez to the crime. The key in his pocket fit a complicated lock to a suitcase filled with stolen items that officers found in the room. His clothing, including socks and new silk underwear, was identified as items taken from the clothing store. Jailers later caught him trying to exchange this clothing with other prisoners.

Confident that they had at least one of the suspects, officers turned loose a half-dozen other Latinos rounded up in the sweep for the killers after witnesses could not identify one of them as Hernandez's accomplice. The second suspect was never located.

Ogden buried Manzel on May 11. Following a viewing at the family home, funeral services were held in the packed Ogden Tabernacle. Mourners were turned away after even the choir seats were filled. Many stood outside in the cold. Mayor Frank Francis and other speakers lamented Manzel's loss to the community and his family. A cortege escorted the casket to the city cemetery, where Manzel was laid to rest as taps was played and a salute fired over the grave. Marzette Manzel received money from insurance policies, as well as funds collected in a memorial drive started by Seth Thomas, a local jeweler. She raised her children alone, remaining single until 1951, when she married Oscar Bybee. She died in 1955 at her home in Uintah.

On the day of Manzel's funeral, Hernandez admitted who he was when detectives confronted him with photographs and fingerprint information received from California. He first claimed that the photograph was of his brother, but confessed when his fingerprints matched records at the California prison where he was released in January. Identifying marks included two bullet scars in his leg, received during the burglary for which he was convicted.

Through an interpreter, Hernandez insisted that he had nothing to do with the murder. On May 20, he was arraigned in city court, where he pled not guilty to a charge of first-degree murder and waived a preliminary hearing.

Marzette Storer Manzel, wife of the slain officer.
(Carl Manzel)

The murder trial began June 18, before Second District Judge James N. Kimball. Hernandez appeared sullen at the defense table in the clothes he wore at the time of his arrest. Just an hour before, Hernandez had scuffled with jailers who forcibly removed a pair of overalls he wanted to wear to court over his suit.

District Attorney Joseph E. Evans prosecuted the case. A long line of witnesses tied Hernandez to the burglary and the scene of the murder, although none testified that they saw him pull the trigger. Detectives said that at the time of his arrest, Hernandez admitted burglarizing the clothing store and even being in the hallway when Manzel was shot. During the testimony, Hernandez sat passively with an interpreter by his side. His only sign of emotion was an outburst in Spanish when hotel chambermaid Rosatta Cedra testified that on May 8 she overheard Hernandez and another man planning a "robbery." Hernandez's lawyer, former judge A.E. Pratt, defended his client by claiming that his confession had been obtained through beatings by police. He further maintained that all of the witnesses who identified Hernandez were mistaken.

On June 23, Hernandez took the stand in his own defense, testifying that he had come to Ogden from Los Angeles to seek work on the railroad. He claimed to have walked from Salt Lake City to Ogden, but could not explain the lack of wear on his new shoes or describe any of the scenery or the towns he would have had to have passed through. Finally, Hernandez testified that officers planted the key to the suitcase on him.

After deliberating most of the following day, the jury reported that they were unable to reach a verdict. Eleven jurors wanted Hernandez convicted of second-degree murder, while a twelfth held out for full acquittal. Kimball discharged the jury and a second trial was immediately scheduled for July 28.

Francisco Hernandez was acquitted of the murder of Manzel but sent to prison for the burglary of an Ogden store. (Utah State Department of Corrections)

The second trial was almost identical to the first. Witnesses for the prosecution placed Hernandez at or near the scene of the crimes. His claim that he arrived in Ogden minutes before being arrested was refuted by several who saw him in town days before the murder. Hernandez took the stand again and stuck to his alibi. This time it worked. After talking it over for two and a half hours, the second jury acquitted Hernandez of murder. The acquittal occurred in large part because of Kimball's instruction that jurors could either convict Hernandez of first-degree murder or acquit him. Several jurors thought that Hernandez was guilty, but not of first-degree murder.

Furious at the decision, officers immediately charged Hernandez with the clothing store burglary. Whereas evidence of his guilt in Manzel's death was not conclusive, Hernandez's third jury found the burglary evidence ironclad. On August 24, he was sentenced to prison on a charge of second-degree burglary.

On May 7, 1924, Hernandez was released from the Utah State Prison and immediately turned over to immigration officials for deportation to Mexico.

Gordon Stuart

Salt Lake County Sheriff's Office
April 15, 1922

Shortly before sunrise on August 31, 1923, George H. Gardner stepped out into the Sugar House prison yard, led by Salt Lake County Sheriff Benjamin R. Harries. Eerie shrieks and moans from prisoners still locked in their cells followed the forty-year-old condemned man into the last morning he would ever see. Although just minutes away from death, Gardner showed no emotion as he limped on a malformed leg to the waiting death chair. He paused and made his final statement.

"The killing of Gordon Stuart was accidental," Gardner said calmly. "I have no apologies to make for the killing of Irvine. I hope the public will have sympathy for Mrs. Stuart. I want everyone to know that I wish for this and that I never injured or wronged anybody intentionally in my life."

Following his final statement, Gardner allowed Harries to tie a hood over his head. Officials then strapped his arms and legs to the chair. Harries pinned a paper target over Gardner's heart and stepped back. Watching from the west wall of the old prison were fewer than fifty spectators, mostly newspaper reporters, police officers, and government officials. Among them was Norval Stuart, father of Gardner's first victim. The waiting crowd tensed as commands to the firing squad rang out.

Thirty seconds later, at 6:32 a.m., four high-powered rifle bullets slammed into Gardner's chest. Despite the lethal volley, it was more than three minutes before Gardner's heart ceased beating and a county physician finally declared him dead. Although he died calmly, few mourned Gardner's death. His execution for most was nothing more than the final chapter in a senseless tragedy that occurred on a small farm in Welby.

On April 15, 1922, Gardner shot and killed Salt Lake County Deputy Sheriff Gordon A. Stuart before turning the gun on his own brother-in-law, Joseph W. Irvine, 46, of Salt Lake City. Gardner's common-law wife, Martha Gerrans, was charged as an accomplice in the bloody affair that captured the attention of Utah for more than a year.

Before leaving for work on that clear April morning, Gordon Stuart, 27, prepared breakfast for his wife, Florence, in the couple's small Sandy home. Married for two years, the Stuarts were the proud parents of a two-month-old baby boy, Gordon Hal. The pregnancy and delivery had been particularly hard, and Florence, 24, was only now recovering. Two weeks before, the couple had gone to the First Congregational Church in Salt Lake City, where Gordon Hal was christened. Things in the Stuart home were finally returning to normal, in large part because Stuart doted on his wife. In addition to assuming many of the evening household responsibilities, the deputy hired a neighbor girl to help out during the day. While the couple talked over breakfast, the girl arrived to help with the laundry. When the time came for him to go to work, Stuart donned his badge and slipped a pistol into his belt. Later, when the full shock of his death settled on her, Florence Stuart recalled that her husband broke a family routine for the first time in their short marriage. A shy man, Stuart decided not to kiss his wife goodbye in front of the neighbor girl. "I'll meet you in the gloaming, dear," he said cheerfully, meaning that he intended to return home at twilight.

Considered one of Salt Lake County Sheriff C. Frank Emery's more reliable deputies, Stuart had been with the office since his appointment in January 1921. He was quiet, cheerful, good-natured, and full of fun. Born in Helena, Montana, Stuart came to Salt Lake City with his family at the age of eight. He attended Salt Lake High School, playing in the band. The family later relocated to Sandy, where Stuart attended Jordan High School. After serving in the army during World War I, Stuart returned to Sandy, where he courted Florence E. Jackson; they married on October 12, 1918. When Emery hired Stuart as a deputy, he assigned the young man to work in Sandy and other areas at the south end of the county.

After leaving his home, Stuart contacted Chief Civil Deputy Frank M. Matthews, who asked him and Deputy Don Gardner (no relation to the killer) to help serve a court-ordered attachment on some stock at the home of George Gardner. Gardner's farm was located a half mile southeast of Welby, a small ore terminal located on the highway between Midvale and Bingham. Matthews wanted the extra help because of George Gardner's well-known reputation for behaving irrationally during times of stress. Two weeks before, deputies had raided the Gardner farm and located an illegal still in some trees. Gardner claimed the still belonged to a group of men he allowed to loiter on the property and that he was not involved in the manufacture himself. Gardner was not arrested and deputies took the opportunity to discuss the pending attachment with him. Gardner's response was to fly into a rage and threaten to "kill any — — that comes on this place to take my property."

It wasn't an idle threat. By the age of thirty-eight, Gardner, whose legal name was George Henry Williams, had reached the end of his rope. A gaunt, humorless man with a deep-rooted persecution complex, he was born January 10, 1884, in Mendon, to Frank and Mary Williams. His mother had married Williams following the death of her first husband, Henry Gardner, in 1881. A few months before the birth of George, Frank Williams deserted the family, and Mary resumed using the Gardner name. In 1911, George Gardner married a woman from Preston, Idaho. The couple lived in Logan and had two children before divorcing in 1914. Both children died in infancy. Born with a malformed leg, George Gardner later said that he grew up friendless and tormented by other children, and that for the last few years he had lived "a dog's life."

The dog's life apparently coincided with the beginning of Gardner's relationship with Martha Stirling Gerrans, the divorced mother of several children. Living together as man and wife, the couple settled on "the old Meek

Salt Lake County Deputy Gordon Stuart in his
World War I army uniform. (Salt Lake County
Sheriff's Office)

place" near Welby, where their frequent fights led Martha to tell neighbors
that her husband was "insane."

In truth, Martha was suspected of being more than a little crazy herself.
Three years before, Martha and her brother operated a small store on 500
South in Salt Lake City. When her brother got into a fight with a bill collector,
Martha rushed to his aid with a meat cleaver. She later admitted to swinging
the cleaver at the bill collector's head, intending to brain him with the flat
side. However, she missed and severed her brother's nose instead.

Martha introduced George to Joseph W. Irvine, the husband of her sister
Margaret. Irvine and Gardner entered into several business arrangements, which
for whatever reasons proved unprofitable. Gardner soon developed an intense
hatred for Irvine, who he claimed had tricked him out of money. Irvine, a
forty-two-year-old family man and foreman for Utah Power and Light,
eventually took Gardner to court, where a judge ordered Gardner to surrender
some farm stock. When Gardner failed to comply, Irvine got a court order and
sought the sheriff's assistance in serving it.

Irvine and the earlier liquor raid by deputies were not the only pressures
Gardner was feeling on the morning of April 15. Minutes before the homicides,
his wife had delivered some disturbing news that likely pushed him over the
edge. On April 14, unbeknownst to Gardner, Martha and her fourteen-year-
old daughter went to Salt Lake City and met with a sheriff's detective to discuss
the girl's allegations that Gardner had sexually abused her. The young girl
said that Gardner had assaulted her on a number of occasions and had also
made improper advances to her friends. Although Martha claimed that her
daughter might be fabricating the charges, the detective thought differently.

He decided to place the girl in a juvenile home until the matter could be sorted out by a more thorough investigation. The girl was released a few hours later and taken to her grandmother's home in Salt Lake.

Knowing that her husband would fly into another of his infamous rages upon learning of the allegations, Martha returned home the following morning with considerable apprehension. She stopped at the general store in Welby, where she told owner Fred Stroshahl about the allegations and said that she was going home to order Gardner to "get out."

At noon, Gardner and Martha were standing outside their home when they saw Irvine and the deputies coming up the lane. In addition to Matthews and Stuart, there were deputies Don Gardner and T.A. Herringer. Irvine also was accompanied by a friend, J.C. Cannon. Martha later claimed that she did not realize the deputies were there simply to seize the stock. "When the deputies came toward the house I waved them away," Martha said. "Then I told Gardner that ... my fourteen-year-old daughter by a former marriage had accused him of having improper relations with her. He seemed to go into a frenzy."

Telling Martha to inform the deputies that he was not at home, Gardner went into the house and slammed the door. Martha initially told the deputies that Gardner had gone to Midvale. When they gave her the court papers authorizing the seizure of the stock, she admitted that Gardner was inside.

At this point, the deputies split up. While Don Gardner remained with Martha, Matthews and Stuart went to find Gardner. Herringer accompanied Irvine and Cannon into the barn to look for the stock. Martha tried to follow them, gathering rocks and spitting curses at her brother-in-law. "I walked towards the barn and threw rocks at Irvine," Martha said later from a county jail cell. "I wanted to drive him away so that he would not be hurt." A few minutes later, however, her actions would indicate that she wasn't interested at all in Irvine's well-being.

During the commotion at the barn, Matthews and Stuart were speaking to Gardner at the back door of the home. Gardner invited them inside "to talk it over." Matthews testified later in court about what happened next. "[Gardner] said in quite a friendly way: 'Come in and we'll settle it,' or 'come on in and we'll talk it over.' When Gardner got to the door leading to the dining room, he turned quickly with an automatic shotgun in his hands and fired twice, shooting Stuart in the abdomen. Stuart turned to his left and ran out of the house, pushing me in front of him."

The first shot struck Stuart in the left arm before passing into his left side. In all probability, Gardner's second shot was intended for Matthews but was blocked by Stuart when the young deputy staggered under the effects of the first. The second blast struck Stuart in the right arm and chest. Stuart stumbled back toward the door leading to the porch, calling his last words to Matthews. "He's got me, Frank. You duck."

Stuart collapsed about fifty yards from the home, where he bled to death in a matter of seconds. Gardner appeared on the porch and covered Matthews with the shotgun. His pistol buttoned under his coat, the deputy had no choice but to raise his hands. "I looked up and Gardner was ten or twelve feet from me, pointing the gun at me," Matthews testified. "He said: 'Back off or I'll kill you, too.' I saw Irvine by the barn and yelled to him to get off the place. He started to run to the southwest."

Leaving Matthews, Gardner went to the barn, where he cornered Don Gardner and Herringer with the shotgun. Holding them at bay, he ordered Martha to bring a horse from the barn. When she did, he handed her the shotgun, which she used to cover the deputies while Gardner mounted. "Go get Irvine," Martha said to Gardner. "He's the dirty dog you want."

Gardner overtook Irvine in a brushy ravine near a creek several hundred yards from the house. When Irvine attempted to hide in the brush, Gardner ordered him to come out and "tell the truth" about the whole matter, referring to the court case. Irvine refused. "I told him to come out of the hollow, and I shot when he didn't," Gardner later related.

Gardner fired twice, hitting Irvine in the neck and blowing away his jaw. Without waiting to see if Irvine was dead, Gardner rode back to the house and told Martha to inform the deputies where to find Irvine. By then, Matthews and the other deputies had removed Stuart's body to Welby and spread the alarm. Cannon made his way to the ravine and found Irvine barely alive, groping blindly about in the mud. Unable to move the bigger man alone, Cannon ran for help. Irvine was taken to the county hospital and eventually transferred to Holy Cross Hospital in Salt Lake. On April 19, despite receiving several blood transfusions and round-the-clock care, Irvine died. He was buried in the Salt Lake City Cemetery.

Police response to the shooting nearly resulted in additional deaths. At 1300 South on State Street, a Utah Light and Traction Company repair truck turned in front of a southbound, fast-moving sheriff's car. The collision seriously injured deputies Dick Giles and Ben Nickerson. Although suffering from internal injuries, Giles got into a trailing car and went on to the Gardner farm. Nickerson, who suffered severe facial lacerations that nearly cost him an eye, was taken to the hospital. Giles was present at the arrest of Gardner but collapsed immediately after. Rushed to the hospital, he underwent immediate surgery. Both deputies eventually recovered.

Meanwhile, the scene at the Gardner farm was one of chaos. Gardner barricaded himself in his home with a rifle. Deputies surrounded the home,

George Gardner was executed for the murders of his business partner Joseph Irvine and Deputy Gordon Stuart. (Utah State Department of Corrections)

and a temporary command post was set up at the general store in Welby. Salt Lake County Sheriff C. Frank Emery arrived and was preparing to lead his men in an assault on the Gardner home when the store owner's wife asked if she could try and talk the Gardners into giving up. With one deputy dead and two others possibly dying, Emery agreed. Mrs. Stroshahl went into the home and returned with the Gardners a few minutes later. (The name Stroshahl alternately appears in newspapers spelled as Droshel, Droshall, Trohfahl, Stroshal, and Strohsahl.)

The Gardners were taken to the county jail. Martha wept silently during the drive. Gardner admitted shooting both men, claiming that Stuart had "forced" him to shoot by rushing him. Regarding Irvine, Gardner said: "Well, there is one consolation. There is one man who won't steal anymore."

The Gardners were placed in separate cells. George complained about the accommodations, while Martha continued to weep, claiming that the shootings were all a terrible misunderstanding. She told jailers that Gardner would not have attacked the deputies had he known that all they wanted was the stock.

On April 19, the same day that Irvine died, Stuart was laid to rest in the Sandy City Cemetery. Because of the number of people attending, funeral services were held in the LDS Sandy Ward amusement hall and overseen by Reverend Elmer I. Goshen of Salt Lake's First Congregational Church. Goshen, Emery, and others eulogized Stuart and called for financial assistance for his widow and son. After the services, several hundred people followed the hearse to the cemetery for graveside services. All were dumbfounded by what happened next.

The mourners had just bowed their heads for the final prayer when two vehicles pulled up to the cemetery and eight men in full regalia of the Ku

Klux Klan stepped out. Hoods covering the men's faces and mud smeared across the license plates of the cars prevented anyone from determining who they were. As the robed figures formed into the shape of a cross and silently marched through the crowd of mourners, a *Salt Lake Telegram* photographer snapped a picture of the first public appearance by the Utah Klan. The Klansman placed a large floral cross at Stuart's grave. A tag on the cross read: "Knights of the Ku Klux Klan, Salt Lake Chapter No. 1, April 19, 1922." Turning to the west, the Klansmen raised their left hands in silent salute before departing as quietly as they had come. The ceremony at the cemetery was not the only display of Klan support. The organization was also the single largest contributor to a fund set up to aid Stuart's widow, donating $150 of the $1,217 eventually collected.

No evidence exists that Stuart was a member of the Klan. It is important to note, however, that the Klan failed to make similar appearances at the funerals of other police officers killed in the line of duty. Still, at the time, the Klan was just beginning to emerge in Utah, and many felt that the demonstration at the Sandy cemetery, which occurred in conjunction with the appearance of Klan-related advertisements in newspapers, was more a demonstration of support for law and order than to honor Stuart in particular.

Whatever the reason, the community did not need the help of the Klan to whip feelings about Stuart's murder to a volatile level. Following the funeral, a number of mourners stopped off for refreshments at a Sandy pool hall. An argument between pool hall employee Frank Bagley and H.H. Roscher resulted in Roscher's threat to kill the employee. Bagley responded by telling Roscher that he was as bad as Gardner. "Gardner certainly was justified in shooting Stuart," Roscher reportedly replied. "Gardner was a high class man and was justified in doing what he did."

Unfortunately for Roscher, the murdered deputy's uncle Moroni Stuart was sitting a few feet away and overheard the remark. A fight started, and it ended with Roscher being badly beaten and chased through town by a furious mob of more than two hundred men. Only the intervention of the Sandy marshal prevented Roscher from being lynched. He was later fined fifty dollars for disturbing the peace. "They were beating the wadding out of him," said Marshal C.M. Anderson. "I took him away from them into my car and brought him to Salt Lake." Although Roscher denied making the statement, several men later testified that they had heard it.

On April 18, Gardner was arraigned before Salt Lake City Judge Ben Johnson. He refused to enter a plea to a charge of first-degree murder in connection with the death of Stuart. Gardner exhibited such indifference to the proceedings that the court was forced to enter a not-guilty plea for him.

Following the testimony of witnesses, trial dates were set for George Gardner on May 8 and for Martha on May 22. Two days later, both were back in court to answer another first-degree murder charge in connection with the death of Irvine. This time, Gardner and his wife pleaded not guilty.

By the time of his trial before Judge Ephraim Hanson of the Third District Court, Gardner's account of the Stuart murder had changed along with his demeanor. He took the stand on May 10 and sobbed as he recounted the hardships of his early life in Cache Valley. Although he admitted to picking up the shotgun to "settle" Irvine's claim to the stock by killing him, he insisted that Stuart's death was accidental. "When I was coming through the dining room, I felt to see if the safety was on, and in my anger of Irvine coming to the place, I pulled the trigger," Gardner testified, contradicting the testimony of a string of officers who claimed the shooting of Stuart was premeditated. "Then the door between the dining room and the kitchen was closed against the gun and it was discharged again."

Under cross-examination Gardner admitted that on April 9, nine days before the murders, he had threatened to kill Irvine or anyone else who came to get the cattle. He also admitted that he had gone into the house to get the shotgun to kill his brother-in-law.

After deliberating for six hours, the jury returned a verdict of guilty without recommendation for mercy. Gardner, pale and worn, received the news without emotion. On May 20, Hanson sentenced Gardner to death and offered him the option of hanging or firing squad. Gardner chose "shooting." "It is always an unpleasant duty to inflict the death penalty," Hanson told Gardner, "but if ever there was a case that justified it, yours is that case." He ordered Gardner shot to death at the Utah State Prison on July 14.

Several attempts were made to spare Gardner's life. His sentence was immediately appealed to the Utah Supreme Court, which affirmed the lower court's sentence. On March 23, 1923, Gardner was again sentenced to die. However, just days before the execution, Governor Charles R. Mabey granted a reprieve to investigate the possibility of Gardner being insane, a claim made by Gardner's attorneys and several citizens opposed to the death penalty. Specialists determined that, while Gardner was "subnormal," he was not nor ever had been insane. His date with the firing squad was set and eventually carried out, appeals for clemency continuing up to the final hours.

On the evening of his execution, Martha, free on bond, visited her husband at the county jail, encouraging him to be brave. He promised that he would. His final request to Sheriff Harries was that he be buried in Mendon next to his mother. Harries agreed, paying the costs over and above the county allowance for the burial out of his own pocket.

Six weeks after Gardner's execution, Martha Gerrans married L.D. McAdams in Ogden, Utah. Mired deep in her own legal troubles, she tried to keep the wedding a secret. From June 1922 to February 1924 she stood trial four times on charges of first-degree murder for her participation in the killing of her brother-in-law.

At the first trial, police officers testified that she had cursed Irvine, pitched rocks at him, and, following the death of Stuart, brought a horse to her husband and held deputies at bay with the shotgun while urging Gardner to hunt Irvine down and kill him. Mrs. Otto Ashbridge testified that at an unspecified time prior to the murders Martha had said to her, "George pulled a gun on Joe this morning. It's too bad he didn't kill him."

On June 15, 1922, Martha took the stand and admitted having told her husband to go get Irvine, but claimed she did so to prevent him from shooting any more "innocent" men. Her attorney, J.E. Darmer of Salt Lake City, attempted to show the jury that Martha was not rational at the time, that the murder of Stuart and fear for her own life had momentarily unhinged her mind.

The case was submitted to the jury on June 16. After deliberating for twenty-eight hours, the jury returned to court and announced that it could not settle on a verdict. Several days later, Martha was released on a $5,000 bond so that she could assist in the wheat harvest on her farm.

A subsequent retrial ended with Gerrans's conviction of voluntary manslaughter and a ten-year prison sentence. The verdict was immediately appealed to the Utah Supreme Court, which reversed the conviction, citing the trial court's failure to allow the jury to pass upon the plea of former jeopardy. A third trial before Hanson began November 17, 1923, and ended in another hung jury.

On January 24, 1924, Gerrans (now McAdams) faced her fourth and final trial before Third District Judge L.B. Wight. After a week of testimony, interrupted briefly by the death on February 4 of former president Woodrow Wilson, a jury acquitted McAdams. She subsequently moved with her husband to Brookings, Oregon, where she died in 1971.

Margaret Irvine eventually remarried. She died in 1944. Joseph Irvine's remains were subsequently reburied next to her in the Salt Lake City Cemetery. In addition to the public fund collected following the death of her husband, Florence Stuart received $5,000 from the County Workmen's Fund at sixteen dollars per week. She later remarried and moved with her new husband to Colorado. Her son Gordon Hal currently lives in southern California.

Nephi P. Pierce

Salt Lake City Police Department
March 26, 1923

During the early morning hours of November 18, Denver & Rio Grande Western special agents John Pennunzio and Albert Pezoldt were patrolling the Pueblo, Colorado, rail yard when they encountered two men walking down the tracks. Pennunzio and Pezoldt stopped the men and were in the process of questioning them when a third man came up behind them with a pistol. The officers were robbed before being bound, gagged, and thrown into a boxcar. Laughing at the struggling railroad agents, the suspects then caught a westbound freight. Among the items taken in the robbery was Pezoldt's .38-caliber Colt "Police Special." A month before, Pezoldt had used the pistol to kill a car thief who resisted arrest. After the shooting, Pezoldt proudly notched the wooden grip of the pistol. The mark would later help identify the pistol after it was used to murder Salt Lake City Police Sergeant Nephi P. Pierce.

Although lawmen did not know it at the time, the three suspects were Henry C. Hett, his brother Lawrence, and Arthur Hayes. The robbery of the D&RGW agents was just one in a series of hold-ups the gang committed in their travels across Colorado and Utah. Hayes, 18, was from Chicago, where he had lived with a sister before hearing the call of California. Like thousands of young men of the time, he crossed the country by hopping freights. He made it to Denver and then south to Colorado City, where he was jailed for vagrancy. There he met the Hett brothers. Lawrence, 18, and Henry, 20, were from Milwaukee, Wisconsin, where they had been orphaned by the death of their parents ten years before. Upon reaching legal age in August the two brothers received several thousand dollars from their parents' estate. They used some of the money to buy a car. After traveling erratically around the country, the two ended up getting tossed into the Colorado Springs jail when Henry lost a fight with a police officer during a robbery investigation.

On November 17, the Hetts were released from jail. They went to Pueblo, where they met up with Hayes and immediately set out to work their way across the country by robbing those they encountered. For that purpose, Henry had a .38-caliber pistol. Their first victim was a Pueblo high school student whom they robbed, beat unconscious, and left bound and gagged in the cellar doorway of a church. Three hours later, they robbed the D&RGW agents.

The affair with the railroad agents put Colorado authorities on the alert. When their freight arrived in Canon City, the three robbers had a brief run-in

Salt Lake City Police Sergeant Nephi Pierce died four months after being gunned down without warning near 500 South Main. (Salt Lake Police Museum)

with the local sheriff, which ended when Hayes got the drop on the lawman and forced him to retreat. From there, the three continued into Utah, eventually losing track of each other.

On November 26, Hayes and Henry Hett encountered each other again in downtown Salt Lake City. Hett was broke and Hayes was down to spare change. The two went to Hayes's room in a boardinghouse and hatched the idea of a crime spree.

That night, Salt Lake City police officers were kept busy by a sudden string of armed robberies committed by two unmasked young men. Most notable was the attempted hijacking of a car driven by twenty-six-year-old Douglas H. Murphy near Beck's Hot Springs. Hayes and Hett jumped on the running boards of Murphy's car and tried to force him to drive out of the city. Murphy, who feared for his own life as well as that of his date Alice Green, complied just long enough to find a streetcar to crash into. The collision, which demolished the car and injured both Murphy and Green, threw the bandits off. They escaped into the night. Despite the severity of the crash, Hett and Hayes suffered only minor injuries. Both Murphy and Green were treated at the emergency hospital and released. Murphy later identified Hett and Hayes as the men who tried to hijack his car.

A few minutes after midnight, Officers Nephi Pierce and George Watson were patrolling Main Street near 500 South. Although much larger than Pierce, Watson was pleased to be working with Salt Lake City's "fighting sergeant." At fifty-three, Pierce was a seasoned veteran of hundreds of scraps with the criminal element. If anyone could track down a pair of robbers, it would be Pierce, who was considered unusually fearless and daring.

Henry Hett managed to turn his life around in prison but was executed for the murder of Pierce. (Utah State Department of Corrections)

Born May 9, 1869, in Sweden, Pierce immigrated to Utah with his family two years later. The family homesteaded in Emery County for years. He married Marie Lorentzen in 1898. The couple later moved to Salt Lake City, where Pierce worked as a conductor and motorman for the Electric Railway Company. He joined the police force in 1906 and was appointed sergeant ten years later. Pierce lived with Marie, by then nearly an invalid, at 1035 Bryan Avenue. The couple attended St. Paul's Episcopal Church.

Pierce and Watson stopped briefly at the Auto Supply Company, 426 South Main, and advised the night clerk to be on the watch for any suspicious characters. Proceeding south on the west side of Main Street, they crossed 500 South and spotted two young men walking furtively in their direction. The two men were Hett and Hayes. As they passed the officers, Watson called to them: "Which way are you fellows going?"

Hett's response was to pull his gun and spin around. Pointing it at the officers, he ordered them to get their hands up. Stunned, Watson complied. Pierce, however, ducked toward a tree and reached inside his coat for his revolver. Hett fired once, striking the sergeant in the left side. Pierce collapsed in a heap on the sidewalk.

At the sound of the shot, Hayes opted for discretion and raced off into the night. He told officers later that he hadn't expected Hett to shoot anyone. Robbing passersby was one thing, shooting cops was something else.

Still covering Watson, Hett ordered the patrolman into a vacant lot and forced him to lie face down. Taking Watson's pistol, Hett savagely bludgeoned the officer unconscious. Believing Watson dead, Hett rejoined his partner at Main and Broadway, chiding Hayes for his lack of nerve. Realizing that having

Arthur Hayes, an accomplice of Henry Hett.
(Utah State Department of Corrections)

"croaked the bulls" would start a manhunt, the two men decided to cache the guns before they were stopped and searched. Wrapping them in an overcoat, they hid their pistols under a platform in the alley behind the post office. Then they headed back to their room at the boardinghouse.

Pierce was not dead. A citizen attracted by the sound of the shot found him on the sidewalk alive but unable to move. A few minutes later, Watson staggered out of the lot, his gashed head pouring blood. Despite their injuries, both of the officers were able to give descriptions of their assailants.

Pierce was taken first to the emergency hospital and then to Holy Cross Hospital, where an x-ray showed that the bullet had cut his spinal column. Even if he lived, he would be permanently paralyzed. Pierce mustered enough strength to tell co-workers to keep news of the wound from his wife until the following day. Knowing that she was emotionally frail, Pierce was afraid the news would cause her to suffer a mental breakdown.

Furious police officers began searching for the gunmen in the time-honored manner of arresting everyone who even remotely resembled the suspect. Nearly fifty men were tossed into jail within a few hours of the shooting, their alibis methodically examined by detectives as the hours dragged into morning. It was a slow process. Fortunately, however, the process was cut short when a citizen came to the station after sunrise and reported finding some guns stashed near the post office.

Rather than move the guns, detectives set up surveillance with the hope that the suspects might return. A few hours later, Hayes was arrested as he tried to remove the bundle from under the platform. Hett, who was watching from a distance, was also picked up.

Watson identified Hett as the man who beat him. Questioned at length by detectives, Hett at first blamed Hayes for everything. Finally, on December 5, Hett broke down and gave a full confession to the killing, though he claimed an unidentified stranger rather than Hayes was with him during the attack. The case against the two was clinched when Hett and Hayes were taken to the hospital. Pierce identified them from his bed. Hett apologized to both officers, who forgave him for his actions.

"I'm sorry, too," Watson replied. "I hope you'll be a better man when you come out than you are now."

"I'll try to be," Hett replied, as he was led away.

A few weeks later, Hett and Hayes pled guilty to attempted murder and highway robbery charges and were sentenced to prison. However, everything changed on March 26, 1923, when Pierce suddenly died. The medical certificate of death lists the cause as "septicaemia ... traumatic myelitis due to spinal cord section from bullet." Funeral services for Pierce were held at Salt Lake City's Masonic Temple under the direction of officers of the Mount Moriah Lodge, No. 2. Because there wasn't enough room inside, hundreds of people gathered on the lawn to pay their respects. Pierce was laid to rest in Mount Olivet Cemetery.

Pierce's concerns about his wife's ability to handle tragedy proved justified. On July 5, 1923, three months after the death of her husband, Marie hanged herself in the basement of the couple's home. Although neighbors had maintained a watch over Marie since the death of her husband, she was apparently determined to end her life. She slipped away for a few minutes and was later found hanging from a beam in the basement. The cause of death was determined to be suicidal intent due to "melancholia." She was buried next to her husband.

In May, Hett and Hayes appeared before Judge G.A. Iverson and pleaded not guilty to charges of first-degree murder. The trial was held January 7, 1924. It took a jury a matter of a few hours to find them guilty. On January 16, Hett was sentenced to death, while Hayes received life in prison.

During the following year, Hett's close association with Catholic prison warden Father William T. Hart brought about a significant change in him. Hett accepted full responsibility for his actions and frequently counseled other prisoners against a life of crime. But despite repeated appeals from Hart, the Utah Supreme Court upheld Hett's death sentence.

Hett's life ended at sunrise on February 20, 1925, when he calmly faced a firing squad. In the next cell, Hayes sobbed uncontrollably as his friend was led away by the prison warden. On the way to the prison yard, Hett was allowed to pause at each tier of cells and shout, "Goodbye, boys." A few minutes later, he was strapped to a chair. Holding a rosary, Hett kept repeating, "I'm sorry, I'm sorry," until the bullets ended his life.

In 1926, the Utah Supreme Court overturned Hayes's murder conviction, and he was resentenced for armed robbery. On October 16, he was paroled.

David H. Crowther
Salt Lake City Police Department
October 12, 1923

On the morning of October 13, Anna Crowther called the Salt Lake City Police Department to inquire why her forty-five-year-old police officer husband had failed to return home from work the previous evening. Detectives determined that Crowther left police headquarters at 2:00 p.m. on October 12, ostensibly to patrol the west-side rail yards and hobo jungles in his own car. He was last seen at approximately 4:00 p.m., driving along 900 West near North Temple. A search began that lasted through the day and night but failed to produce any sign of Crowther.

At 10:00 a.m. the following day, a man walking his dog along the west bank of the Jordan River a short distance north of South Temple discovered a patch of blood and a spent cartridge casing in the middle of the dirt road. A brief search of the area revealed Crowther's body hidden in some weeds on the bank of the river, just three blocks from his home at 1027 West on North Temple.

A medical examination revealed that Crowther had been shot once in the back of the head with a .32-caliber automatic pistol. He had been dead for approximately eighteen hours. Officers found the misshapen bullet that killed Crowther on the road. Missing, however, were Crowther's .38-caliber Colt revolver, watch, money, and 1920 Studebaker Special Six touring car.

Police attention immediately focused on Salt Lake City's transient population. The area where Crowther's body was found was a notorious "jungle," a place where hobos camped while waiting to catch a freight train out of town. Crowther, a fifteen-year police veteran, had a reputation for moving tramps along in this particular area, perhaps because it was so close to his home. At the end of his shift each day, Crowther customarily made a tour along the banks of the river to roust the transients, often giving them a ride in his car to a location where they could jump on a boxcar.

Police Chief Joseph E. Burbidge knew immediately that the key to solving Crowther's murder was the Studebaker. The killer had numerous routes available to him once out of town. Finding him depended primarily on alerting law enforcement agencies along all highways leading away from Salt Lake. News of the crime was therefore immediately broadcast from the radio at the United States Air Mail field. By evening, a thousand circulars describing Crowther's car and property were in the mail to police agencies throughout the western states. "The murderers left with the automobile and will no doubt cache it along the highway or drive it through to some city," the circular read. "Please notify all your gas stations and garages to be on the lookout for this automobile or anyone in possession of it."

Acting Governor H.E. Crockett offered a reward of $500 for the arrest of Crowther's killer. Meanwhile, Burbidge put every available man on the case. Officers immediately began arresting hobos and questioning them at length about the killing. However, while some of the transients were booked for carrying concealed weapons, none of their guns matched the murder weapon, and no one had any pertinent information regarding Crowther. It became apparent to officers that they would have to wait until the car turned up.

Shortly before 4:00 p.m. on October 16, detectives received a telegram from San Bernardino County Sheriff W.A. Shay, informing them of the arrests of three men caught driving Crowther's bloodstained car at Ludlow, a small Mojave Desert town fifty miles west of Barstow, California. The men gave their names and ages as Fred Dupond, 20, Robert Sanders, 20, and George Williams, 19. All three were booked for suspicion of murder and violation of the Dyer Act—the transportation of a stolen car across state lines. Because of the paperwork and distances involved, it would be at least a week before Utah authorities could get custody of the killers. Utah detectives headed south while extradition papers were prepared.

Sanders immediately confessed to San Bernardino County deputies that he was the triggerman. In his possession was a .32-caliber Mauser pistol that turned out to be the murder weapon. He claimed that his companions were not involved and that he shot Crowther when the officer resisted a robbery attempt. Sanders would, however, change his story many times before officers were able to determine what really happened.

Although authorities would not find out until later, Sanders was actually Ralph Seyboldt, released September 14 from the Wyoming State Prison in Rawlins after serving two years for grand larceny. In Rawlins, Seyboldt hooked up with another ex-con, Joseph E. Marenger (alias Dupond), and the two went to Evanston, where they fell in with Noel E. White (alias Williams). Before proceeding on to Salt Lake City, Seyboldt stole the murder weapon from another hobo. On October 8, the three men arrived in Salt Lake City hungry and broke. Three days later they attempted to raise some traveling money by robbing a

Salt Lake City Officer David H. Crowther was murdered just blocks from his home while showing a group of transients where to catch a train. (Salt Lake Police Museum)

man at gunpoint, but the victim was able to get away. On October 13, they were more successful, knocking a man down and robbing him.

When they were arrested in California, Seyboldt told deputies that he had killed Crowther in a fit of anger. When asked why, Seyboldt replied, "I guess I must have lost my head." Seyboldt wasn't as eager to talk when Utah authorities arrived a few days later. Although he first admitted the killing to them, he then recanted his confession and stopped talking. All detectives could get out of him was that "something" had happened.

On October 18, Crowther was buried in the Salt Lake City Cemetery. More than two thousand police officers and citizens filled the police department gymnasium for the funeral services. Trustees and members of the city's chain gang provided the decorations. Crowther had joined the department in 1908 and served as a mounted patrolman before being assigned to supervise the chain gang and vagrancy detail. He was survived by his widow and three teenage children.

Three days later, Seyboldt, Marenger, and White were brought to Salt Lake City by train. By the time he reached Utah, Seyboldt had clammed up. It was Marenger doing the talking, and he gave detectives a detailed account of Crowther's murder. Marenger said they first met Crowther on 600 West between South Temple and 100 South. When the three men told Crowther that they were headed to Reno, he offered to give them a lift to a place where they could hop a train. Marenger admitted that he knew Seyboldt had a gun but thought Seyboldt had left it hidden in his bedroll. Crowther first took the three vagrants to a home where they got some food. He then drove them to a spot 250 yards south of North Temple.

Ralph Seyboldt claimed he shot Crowther in the head because the officer tried to kiss him. (Utah Department of Corrections)

It was recorded that, as the car was coming to a halt, Seyboldt, who was sitting beside Crowther in the front seat, "is said to have stealthily reached around the back of the officer, and with the revolver in his left hand, fired into the back of Crowther's head as he was leaning over in the act of turning the ignition key on the instrument board of the automobile."

The three men dragged the body into the weeds and then took off in the automobile. They stopped at a gas station and then sped south out of town, trying to put as much distance between themselves and the crime as possible. Seyboldt repeatedly threatened White and Marenger along the way, telling them to keep their mouths shut about what happened. At Cedar City, the killers sold Crowther's gun for five dollars; they pawned his watch in St. George for ten dollars and some groceries. In Las Vegas, they got five dollars for the car's spare tire and wheel. In Amboy, California, just hours before their arrest, they sold the car's spotlights.

Seyboldt was furious when Marenger "squealed" on him. He immediately broke his silence and blamed Marenger for the murder. When asked why he first confessed to the murder and was now blaming Marenger, Seyboldt said he thought Marenger and White would be released by California officers and would then break him out of jail. Pinning the murder on Marenger was just the next in a series of Seyboldt's versions of what happened on the night of October 12. The constantly changing stories served only to further erode his credibility and eventually put him in front of a firing squad.

On October 26, Seyboldt pled not guilty to a charge of first-degree murder before Judge Noel S. Pratt. The following March, he stood trial for the murder of Crowther. On the stand, he admitted killing Crowther but claimed he did it in self-defense. He said Crowther was drunk and made homosexual advances toward him. When Seyboldt resisted, Crowther allegedly flew into a rage and pulled a gun. Seyboldt knocked it out of his hand. When the officer bent over to retrieve the gun, Seyboldt said he accidentally shot him in the back of the head while aiming for his shoulder.

The jury didn't buy it. On April 1, 1924, they deliberated for fifteen minutes before finding Seyboldt guilty of murder, a record time for jury deliberation in a capital case in Utah.

On September 4, 1924, Marenger and White appeared in Third District Court, where they were each sentenced to twenty years in prison for second-degree murder. Marenger was paroled in 1930, White in 1934. Seyboldt wasn't so fortunate.

At 8:01 a.m. on January 15, 1926, Seyboldt was shot to death by a firing squad in the snowy yard of the Utah State Prison. At the time of his death, he was the most reprieved condemned prisoner in Utah, having lost his seventh appeal just two days before he was executed.

Minutes before the rifles spoke, Seyboldt had one more version of what happened the night Crowther was killed. "Crowther did not have a gun in his hand when I shot him," Seyboldt said to Warden Richard E. Davis. "That statement was not true." Seyboldt's last words were short and to the point. "I haven't much to say. I want the public to know that I have told the truth all the way through. I regret very much this unfortunate affair. My conscience is clear."

The Crowther family would contribute again to the Utah law enforcement community. David Crowther's sister Caroline Kelly died in 1897, leaving her husband alone with an infant son. Raised primarily by his maternal grandparents, Leonard C. (Kelly) Crowther was twenty-seven when his uncle was murdered. "Len" Crowther subsequently joined the Salt Lake City Police Department, rising through the ranks until he became chief of police from November 1945 to January 1952, and again from 1960 to 1962.

Brigham Heber Honey Jr.
William Nolan Huntsman

Salt Lake City Police Department
February 15–16, 1924

Every day hundreds of people pass the alcove of 307 South Main in downtown Salt Lake City. Located in the Judge Building, the door leads to a small shop

Salt Lake City Patrolman Brigham H. Honey
died the day after being shot by a robbery suspect
who then turned the gun on himself and his
girlfriend. (Salt Lake Police Museum)

space that was once a fur store. In 1924, the bloodiest episode in the history of
the Salt Lake City Police Department came to an end in this nondescript
doorway. The murders of Officers Brigham H. Honey and Nolan W. Huntsman
occurred during an especially dark period for the police department. Of the
thirteen Salt Lake City police officers murdered in the line of duty, five were
killed between 1921 and 1924.

On February 15, 1924, William Lee, a parole violator from California, hid
in the doorway after murdering the two Salt Lake City police officers. Wounded
and surrounded by a growing crowd, Lee shot his girlfriend and then himself.
(It is possible that William Lee was an alias. San Quentin prison, where Lee
allegedly served time, does not have a listing for a William Lee paroled during
this period.)

William Lee, 24, and Beatrice Hunter, 25, arrived in Salt Lake City from
Ogden on the evening of February 15. Hunter later told officers that the two
had met in San Francisco, California, less than a month before and only days
after Lee claimed to have been paroled from San Quentin Prison after serving
a term for forgery. Lee reportedly worked at a Susanville fruit company for
three days before deciding he had had enough of California. He jumped parole
and, together with Hunter, headed east.

On February 13, Hunter pawned two silver rings in Reno, Nevada. The
money allowed the couple to buy a single train ticket to Ogden. Hunter used
the ticket, while Lee hitchhiked and met up with her in Ogden on February 15.
After briefly looking for work in Ogden, the two traveled to Salt Lake City by
rail, arriving at 9:00 p.m. The weather was cold and the two had no money for
lodging. For two hours they wandered the streets.

Salt Lake City Patrolman Nolan F. Huntsman, killed in the shootout with the robbery suspect. (Salt Lake Police Museum)

Patrolman William Nolan Huntsman was working that night. Huntsman was born May 12, 1897, in Egin, Idaho, to Lafayette and Elizabeth McMahon Huntsman. The twenty-six-year-old officer married Lucy Lamb Robinson on June 23, 1920. The young couple lived with their infant daughter at 238 South 200 East. Huntsman was an army veteran, having served in the U.S. Army Medical Corps during World War I. He joined the force on May 18, 1923, just nine months before the day he died. His foot beat was on Broadway (300 South).

Huntsman's beat that night adjoined that of Patrolman Brigham Honey, a six-year veteran of the force. Born December 9, 1889, in Kanab to Brigham H., Sr., and Margaret Jackson Honey, he married Helen Pauline Lund on November 17, 1910. He joined the police department on July 1, 1918. The couple lived with their two children at 426 Cottage Avenue. For the past several weeks, Honey's foot beat had been on West Temple. But minutes before leaving the station that evening, the shift sergeant ordered him to switch with rookie officer Jennings "Sparky" Ipson and walk the Third South beat instead.

Shortly after 11:00 p.m., Lee and Hunter stopped near the State Cafe, 46 West Broadway. Hunter later claimed that Lee said only that he was going into the restaurant to buy cigarettes and asked her to wait for him on the corner of Main Street. The cashier, Mrs. A.M. Pistolas, was reading a magazine when Lee walked in and began rifling the register. When Pistolas jumped up to stop him, Lee stuck a .32-caliber Colt automatic in her face and quietly said, "Stick 'em up or I'll kill you." So casual was Lee's demeanor that the few customers sitting in booths failed to notice the robbery. Lee took approximately fifty dollars and left the store.

As soon as Lee was outside, waiter Frank Regis grabbed a .32-caliber pistol from a drawer and gave chase. Regis watched as Lee rejoined Hunter and turned south on Main Street. Regis ran to the corner and fired two shots as the couple crossed to the east side of Main Street. The shots alerted Honey and Huntsman, who came running. When Regis told the officers about the robbery and pointed out the fleeing couple, the officers gave chase. Honey's route took him down the east side of the street behind Lee and Hunter, while Huntsman took the west side, running to get ahead of them.

Knowing that he was being overtaken, Lee told Hunter to wait for him in front of Leffs Fur Store, 307 South Main. He then ran down the block to Boes Jewelry, 337 South Main, where the officers closed in on him. Approaching from across the street, Huntsman ordered Lee to throw up his hands. Instead, Lee ducked behind a parked car and fired several shots at the officer. Struck first in the left leg, Huntsman fell across the curb, where Lee then shot him through the heart.

Closing in from the north, Honey saw his fellow officer fall. He fired at Lee and hit the bandit in the side, the bullet cutting through his liver. Unfortunately, the standards of the police department may have unwittingly worked against Honey. At the time, Salt Lake City police officers carried revolvers chambered for a .32-20 cartridge. Originally developed as a varmint cartridge that would conveniently chamber in both a rifle and pistol, the .32-20 was not much of a man-stopper.

Although badly wounded, Lee still managed to return fire and shoot Honey twice. Hit in the stomach, the officer collapsed on the sidewalk at 327 South

Police officers carry Brigham Honey's casket from the LDS Assembly House on Temple Square. (Salt Lake Police Museum)

Main. Bystander G.H. Davis narrowly escaped being shot during this exchange of gunfire when a bullet passed through his coat.

With a bullet in him, a crowd gathering, and additional officers converging on the scene, Lee was out of options. He staggered back north on Main Street. Witnesses say he rejoined Hunter near the doorway of the fur shop. ZCMI salesman J. Byron Reid saw Lee pull Hunter into the darkened doorway and then heard two shots. He stopped his car and cautiously went to investigate. He found the couple slumped near the door of the fur shop, bleeding profusely from bullet wounds in their heads. Loading Hunter into his car, Reid drove her to a hospital. Lee was taken to the same hospital but died at 5:50 a.m. without regaining consciousness.

Honey was taken to Holy Cross Hospital, where assistant city health commisioner J.J. Galligan operated on him. Galligan removed part of Honey's intestines perforated by Lee's bullet. By then, Honey was already in shock from hemorrhaging. He died at 8:10 a.m.

The lone survivor of the gunfight was Hunter. She told officers that when Lee dragged her into the darkened doorway of the fur shop, he placed the gun against her face and pulled the trigger before turning it on himself. Miraculously, the bullet only pierced Hunter through both cheeks, ripping away part of the roof of her mouth. She was able to answer questions from detectives only hours after being shot.

Hunter initially claimed that she barely knew Lee, but later changed her story and said that they were going to get married. She insisted that she knew nothing of the robbery beforehand or even that Lee had a gun when he entered

Hearses surrounded by a police procession escort fallen officers Brigham Honey and Nolan Huntsman to the Salt Lake City Cemetery. (Salt Lake Police Museum)

the cafe. Officers doubted Hunter's story after finding several .32-caliber cartridges in her purse. She said that Lee must have placed them in her purse after shooting her. When asked for Lee's motive in shooting her, Hunter said she didn't know, "unless he was crazed."

Police Chief Joseph F. Burbidge pressured the county attorney to file murder charges against Hunter as an accomplice. On February 26, Hunter was charged with first-degree murder. When blood poisoning set in, she remained at the hospital under guard.

The day after the murders, a trust fund was set up for the widows of Honey and Huntsman. Within two weeks, the fund contained $8,048.51 and was still growing. In a rather macabre twist, the State Cafe donated the blood-soaked bills taken during the robbery and later recovered from Lee's body.

On February 20, a joint funeral service for the slain officers was held in Assembly Hall on Temple Square. Mayor C. Clarence Neslen and LDS apostle Melvin J. Ballard eulogized the officers as heroes and called for citizens to renew their commitment to law and order. Police officers and firemen lined South Temple as two hearses traveling side by side carried the bodies to the Salt Lake City Cemetery. More than 150 cars followed behind. In sharp contrast to the mourning for the officers, Lee's body lay unclaimed in the O'Donnell Mortuary.

Having lost five officers in four years, Burbidge set about trying to stop what some were calling a slow massacre of Salt Lake police officers. He issued a "shoot to kill" policy regarding some actions of hoodlums and told the press that he wished every member of the police department would comply with it.

Whether Burbidge's order changed the department's attitude about dealing with the criminal element is not known. What is certain is that despite future shootouts with lawbreakers it would be twenty-seven years before another Salt Lake City officer died in a gun battle. In 1927, the Salt Lake Police Department again standardized the sidearm carried by all officers, formally adopting the Colt .38-caliber Army Special.

Hunter never stood trial. Unable to prove that she played an active role in the murders, the county attorney dropped the charges in March. A few days later, Hunter quietly checked out of the hospital and disappeared.

Both Lucy Huntsman and Helen Honey remarried. Lucy died of Addison's Disease in 1938 and was buried next to Nolan. Although she lived another sixty-four years, dying in 1986, Helen is buried next to Brigham in the Salt Lake City Cemetery.

James Milton Burns
Castle Gate Police Department
June 15, 1925

Thirty-one years after rustlers gunned down his father, Castle Gate Officer J. Milton Burns also died from gunshots received in the line of duty. However, unlike his father's murderers, who were never brought to justice, the killer of "Milt" Burns met his fate in one of the most shameful incidents in Utah history.

Born April 28, 1873, in Mount Pleasant, Burns was twenty-one when his father was murdered. As a young man, Milt herded sheep in the Robber's Roost country. Two years after the death of his father, Burns married Olivia Peacock in the Manti LDS Temple. The couple settled in Manti, where in 1904 Burns accepted a job as the city marshal. He served that community until 1906, when he was appointed deputy sheriff of Sanpete County. In 1914, Burns followed in his father's footsteps and was elected sheriff of Sanpete County. He remained in this capacity until 1920, by which time most of his six children had grown and left home.

In 1922, Burns and his wife relocated to Castle Gate, a coal mining community of approximately eight hundred residents. The couple took up residence in the first home located north of the Castle Gate Hotel. Burns accepted a job as special agent with the Utah Fuel Company and an appointment as the city night marshal.

On the evening of Monday, June 15, Burns made his rounds of the town and the mine buildings on the west side of the Price River. After checking the fan house of the No. 1 Mine shortly after 7:30 p.m., Burns proceeded back across the bridge toward town. There he saw Robert Marshall, an itinerant black miner, standing near the end of the bridge. Two weeks before, the officer had taken a pistol away from him in the town post office. On the day of the killing, Marshall allegedly had quit his job in the Castle Gate Mine, obtained another pistol, and waited along the officer's route to ambush him.

When Burns spotted Marshall on the bridge, the man was leaning over the railing with one hand in a paper sack. As Burns approached to question him, Marshall spun around and shot the officer twice in the abdomen with a pistol concealed in the sack. Burns fell, and Marshall quickly shot him three more times, two of the bullets striking him in the thighs, the last in the stomach. Marshall reportedly then beat the fallen officer on the head with his pistol, ground the heel of his boot in the officer's face, and robbed the dying man of forty dollars and his sidearm. The only witnesses to the murder were several young boys standing aghast at the opposite end of the bridge. As Marshall disappeared into the hills, they ran for help. (Another version of the story regarding Marshall's motive claims that the young boys had taunted him shortly before the arrival of Burns, who was then murdered in a fit of rage.)

Several citizens arrived minutes later and found Burns still alive but motionless. Taken to Castle Gate Hospital, he underwent a two-hour surgical procedure performed by Dr. C.E. McDermid, who found the marshal's intestines and organs badly lacerated. Little hope was held out for his recovery. Burns rallied after the surgery long enough to identify his assailant and explain what he believed to be the motive. But shock from a massive loss of blood soon set in and Burns slipped into a coma. He died at approximately 10:00 p.m. the following day.

After crossing the river, Marshall climbed up the mountain through a steep and narrow draw two hundred yards from the bridge. By the time Deputy Sheriff Henry East arrived on the scene, Marshall had disappeared into the cedars. Rounding up a posse, Sheriff Ray Deming tried to track the killer, but night soon fell and ended the search. Deming then posted guards at strategic locations, hoping one of them would spot Marshall as he tried to slip through the cordon in the morning.

Just before daybreak, Deputy Mack Olson spotted a shadowy figure skulking through the brush near Hiener, a small town at the mouth of Panther Canyon between Helper and Castle Gate. When Olson challenged the figure, it turned and opened fire on him. Marshall and Olson traded several shots without effect before the killer slipped away in the darkness.

For two days, lawmen combed the hills between Helper and Castle Gate, closing off the roads and guarding known avenues of escape. But as the hours passed, many began to believe that Marshall had escaped. Deming decided to dramatically widen the scope of the search. Before leaving for Green River, Utah, and Grand Junction, Colorado, to put authorities there on alert, Deming offered a personal reward of $250 for the arrest and conviction of Marshall.

On Thursday morning, George Gray came into Castle Gate for supplies. After making his purchases, Gray entered the offices of the Utah Fuel Company and informed night watchman John Daskalakis and company clerk Joseph Parmley that Marshall was hiding out in a cabin the two men had once shared in the mouth of Willow Creek. Gray said that Marshall came to the cabin during the night for food and was still there in an exhausted state. After arranging a series of signals to communicate with officers, Gray was sent back to his cabin. Parmley and Daskalakis then notified Deputy East, who quickly formed a posse and surrounded the cabin.

After receiving a signal from the window of the cabin, East and Daskalakis

Castle Gate Officer James Milton Burns. His affiliation with a secret society may have contributed to the fate of his killer. (Sanpete County Sheriff's Office)

crept to the side door and waited. When Gray opened the door and stepped out, the two men rushed inside and pounced on Marshall, who was still in bed asleep. Pinning his arms, the officers stripped two pistols away from him, one of which belonged to Burns. In response to an accusation that he had killed Burns, Marshall sullenly admitted his guilt.

The posse placed Marshall in the backseat of East's car and drove him to Price. Along the route, several cars filled with volunteers still out looking for the killer joined the column. As word spread of the capture, additional vehicles swung into line, until by the time it arrived at Price the column contained nearly twenty vehicles loaded with grim men. At approximately 10:00 a.m., East stopped in front of the courthouse and went inside to report the capture, leaving Marshall in the car surrounded by a growing crowd.

Several factors contributed to what happened next, not the least of which was Burns's membership in a secret organization. Although an active Mormon and widely respected in the community, Burns reportedly was also a member of the Ku Klux Klan. Since 1924, the Klan had actively recruited in Carbon County and numbered among its members many of the community's most prominent citizens. The Roaring Twenties were a particularly lawless time in Utah, and many residents were initially more attracted to the Klan by the organization's patriotic and crime-fighting claims rather than because of racial prejudices. However, many were fed up by the Klan's alarming intolerance and arrogance, and interest in the organization was already waning by the time of Burns's death.

Unfortunately for Marshall, six members of the posse that captured him were not only close friends of Burns but fellow Klansmen as well. Whereas

Marshall's color was not a significant factor when he was being chased, it undoubtedly meant something when those doing the chasing finally got their hands on him.

As East made his report inside the courthouse, the crowd quickly grew into a mob of approximately 150 men. One man suddenly jumped behind the wheel of East's car while others stepped onto the running boards and subdued the posse members. The car quickly swung into a caravan of approximately fifty other vehicles and drove three blocks east of the courthouse, then south on the Wellington road for three miles to a ranch owned by A.W. Horsley. There they stopped in a grove of cottonwoods. Someone took out a rope and tossed it over a branch. The mob dragged Marshall over to the tree, untied his hands, and fastened the noose around his neck. "Don't you dare put your hands up to your neck to ease that rope," Marshall was told. "Just as sure as you make a move to do that we will cut your hands off. You are going to suffer a long lingering death for what you have done."

A dozen pairs of hands reached for the rope and hoisted Marshall thirty feet into the air. He struggled briefly and then started to twitch. Someone in the crowd began calling off the passing time. Someone else suggested that they speed the process along by shooting him. Others wanted him to suffer.

The mob's desire to make him suffer almost saved Marshall. About nine minutes after he was hung, deputies Sam Garrett, Mack Olson, and Lee Bryner arrived at the lynching site with Price Police Chief Warren Peacock. Garrett ran to the tree and cut the rope, lowering Marshall to the ground. The crowd made no move to interfere with the officers until someone noticed that Marshall showed signs of life. As the officers carried him to their car, a shout went up: "Lynch him, he's still alive."

The mob swarmed over the officers, disarming them and taking away their prisoner again. This time, however, they took no chances that Marshall would escape death. Placing the noose back around his neck, they lifted him three feet off the ground and tied the rope to hold him in position. Then they lifted him thirty feet into the air and dropped him. Marshall died of a broken neck.

Marshall was left in the tree while an estimated eight hundred men, women, and children drove by the lynching site to view his body. A local photographer snapped a picture of the dead man. Deming eventually arrived at the scene, having been delayed by a broken axle on his vehicle. He cut Marshall's body down and transported it to an undertaker.

Earlier that same morning, the body of Milt Burns was placed aboard a train and shipped to Mount Pleasant for burial. On June 20, following funeral services in the town's social hall, Burns's four sons and two brothers carried him to a resting place near that of his father in the Mount Pleasant Cemetery.

Robert Marshall was lynched by Carbon County residents, some of whom may have belonged to the Ku Klux Klan, for the murder of Castle Gate Marshal Milt Burns. (Utah State Historical Society)

Money to bury Marshall in the city cemetery was raised among the African-American residents of Price. On June 28, Reverend M. Gregory, the leader of a black congregation in Sunnyside, conducted a simple funeral ceremony. Shortly before the burial, the Price postmaster received a letter from Pearl Marshall, living in Van Buren, Arkansas. The letter, in which Pearl referred to herself as Marshall's widow, asked for contact with anyone who knew her husband. The letter was passed on to members of the black community.

Governor George H. Dern learned about the lynching the following day when he returned from the season opening of Yellowstone National Park. He immediately demanded an investigation, seeking help from the U.S. Attorney for Utah. Within days, eleven Carbon County men were arrested and jailed on charges of murder. Among them were Peacock, East, Parmley, and Daskalakis.

A subsequent grand jury inquiry went nowhere. On August 18, after interviewing more than one hundred witnesses who refused to testify against friends and neighbors, the grand jury reported a lack of evidence necessary to return an indictment. On September 8, charges against the eleven men were dismissed.

If the lynching of Marshall had any positive effect, it perhaps sealed the fate of the Carbon County Klan. The murder stunned a community already weary of the Klan's arrogant bullying. Affiliation with the Klan quickly became a political and economic liability, as many residents ceased doing business with or voting for those suspected to be members. Although the Klan continued to exist in Carbon County for years, its acts of overt vigilantism all but ceased.

Still, the shame of the lynching haunted many Carbon County residents. On April 4, 1998, a group of citizens and local religious leaders dedicated a headstone to Marshall in the Price Cemetery. The inscription reads: "Robert Marshall. Lynched June 18, 1925. A Victim of Intolerance. May God Forgive."

Chapter 3 _____

1926–1960

With the introduction of the automobile in police work, officers were able to increase their reach, but communication with police officers soon posed a problem. Prior to the advent of the radio, communities had to improvise when it came to alerting their police forces. As reported in *A History of Washington County* by Douglas D. Alder and Karl F. Brooks, a St. George telephone operator during the 1930s recalled, "When there was a call for the police, we put a red light on at the Tabernacle and they would see it from wherever they were patrolling and call us for information."

The exigencies of World War II resulted in lighter and stronger radios. In the late 1940s efforts were made to equip all police departments with radios; however, early models could only transmit or receive, not both. As the technology improved, radio eventually became among the most important tools a police officer could have.

First used in 1902, fingerprinting soon became a mainstay of identifying lawbreakers. In 1927 the Utah State Bureau of Criminal Identification and Investigation was formed. In the age before computers, a warehouse and a staff of clerks were needed to comb through the hundreds of thousands of fingerprint cards.

Utah police officers also took to the skies during this period, using aircraft to increase their reach into isolated areas. The first Utah aircraft-related police death occurred October 14, 1960, when San Juan County Sheriff Seth Wright died during the extradition of a prisoner from Texas. Wright, the prisoner, and the pilot were killed when their aircraft struck the edge of Black Canyon after taking off from Monte Vista, Colorado. The day before Wright died, four off-duty Salt Lake City officers were killed on a flight to Las Vegas, when their aircraft struck a mountain in bad weather near Eureka.

This period also marked the first death of a Utah Highway Patrol trooper. Formed as the state road police patrol in 1923, the thinly spread organization had just seven patrol officers for the entire state when Patrolman George E. VanWagenen died. On May 23, 1931, VanWagenen was killed when he fell into a saw blade while searching for an escaped prisoner near Provo.

A decline in the national homicide rate, particularly during the 1940s, was paralleled by a decline in the murder of police officers. In 1943, seventy-five police officers were killed in America, a decline in numbers not seen since 1914, when seventy-five died. Of the twenty Utah officers killed during this time period, only eight would be murdered.

Willard R. Dahle
Logan Police Department
May 4, 1929

A newspaper editorial called the murder of Officer Willard R. Dahle on May 4, 1929, "Logan's catastrophe." The crime stunned the quiet community and proved that Prohibition violence was not just an ugly fact of big-city life.

Dahle was born in Logan on April 5, 1876, the son of John and Jeannette Engermont Dahle. He married Vilate Barson of Clarkston on February 27, 1907. In 1918, Dahle joined the police department, where he worked as a uniformed officer. The couple had three children.

Events leading up to Dahle's murder began on May 1, when Logan officers raided the Carlson home, 367 East 500 North, and seized a five-gallon keg of moonshine whiskey. The owner of the home was an elderly woman, but officers knew the moonshine did not belong to her. They were after her son, forty-six-year-old Oliver Carlson, a known bootlegger who made a lot of money selling whiskey to local residents.

Carlson, a lifelong bachelor, lived in his mother's home, from which he ran his bootlegging operation. He had troubled the police for years with violations of the Prohibition Act, and Wednesday's raid was just the most recent of his troubles with the law. But, if the police had long since grown weary of his behavior, Carlson was completely fed up with theirs.

The day after the raid, Officers James Smith and Job Larsen returned to the home and arrested Carlson for yet another violation of the Prohibition Act. They took him to the First National Bank, where Carlson obtained a $1,000 cashier's check and handed it to Larsen for bail. At the time of his arrest, Carlson was armed with a .380-caliber automatic pistol. Upon his release, Smith and Larsen gave him back the pistol, but not before they took out the loaded clip. Carlson took the gun and bitterly told the two officers that it wouldn't be healthy for them to come after him again. Carlson went straight back to his mother's home, where he shut himself up in his room and began drinking. It wasn't until later in the day that someone at the police department noticed that Carlson had failed to endorse the check. Efforts made to communicate with him got nowhere.

Shortly after 4:30 p.m., Dahle was instructed by Chief Gilbert Mecham to obtain Carlson's endorsement on the check. Mecham's choice of Dahle was

Logan City Police Officer Willard R. Dahle died
while trying to get a bootlegger to endorse a
check. (Doris Dahle Jones)

logical. The fifty-three-year-old officer was one of the most even-tempered
members of the police department. If anyone could reason with "Ollie" Carlson,
he would probably be the one.

Officer C.S. Amussen drove Dahle to the Carlson residence and waited
outside while Dahle entered the home. Amussen later testified before a
coroner's jury that Dahle was in the home for fifteen minutes when Carlson's
mother suddenly ran out the front door screaming, "Oh, this is terrible! They
are both shot!"

Amussen and a neighbor went into the home and found Carlson and Dahle
in a bedroom. Dahle was facedown on the floor, shot twice in the chest with
the same .380 automatic pistol officers had returned to Carlson that morning.
A third shot had apparently struck the officer's watch. An autopsy later revealed
that one of the bullets had hit him in the heart, causing death within seconds.

Carlson was face up on the bed, the gun still in his hand, a bullet wound in
his right temple. The bullet had traveled completely through his head and
lodged in a wall. Despite this gruesome wound, Carlson was still alive. He
was taken to the hospital, where he died nine hours later without regaining
consciousness.

Evidence in the room and a statement by Mrs. Carlson indicated that things
initially had gone well. Dahle entered Carlson's bedroom and sat down on a
chair near the bed. The two men talked while Carlson continued to lie on the
bed. There were no shouts or signs of a struggle, but at some point Carlson
snapped. He brought out the pistol and shot Dahle before the officer had a
chance to react. The cashier's check was on the floor near the chair and Dahle's
pistol was still strapped in its holster.

Dahle's funeral on May 7 completely shut down Logan. Businesses closed and homes emptied, as nearly the entire town went to the funeral. Officers from around the state arrived to pay their respects. Officials who spoke at Dahle's funeral lamented the fact that big-city violence normally associated with Prohibition in such places as Chicago had finally come to Utah. A newspaper editorial blasted the citizenry of Logan for the murder, citing residents' patronage of Carlson and his moonshine as a contributing factor: "No one now would want to be known as a patron of Ollie Carlson, whose career was stimulated by the extensive patronage he received, and who, driven mad by resentment against the officers who interfered with his profitable business, and by over-indulgence in his own stock in trade, performed the deed that caused Logan to mourn today."

Vilate Dahle never remarried. She died April 26, 1964, and was buried next to her husband.

Richard D. Westwood

Grand County Sheriff's Office
September 5, 1929

On a sweltering September afternoon, two young men entered the Moab Co-op and thumped a cotton sack of silver coins onto the counter, demanding that it be changed into bills. While the clerk laboriously counted the coins, the two young men wandered around the store selecting items from the shelves. Something about the young men made a second clerk nervous. He slipped out of the store and went to a neighboring shop, where he called the sheriff's office. Grand County Sheriff J.B. Skewes and his deputy Richard D. Westwood answered the call. The two officers had spent most of the morning on the lookout for a car stolen in Colorado, allegedly by two men who had committed a string of burglaries near Grand Junction. Within minutes of the call, Skewes and Westwood pulled up in front of the co-op.

"Just a minute, boys," Skewes said, as the two strangers were reaching for the bills in the clerk's hand. "Is that your Chevrolet outside with the Colorado plates?" "It is," replied one of the men. "What of it?"

Before the conversation went any further, Skewes and Westwood frisked the two suspects. They had already recognized the car and plates from the report. When the search of the suspects turned up nothing but an unusually large amount of cigarettes and cigars, the officers took the suspects outside and searched the car. Camping gear and automobile accessories were found and recognized as loot from a series of service-station burglaries. Skewes also found a box of .32-caliber bullets but no pistol.

The suspects were placed under arrest and escorted to the county lockup, a small facility used to house the occasional drunk. While being booked, the suspects laughed about the quaintness of the jail and told the officers that they were making a mistake, claiming that they were just passing through Moab on a camping trip. Although they gave false names to Skewes and Westwood, the two suspects were in fact Delbert W. Pfoutz, 21, of Dayton, Ohio, and Robert J. Elliott, 22, of San Francisco, California. Despite their young ages, both were hardened criminals. Pfoutz had served time for auto theft in an Ohio state boys home, a federal prison in Atlanta, Georgia, and finally in the Ohio State Penitentiary, where he bounced in and out on parole violations. Elliott had a criminal record in California, Louisiana, Texas, and Montana, primarily for carrying a concealed weapon; and it was for that crime that he served a short stretch in the Montana State Penitentiary in 1924.

Had Skewes and Westwood known any of this, things might have turned out differently. From all appearances, however, the two appeared to be a couple of young men on a bumbling crime spree. There was one more thing the officers didn't know: despite the cursory search at the co-op, one of the suspects still had a .32-caliber pistol hidden on him.

After Pfoutz and Elliott were locked in a cell, Skewes sat down and called Sheriff Charles Lumley of Mesa County, informing him of the capture. Lumly happily dispatched two deputies from Grand Junction to pick up the suspects.

After his call to Colorado, Skewes talked to his sixty-six-year-old deputy, telling Westwood to watch the prisoners while he went home to get something to eat. "I'll hurry back. Maybe we can get a confession out of them while we're waiting for Lumley's men." Westwood agreed to what would be his last assignment in a long and distinguished police career.

Westwood and a twin sister, Anthear, were born August 9, 1863, in Springville, Utah. Their mother was Catherine Dallin, an aunt to the famous sculptor Cyrus Dallin. On May 23, 1887, Westwood married Martha Wilcox at Thistle. The couple later moved to Moab, where Westwood at various times operated a freighting venture, a logging business, a mine, orchards, cattle herds, and a ferry. The couple eventually had twelve children, four of whom died in infancy.

In addition to his business pursuits, Westwood was twice elected sheriff of Grand County. However, his first law enforcement job was an appointment to complete the unfinished term of the county's first sheriff, who resigned in 1890 after just six months. Although Westwood frequently became disgusted and quit police work because of low pay and public apathy, he always stepped

Grand County Sheriff's Deputy Richard
Westwood in his early years. (Dick Westwood)

forward when called upon to fill positions left vacant by other officers who
were killed, including Sheriff Jesse Tyler, murdered in 1900, and Deputy Joe
Johnson, accidentally killed in 1927 when a horse fell on him.

All told, Westwood's law enforcement career spanned nearly forty years
and involved a number of hair-raising experiences, including a gunfight with
members of Butch Cassidy's Wild Bunch. During the later years of his career,
Westwood broke up stills and enforced Prohibition in Grand County. The people
of the county knew him as someone who could be counted on in a pinch.

At about 5:30 p.m. Westwood and state car inspector J.W. Johnson brought
food to the prisoners. One of the prisoners asked Westwood to buy a pack of
cigarettes. A few minutes later, witnesses saw Westwood return to the jail
alone with the cigarettes. It was the last time anyone but his killers saw him
alive. Twelve-year-old Claron Bailey was seated in a window of the courthouse
overlooking the jail yard when Westwood went inside. He later told officers
that he heard voices inside the jail, then three shots, followed by someone
shouting, "I got him. Get his gun."

Although Elliott later told several versions of what happened in the jail,
Pfoutz stuck by his statement. He told investigators that as soon as Westwood
opened the door of the cell, Elliott shot him three times. The elderly deputy
was hit in the right shoulder, right side, and through the left arm and into his
heart. Mortally wounded, Westwood grabbed at his killers' legs as they ran
over him and out into the rainswept street.

Whether by intent or design, Pfoutz and Elliott split up almost immediately.
Pfoutz ran through the courthouse lot and toward the cliffs south of town.
Elliott headed east through the rain.

Robert Elliot smuggled a gun into the Grand County jail and used it to shoot Deputy Richard Westwood. (Utah Department of Corrections)

Within minutes, Skewes and a crowd of onlookers had gathered at the jail and found Westwood dead. The sheriff wasted no time sending men to watch the roads leading out of town. However, by the time a posse was organized, it was too dark and was raining too hard to track the killers. It wasn't until early the following morning that the manhunt began in earnest.

At dawn, Pfoutz's tracks were located and followed to the mouth of Mill Creek and down the Colorado River for five miles to Kane Springs Wash, where lawmen found evidence that he had fashioned a crude raft. Skewes sent for a motorboat and used it to scour the river. Pfoutz was located about ten miles farther downriver. Soaking wet and exhausted, he begged officers not to shoot him, saying that it was Elliott who had killed Westwood.

Elliott was harder to catch. In fact, if not for the vigilance of a citizen, the killer might well have gotten away. While searchers combed Moab for him, Elliott tried to scale the cliffs above town during the night. He fell and lost his gun, found later by searchers. On September 7, two days after the murder, Elliott was walking south on Highway 191 near Blue Hill, thumbing for a ride. Driving past, V.R. Johnson recognized Elliott but did not stop. He continued on a short distance until he spotted Edward Beach heading toward Moab. He flagged Beach down and told him about the killer. Beach had a .22-caliber rifle, and so the two men returned and Beach held the killer at gunpoint while Johnson sped to Moab for help.

When deputies arrived and handcuffed him, Elliott's first words were, "Did I get the old man?" When told that he had, Elliott tried to pass it off as self-defense. A search of his clothing turned up a butcher knife stolen from a cabin. Elliott grinned and said that Johnson was lucky he had not stopped to give

Delbert Pfoutz tried rafting the Colorado River
following the murder of Deputy Westwood.
(Utah State Department of Corrections)

him a ride, because he intended to use the knife to kill the driver and steal the
car.

On September 9, Westwood was laid to rest in the Moab City Cemetery.
Hundreds of relatives and county residents gathered to pay their final respects
to a man who spent a lifetime protecting them.

Four days later, Elliott and Pfoutz appeared before a judge and pled not
guilty to charges of first-degree murder. The judge ordered them to stand trial
on December 6. Knowing that the odds of a jury finding them guilty were
great, the suspects opted not to wait for the wheels of justice. On November
14, Eliott and Pfoutz escaped from the Grand County jail a second time. Shortly
after 7:30 p.m., a routine check of the jail revealed the door open and the two
killers gone. On the run for thirty-six hours, Elliott and Pfoutz got no farther
than they had the first time. Officers tracked them to a cabin near Wilson
Mesa, ten miles east of Moab. The two started to run but surrendered when
officers opened fire on them. Both were found to have armed themselves with
butcher knives.

Westwood's son Neil was part of the posse that captured Elliott and Pfoutz.
He had sworn to shoot them on sight. Although no one was ready to stop him
from pulling the trigger when he finally got his chance, he couldn't do it. His
murdered father had stood for law and order, and killing Elliott and Pfoutz
would have shamed the old man's memory.

Elliott and Pfoutz claimed that they had found a key lying around the jail
and used it to unlock the door. Embarrassed lawmen decided that they had had
enough of the two. That evening Pfoutz and Elliott were driven to Price, where
they were turned over to Carbon County Sheriff Marion Bliss and locked up

in a stronger jail. On December 9, they appeared in Moab before Judge Dilworth Woolley. After a short trial, Elliott and Pfoutz were each convicted of first-degree murder and sentenced to life in the Utah State Prison. Two years later, the two tried to break out of the prison but failed.

Elliott's mind eventually gave out. He became increasingly delusional and in 1937 he was committed to the state mental hospital in Provo. Diagnosed a schizophrenic, he spent the remainder of his life there. Over the years, his weight ballooned and contributed significantly to his death from a heart attack on February 19, 1963.

On September 24, 1940, the Seventh District Court commuted Pfoutz's sentence to twenty years, citing the fact that he had not actually fired the shots that killed Westwood. He was paroled December 8, 1941, the day after the Japanese attack on Pearl Harbor. Pfoutz apparently proved himself worthy of the reduced sentence and parole: he spent the remainder of his life working and raising a family. He died May 5, 1979, at his home in Veyo, Utah.

Joseph H. Quigley

Ogden Police Department
July 12, 1935

In the summer of 1935, bad news was everywhere. Not only was America mired deep in the Great Depression, the winds of a war that would soon sweep over the world were being steadily fanned in Europe. But the city of Ogden was determined to forget its troubles by holding the best Pioneer Days celebration ever. A minor element of that celebration would have disastrous results, however. On a quiet July night, while heading home from his rounds as a residential patrolman, Joseph Horald Quigley, 35, was shot to death by two men he attempted to arrest for siphoning gasoline from a car.

Joseph Quigley was born June 27, 1900, to Joseph and Virginia Whitt Quigley, in Swan Lake, Idaho. He spent his boyhood working on his parents' farm. The Quigley family later moved to Ogden. In 1923, Quigley married Edith Mae Allred, a young woman he met at a dance in the White City Ballroom. The couple lived in Ogden, where Quigley found work as a lathe operator. He participated in the construction of several important local buildings, including the Union Pacific Depot, the Egyptian Theater, and the Ben Lomond Hotel. When local work became scarce, Quigley traveled to jobs in Wyoming and Idaho. In 1930, the family moved to Rock Springs, but they remained just a short time before returning to Ogden.

By the time the Great Depression settled over America, the Quigleys had four children and little work. Quigley worked odd jobs, but times were hard and the family struggled. Rather than go on relief, Quigley decided to make a job for himself. In the early part of 1931, Quigley approached city officials and asked to be hired as a police officer for the residential area of Ogden. Burglary, vandalism, and theft had increased dramatically during the Depression, and east-bench residents wanted something done about it. Quigley was sworn in as a "special officer." Although his wages came from local residents, he worked under the direct supervision of the police department.

It wasn't easy work. Exposed constantly to freezing night temperatures, Quigley contracted a severe case of pneumonia two months later and was confined to the hospital for a month. Soon enough, however, he was back at work arresting thieves and vandals. By the following spring, the steady income allowed the family to purchase a home at 753 Twenty-sixth Street. The couple had five children now, and considered themselves as happy as they had ever been. It wouldn't last.

On May 12, 1934, the Quigleys' two oldest sons were playing in a pond near El Monte Springs when a raft they were on tipped over. Vaun, the elder of the two, made it to shore, but eight-year-old Val drowned. The death of his son profoundly affected Quigley, and he began having premonitions of further changes in the family. One night, he woke his wife to tell her that he felt Val wouldn't be alone much longer.

On the evening of July 11, 1935, Quigley left home on his rounds but returned a short time later to check on Edith, pregnant now with their sixth child. Several hours later, Quigley told a fellow officer that he felt a separation from Edith was looming in the future, but he did not know what to make of the vague feeling.

Quigley did not look like a police officer the night he died. As a way of promoting the coming Pioneer Days celebration, Ogden Mayor Harman W. Peery had ordered all city officers to dress as cowboys. In addition to his Old West costume, Quigley grew a beard. The badge pinned to his shirt was perhaps the only thing that identified him as a police officer.

At 1:30 a.m. Officer Weldon S. Champneys and Sergeant L.M. Hilton were giving Quigley a lift home in a police car. The officers observed two men siphoning gas from a car near the northeast corner of Monroe Boulevard and Twenty-fifth Street. As the police car slowed to investigate, the men got into a roadster and started to drive away. Quigley jumped from the police car and into the rumble seat of the roadster as it sped off.

A block away from the sudden action, Quigley's wife was still awake. She later related: "I went to bed after he left, but I couldn't go to sleep so I turned the light on, got a book and read to the early morning hours. I heard three shots fired while I was reading. It affected me so that I couldn't read anymore, so I got up and dressed and went outside." Edith walked toward Monroe Avenue, but changed her mind and returned home. A short time later, church members arrived with the tragic news. The shots she heard had killed her husband.

The two suspects were Fred John Lund, 24, and John "Jack" Ellis, 21, recently paroled from San Quentin Prison in California. Although both men were from San Diego, Lund had been born in Ogden. Out of work, they lived in a shack behind a home at 336 Fourth Street. Between them, they had a history of arrests for robbery, larceny, burglary, statutory rape, and auto theft.

When Quigley jumped into their car, Lund got out and fled on foot, with Hilton close behind. Champneys accidentally stalled the engine of the police car and struggled to restart it. Quigley was climbing into the front seat of the moving roadster when Ellis turned and shot him three times with a .380-caliber automatic pistol. Struck twice in the head and once in the shoulder, the officer died in the back seat.

Ellis paused two blocks away and dumped Quigley's body in the intersection of Twenty-third Street and Monroe Boulevard. A block and a half later, he tossed Quigley's hat onto Madison Street, between Twenty-second and Twenty-third Streets. Meanwhile, Lund managed to elude Hilton, who flagged down the now-working police car. The two officers drove to the station, hoping to find Quigley there with the suspect. When they did not, they returned to the area and found a group gathered around Quigley's body.

Hundreds of officers and citizen posse members scoured the city for the killers, but Lund and Ellis managed to find their separate ways back to the shack undetected. Quigley's pistol was discovered on the back seat of the roadster. Believing that Ellis's vehicle would increase their odds of being apprehended, they elected to abandon it and steal another. The blood-spattered roadster was left parked at 336 Fourth Street, where sheriff's deputies discovered it the following morning. Inside they found Quigley's flashlight and four .380-caliber shell casings.

In the meantime, Lund and Ellis had hiked to Farr West and broken into a home, stealing food and a car. Shortly before 4:00 p.m., while driving at a high rate of speed north on U.S. Highway 89, Ellis lost control of the vehicle while attempting to pass a truck. The car careened off the road, clipped another vehicle, knocked down a five-year-old girl, and slammed into a peach tree at the Woodland service station in Willard. The two fugitives jumped out and disappeared into a nearby marsh. Items found in the car tied Ellis and Lund to the accident.

Ogden Patrolman Joseph H. Quigley dressed in police costume for the city's Pioneer Days celebration; and this may have contributed to his death. (Glenna Quigley Baker)

The following morning, Brigham City sexton A.M. Nielsen was working in the cemetery when he observed two men in dungarees sneaking into a brushy area near the mouth of Box Elder Canyon. Nielsen alerted Marshal John M. Burt and Deputy William Fife, who located Lund and Ellis hiding in the brush. Lund, who was soaking an injured leg in the creek, offered no resistance. Ellis started to run until Burt threatened to shoot him. The two were arrested and taken to separate jails. A later search of the area turned up the murder weapon and Quigley's revolver.

Quigley was buried in the Ogden City Cemetery on July 14, following services in the LDS Fifth Ward. Because he had no life insurance, a trust fund was begun for Edith and the children. The community rallied around the grief-stricken family. Benefit boxing and wrestling exhibitions were held, dance organizers donated door receipts, and city officials also contributed. The Utah State Industrial Commission eventually awarded Edith Quigley $4,500 plus burial expenses. Two weeks after her husband's murder, she gave birth to their daughter.

Though they readily admitted stealing the car, Lund and Ellis refused to talk about the murder. However, under constant interrogation, Ellis "confessed" that it was Lund who pulled the trigger. Prosecutors focused on Lund as the killer, a move that would come back to haunt them.

In a sweltering courtroom on July 30, Lund and Ellis pleaded not guilty to first-degree murder. Despite their counter-accusations against each other, the two remained on good terms. The trial began October 4 before Second District Judge Eugene E. Pratt. Prosecutors attempted to prove that Lund fired the fatal shots before jumping from the car and eluding Hilton in a lumberyard.

Jack Ellis managed to flee the murder scene but was later apprehended near Box Elder Canyon. (Utah Department of Corrections)

Fred Lund said that he thought the officer was a "cowboy" intent on assault. (Utah Department of Corrections)

A week into the trial, Jack Ellis took the stand and testified that he fired the fatal shot, but did so in self-defense. He claimed the rough appearance of the officers led him to believe that he was being attacked by a group of "cowboys." He claimed that Quigley was attempting to fire at him when he shot first. Subsequent testimony from a ballistics expert revealed that Quigley's revolver had misfired four times, although he was unable to say who pulled the trigger or even when.

Perhaps the most damaging element was the revelation that prior to the trial Sheriff Oscar E. Lowder of Weber County had ordered the law library bugged with a dictaphone transmitter that recorded confidential conversations between the defendants and their attorneys. Parts of the garbled recordings were played for the jury. Although they were aware that history was being made by this, the first use of voice recordings in a Utah trial, the jury members were not impressed with the sheriff's high-handed tactics.

On October 16, the jury deliberated for three hours before acquitting both men of the murder. Principal points for the acquittal were the jurors' belief that Ellis and Lund acted in self-defense when attacked by men whose appearance and behavior failed to identify them as police officers, as well as the intrusive investigation tactics of the sheriff's office.

Minutes after their acquittal, Lund and Ellis were arrested again for the Farr West auto theft. They stood trial in December. This time, it took a jury less than an hour to find them guilty of grand larceny. They received sentences of one-to-ten years and were immediately taken to the state prison.

Ellis was paroled in 1939, Lund in 1942. Neither of them prospered. Both returned to California, eventually lapsing back into crime. Ellis made several attempts to join the Navy during the war but failed. From 1944 until his death, he was arrested for a string of crimes, including immoral conduct, robbery, drunk driving, and vagrancy. In 1949, Ellis was convicted of robbery and sent to prison. Paroled in 1956, he died of acute peritonitis in San Diego on August 16, 1957.

Following his release from prison, Lund worked briefly for the U.S. Army during World War II. In 1949, he was arrested for possession of narcotics, a crime that became part of a pattern for the remainder of his life. Over the following years, he was arrested repeatedly for vagrancy, burglary, auto theft, and possession of heroin. In 1957, he was found to be mentally ill, and was confined to an institution in San Diego, where he later died, on January 27, 1996.

Edith Quigley remarried in 1947. The murder of her first husband gradually faded from the city's memory until it all but disappeared. Finally, in 1995, the Ogden Police Benefit Association added the name of the forgotten patrolman to a granite monument honoring Ogden officers killed in the line of duty.

William Levi Black
Emery County Sheriff's Office
August 22, 1936

On August 22, 1936, a bitter family feud over water rights ended in the murders of a citizen and Emery County Sheriff William L. Black. At 8:00 a.m. LeRoy and Martha Black (no relation to Sheriff Black) arrived at the sheriff's home in Ferron. Martha, 44, claimed that her brother had viciously assaulted her during an argument over irrigation water to their respective farms.

The animosity between Hugh Wayman, 39, and his sister was no secret to the sheriff or the community. The two clashed repeatedly over the parcels of land left to them by their father, following his death the year before. At primary issue was a cistern located on Hugh's property, the water from which flowed over property belonging to the Blacks. Each accused the other of misappropriating the water and failing to keep the ditch clean.

On the morning of the murders, Martha and Hugh had argued until Wayman's temper snapped. Seizing his sister by the neck, he choked and

Emery County Sheriff William Black was
unarmed when he went to settle a water dispute
that turned deadly. (Mrs. Duane Frandsen)

threatened to kill her. Martha fled, but not before telling her younger brother that she would be back with her husband and the sheriff "to settle the matter once and for all."

Sheriff William Black was born May 9, 1888, in Maricopa County, Arizona, but spent his early years in southern Utah. In 1910 Black married Clyda Barton of Ferron in the Salt Lake LDS Temple, eventually settling in Ferron, where he engaged in farming, logging, and sheep raising. The couple had six children, the youngest of whom was fifteen.

In 1934, Black was nominated by Emery County Democrats to run for sheriff. Elected a short time later, Black served the county well for over two years. In addition to being the sheriff, Black was also the mayor of Ferron. Black knew Wayman well. Their children attended the same school. The two men also had competed for the Democratic nomination for sheriff, and Wayman was furious when the nomination went to Black.

Competent and respected, the sheriff had a reputation that was almost always enough to get the job done, and for this reason he may have decided that taking a gun along that morning was more trouble than it was worth. The forty-eight-year-old sheriff told the Blacks that he would follow them back to the Wayman place in his own vehicle.

Unbeknownst to everyone, Wayman had reached a breaking point. After his sister left, the World War I veteran drove into town and purchased some cartridges for his .30-.40 Krag army rifle. Returning home, he sat down in a field near the entrance to his farm and waited. At approximately 8:20 a.m. the Blacks, followed by the sheriff, drove up the private lane that separated the two farms.

Hugh Wayman shot his brother-in-law and
Sheriff Black, claming that he thought both men
were armed. (Utah Department of Corrections)

Wayman later testified that he stepped out into the lane and stopped the cars, commanding everyone in them "to put their hands up while we talk it over." Sheriff Black got out of his car, but changed his mind when Wayman pointed the rifle at him. He was getting back inside when Wayman shot him through the left side of his head. Unaware that the bullet had killed the sheriff instantly, Wayman fired a second shot through the car's radiator, hoping to hit Black as he took cover behind the dashboard.

The Blacks were too stunned to move as Wayman turned the rifle on them, firing two rounds into LeRoy's head, spattering Martha and her nine-year-old stepson with gore. When she attempted to jump out, Wayman told her, "You keep in the car or you'll get yours."

Wayman forced the two survivors to sit in the car for ten minutes, then released them. He went home, put the rifle away, got a drink of water, then calmly walked into town and gave himself up to Ferron Marshal George Duncan. "I've killed two men. Sheriff Black and Roy Black," Wayman said. "Their bodies are in the road near my place."

Wayman was arrested and taken first to Castle Dale. The following day, his fortieth birthday, he was removed to the Carbon County jail in Price for "safe-keeping." Although he would claim later at his trial that he had not recognized Sheriff Black at the time of the shooting, while in Price Wayman admitted to a *Deseret News* reporter that he knew precisely whom he was shooting at: "When Black returned with the sheriff, I decided that I would not go to jail since I had nothing to go there for, and since the sheriff had no warrant for my arrest, and so I told the two men not to come onto my property. They proceeded to come anyway, so I shot."

On August 24, funeral services for LeRoy Black were conducted in Huntington. The following day, Sheriff William Black was laid to rest in the Ferron Cemetery.

Wayman was charged with two counts of first-degree murder. Despite confessing the crime to a number of people, including reporters and a police officer, he pleaded not guilty. His trial for the murder of Sheriff Black began in Castle Dale on November 12 before Seventh District Judge Dilworth Wooley. Noting the deliberate callousness of the crime, prosecutors asked for the death penalty. Defense attorney Lou Larsen sought immediate dismissal of the case on the basis of self-defense, a motion immediately denied by the court.

Wayman took the stand on November 15. He testified that he did not know the sheriff was in the second car, and claimed that he thought both men were armed: "Roy Black's hand," Wayman said, "was at his side as though he was reaching for a gun. The driver of the second machine began to get out of the car. I figured I was trapped, so I let them have it."

On November 20, after deliberating for fifteen hours, the jury found Wayman guilty of second-degree murder. Wooley sentenced the killer to life in prison at hard labor. Wayman was taken immediately to the state prison in Salt Lake.

Wayman's sentence was commuted to twenty years by the state Board of Pardons on January 17, 1942. Wayman, by then a prison trustee, appeared before the board with his attorney, R. Verne McCullough. McCullough told the board that five hundred Emery County citizens had signed a petition urging his client's release.

Clyda Black, widow of the murdered sheriff, sent a letter to the board. "Serving less than five years of a life sentence is certainly not adequate," she wrote. "Petitions signed by various individuals in Emery County are not representative of the sentiment. If there is any question as to how the Black family feels in this matter, we would be glad to appear before the board."

Nevertheless, on June 1, 1943, Wayman was paroled. Two days later, Wayman's brother Daniel drove to Syracuse, Utah, from Blackfoot, Idaho, and confronted Leon L. Waite, a local farmer and church leader, who Daniel believed was having an illicit relationship with his wife. When Waite invited Wayman into his home to discuss the matter, Wayman shot the unarmed man twice with a .32-caliber pistol.

Arrested at the scene, Daniel Wayman told officers that he thought Waite was going for a gun, so he shot him. Charged with first-degree murder, Daniel Wayman was eventually confined to the state mental hospital in Provo, where he died of natural causes in 1958.

Following his release from prison, Hugh Wayman lived and worked in Salt Lake City. He died of natural causes in 1971.

Clyda Black never remarried. She moved to Provo, where she finished raising her children alone. She died in 1963, twenty-six years after the murder of her husband, and was buried beside him in the Ferron City Cemetery.

Hoyt L. Gates
Ogden City Police Department
February 11, 1941

Shortly after closing time on the evening of February 11, 1941, a gunman entered the Ogden Safeway grocery store located at Twenty-fourth Street and Grant Avenue. Store manager R.K. Yeates was talking to his wife on the telephone when the man began rounding up employees at pistol point. Yeates had just enough time to tell his wife to call police before he was forced to hang up by the robber. Not knowing what was going on, Mrs. Yeates immediately called the station and requested that an officer be sent to the store. When asked the nature of the problem, Mrs. Yeates replied that her husband had told her to call, then she disconnected in confusion.

Detective Hoyt L. Gates, 38, had just walked into the station when the call came. Because his partner, Detective George Theobold, was manning the phones, Gates volunteered to go to the store alone and see what was wrong.

At the store, Robert Walter Avery, 31, waited while the manager gathered money from several tills. Avery forced a dozen employees and late shoppers to gather around him and act natural. When Gates arrived, he found the door locked. Unaware of the robbery, he began knocking. Store clerk Richard Hardy recognized the plainclothes officer through the glass. Seeing the robber momentarily distracted, Hardy unlocked the door. "What's going on here?" Gates demanded, stepping inside.

Hardy had just enough time to tell Gates to pull his gun before diving behind some boxes as Avery began firing from a checkout lane. Caught unawares, Gates was struck by two .32-caliber bullets, one in the left arm and another through his left side. Though mortally wounded, Gates refused to retreat to safety. He fired six shots at Avery as the robber fled toward the back of the store. Gates reloaded and fired twice more, then reeled outside, where he encountered nearby resident J.B. Marsh. "Johnny, I've been shot," Gates said. "Call the station."

Marsh ran to another grocery store just east of the Safeway and shouted for employees to call the police, then returned to check on Gates. The detective was leaning against a wall, covering the front door with his pistol. He showed

Ogden City Detective Hoyt Gates was mortally wounded when he walked in on an armed robbery at a local grocery store. (Ogden Police Department)

Marsh the wound in his side. Marsh offered to get a gun and assist the officer. Leaving Gates again, Marsh ran across the street to his home and got a rifle. He returned and found Gates staggering along the side of the store. Marsh put his arm around the detective and tried to support him, but Gates was sinking fast. "I'm getting sick," Gates groaned, and collapsed on the sidewalk.

By this time, other Ogden officers and Weber County sheriff's deputies had surrounded the store, preventing Avery from escaping. Additional special officers from the railroad and the Ogden arsenal rushed to the scene. An ambulance arrived, and the wounded officer was loaded onto a stretcher. Marsh later described the detective's final moments to a jury: "I put his hat on his chest, smoothed his hair from his eyes, said 'God bless you, you did the best you could.' He said, 'So long, Johnny.'"

Gates died minutes after arriving at Dee Hospital. Later, doctors discovered that the bullet in his side had severed an artery, causing an internal hemorrhage. The bullets Avery had used in his revolver were intended for an automatic pistol of the same caliber; they "splattered" when fired, causing them to be less accurate, but capable of inflicting greater damage.

Police Chief C.H. Taylor said that the murdered officer did not seem to know what fear was. "Whenever there was a dangerous assignment, Detective Gates would say 'Let me go.' He was one of the most willing officers in the department. Whenever there was any service to extend, such as a blood transfusion, he was usually the first to volunteer."

Gates was born May 21, 1903, in Fort Madison, Iowa, the son of LeRoy S. and Fannie J. Kinsey Gates. The family moved to Evanston, Wyoming, in 1909, where Gates attended elementary and high school. In 1924 the family

Ex-marine and self-confessed heroin addict
Robert W. Avery claimed he fired in self-defense
during the botched robbery. (Utah State Department of Corrections)

relocated to Ogden. Gates worked on the natural-gas pipeline being constructed between Utah and Wyoming, and later was employed as a conductor for the Utah-Idaho Railroad.

For many years, Gates was a sergeant in Battery B, 222nd Field Artillery, Utah National Guard. In March 1935, he married Irene Fowler in Tooele. Eight months later, on November 22, he was appointed to the Ogden Police Department. The couple had two children, lived at 584 Chester Street, and attended the Episcopal Church of the Good Shepherd. Described as an easygoing but fearless police officer, Gates was promoted to detective two months prior to his death. He was buried in the Ogden City Cemetery.

After shooting Gates, Avery fled to the back of the store and barricaded himself in a room. Dozens of lawmen cordoned off the area and ordered him to come out. Avery refused, saying that he feared officers would shoot him if he surrendered. Officers replied that they certainly would shoot him if he didn't. Finally, Captain Dewey Hawkins and Lieutenant C.K. Keeter went outside, pulled the screen away from the window, and tossed in a tear gas grenade. Blind and in pain, Avery staggered out and gave up. His revolver contained two live rounds, while six empty shell casings were found in the room.

Transported to the station, Avery readily confessed to shooting Gates. When it was pointed out that he hadn't given the detective much of a chance, Avery responded, "He didn't give me any chance. He was pumping lead at me." Avery told officers that two accomplices had abandoned him in the store, but he later admitted that his wife was supposed to wait for him in a car parked on Twenty-fifth Street. Roverda Avery, 32, a native of Price, was still patiently waiting for her husband when detectives arrested her three hours later. A third suspect, William Chapman, 42, gave himself up to Salt Lake City officers the following day. Chapman claimed that his only involvement was riding with the Averys to Ogden on the day of the murder.

Although initially charged with being an accessory to the robbery, Roverda Avery was eventually released. Officers weren't sure about Chapman, however, and charged him with vagrancy while the investigation continued. He pleaded guilty to the charges, and was still incarcerated in Ogden on April 23, when he hanged himself in his cell.

At the time of the murder, the Averys were living in Salt Lake City's Ambassador Hotel. Under questioning, Avery confessed to the January 27 robbery of a First South Safeway. The robberies were the end of a recent string of crimes from California to Utah. The ex-Marine and admitted heroin addict had served time in several prisons, including Leavenworth, Kansas; McNeil Island, Washington; and the Nevada State Prison for counterfeiting, burglary, narcotics, and firearms violations. The gun used to kill Gates had been stolen in San Francisco.

Avery initially pleaded innocent to a charge of first-degree murder but changed his plea on March 4. Appearing before Second District Judge Lewis V. Trueman, Avery pleaded guilty to the murder, later telling reporters that he preferred a death sentence for the crime as opposed to life imprisonment. "I've seen too much of this life imprisonment," he said. "I'm not going to get down on my knees before any judge and beg for mercy."

Nevertheless, Avery changed his plea again two days later, contending that he didn't understand what he was doing when he pleaded guilty. Trueman agreed, and the case went to a jury trial on March 11.

The trial lasted two days. A stream of witnesses identified Avery as the man who entered the store with a gun, told employees that it was a robbery, and fired the bullets that killed Gates. The only main objection occurred when the prosecution attempted to present Avery's initial signed confession. The only witness for the defense was Roverda Avery, who testified that she watched her husband inject "a speedball"—a combination of cocaine and morphine—shortly before the robbery. In closing, the defense attorney asked the jury to consider the effects such a combination of drugs would have on Avery's ability to govern his actions.

The jury deliberated just three hours, finding Avery guilty of the murder. Trueman sentenced Avery to die before a firing squad on April 24, and ordered him taken immediately to the state prison. Avery congratulated everyone for doing their jobs fairly, and blamed narcotics for destroying his life.

The appeals process delayed the execution almost two years. Despite his previous disdain for life imprisonment, Avery attempted to have his sentence commuted to such. The court failed to grant his appeals, and time ran out. At dawn, on February 5, 1943, while war raged in Europe and the Pacific, Avery was led to a chair in the yard of the state prison. When asked if he had any final words, Avery remained silent. Minutes later, four .30-30 rifle bullets ended his life.

Avery was the first person to be sentenced to death by Weber County courts. Ironically, the man who sentenced him would play a part in yet another death sentence from Weber County. On the night of July 23, 1943, Judge Lewis V. Trueman was murdered in his home by Austin Cox., Jr., who claimed the judge had treated him unfairly in a divorce proceeding. Cox, who also killed four other people during his rampage, was executed in 1944.

Alonzo "Lon" Theodore Larsen
Mount Pleasant Police Department
October 15, 1945

Autumn of 1945 should have been a happy time for Mount Pleasant. Japan had surrendered in September. Men whose futures had been in doubt through four terrible years of war were coming home safe. However, on Monday, October 15, the city's peace was shattered by the vicious murder of Marshal Alonzo T. Larsen. The forty-year-old police officer was gunned down on Main Street while talking to the wife of a man he had just evicted from a nearby tavern.

Larsen was born July 23, 1905, the son of Andrew and Christine Mateson Larsen. He graduated from North Sanpete High School. In 1937, he married Helen Jones. The couple had no children. Employed as the city marshal just a month before his death, Larsen had worked previously in Wendover and at Geneva Steel in Provo.

At about 6:00 p.m. on the day he died, Larsen was summoned to the Sparks-Kolstrom Tavern on a report of an unruly customer. Larsen was unarmed but wearing a badge beneath his civilian coat. The unruly customer was Hiram Bebee, approximately sixty-five years old and a short-time resident of Spring City. Bebee, his common-law wife, and a man named Paul Millet had stopped in Mount Pleasant for beer on their way home from a day in Provo.

According to witnesses, including bartender Vadis Johansen, Bebee made loud and vulgar comments to a female customer and threatened two other customers when they objected to his language. Johansen told him to stop or leave, but Bebee refused.

Mount Pleasant City Marshal
Alonzo Larsen was unarmed
when he was shot while evicting
a rowdy patron from a local
tavern. (Mrs. George Cox)

Larsen arrived at the tavern and confronted Bebee. Because the officer was not wearing a uniform, Bebee demanded to know what business his behavior was to Larsen. Larsen reportedly showed Bebee his badge and ordered him to leave. When Bebee loudly refused, Larsen seized him by his coat collar and the seat of his pants and forcibly ejected him. Both men stumbled to their knees in the doorway, but Larsen succeeded in maintaining a grip on Beebe.

Witnesses said Larsen hauled the cursing Bebee out of the tavern, and pushed him into the cab of a red pickup belonging to Millet. At this point, Bebee's wife, Glame, came out of a nearby drugstore and demanded to know what the officer was doing. While the officer's attention was diverted, Bebee pointed a .32-20-caliber Colt Army revolver out the window of the truck and shot Larsen through the right side.

Kanute Kolstrum, owner of the tavern from which Bebee was removed, saw the marshal stagger and fall. Beebe then got out of the truck and walked to where Larsen was struggling to rise. Taking deliberate aim, he fired a second shot into the marshal's body, saying, "Take that, you little pup."

Several bystanders attempted to go to Larsen's aid, but Bebee waved them off with the pistol. The Bebees and Millet then got back into the truck and fled the scene. When a citizen attempted to open the passenger door of the truck and pull Bebee out, Glame produced another pistol and threatened to shoot him.

Larsen was carried into Beck's Barbershop, where he died minutes before the arrival of a doctor. An inquest later revealed that either bullet would have been fatal.

The identity of the killer was not a problem. Most Sanpete County residents were familiar with the Bebees. The skinny, bearded old man had a small following of people intrigued by his pseudo-religious babblings and his supply of bootleg liquor. Recently run out of Fountain Green, the neurotic group had settled in Spring City the week before the murder.

After fleeing Mount Pleasant, Millet and the Bebees traveled to Moroni, where they had a minor altercation with City Marshal Russell Bailey, who took the keys to their truck. Here Bebee brought out the gun again, threatening to "drill" Bailey "like I did that guy in Mount Pleasant." The marshal returned the keys and the trio drove back to their home in Spring City.

Fortunately for Bebee, Sanpete County Sheriff Ulysses Larsen and Utah Highway Patrolman Paul Christison arrived at the Bebees' home just ahead of a mob loosely disguised as a posse. After a brief altercation, the Bebees and Millet were arrested. Several firearms were seized inside the home, including the revolver used in the murder.

Bebee readily admitted to shooting Larsen, but claimed it was self-defense. He said that he was unaware at the time that Larsen was a police officer, and feared the victim was going for a gun when he fired. If he had an excuse for the summary execution part of the shooting, he didn't offer it. The Bebees, Millet, and another occupant of the home, Frank O'Bannion, were taken to Manti and placed in the Sanpete County jail. Glame was charged with assault with a deadly weapon, Millet as an accessory to murder, and O'Bannion for interfering with officers.

Initially, it was hard to figure out exactly who Hiram Bebee really was. Among other things, the wizened old man claimed to be more than a hundred years old, invulnerable to harm, a traveler of the world, and even the Sundance Kid. Bebee's claim of being the Sundance Kid subsequently brought him a great deal of attention from historians, writers, and other enthusiasts of the Old West. Although evidence to support this claim is entirely circumstantial at best and outright fabrication at worst, the story persists to this day.

What officers were able to learn was that Bebee served time in San Quentin for grand larceny in 1919. He was going by the name of George Hanlon then, and using 1877 as the year of his birth. Between the time of his release in California and Larsen's murder, he knocked around the West, eventually settling in Utah during the early forties. He gained some attention as a quasi-religious figure, sold questionable mineral water, and generally seems to have made a nuisance of himself wherever he went. He was unpopular in the small towns

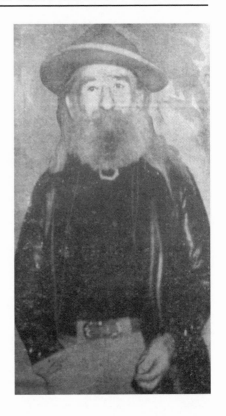

Above: Hiram Bebee when he was a San Quentin Prison inmate. (Richard E. Rose collection)

Right: Newspaper photograph of Hiram Bebee at the time of his arrest for the murder of Marshal Alonzo Larsen. Bebee claimed to be the Sundance Kid. (Author's collection)

where he lived. Though he had money, there is no record of his ever having been gainfully employed while in Utah.

On October 19, Larsen was laid to rest in the Mount Pleasant Cemetery. The entire town closed for the funeral. Feelings against Bebee were so strong within the community that the sheriff hustled the four suspects to the Salt Lake County jail for safekeeping the following day.

Because of delays and legal maneuverings, Bebee's day in court did not come until February 5, 1946. Charged with first-degree murder, Bebee told a Manti jury that he regularly carried a pistol, and that Larsen had been the aggressor by manhandling him into the truck. "I thought he was reaching for a gun and it would either be him or me ... it was then I shot him."

Because he claimed Larsen never identified himself as a police officer, Bebee moved to have the murder charge reduced to manslaughter. Seventh District Judge John H. Hougaard did not agree.

On February 16, it took the jury seventy minutes to find Bebee guilty. Nine days later, he was sentenced to death. When asked how he preferred the sentence be carried out, Bebee replied, "I want to be shot."

The appeals process interrupted the execution, scheduled for April. Eventually, the Utah Supreme Court found mistakes in the original trial — primarily that the judge had allowed the prosecutor to make too much of Bebee's dubious reputation and use of aliases — and ordered a second trial.

With a change of venue to Price, the second trial began June 23, 1947. Four days later, Beebe was again found guilty of first-degree murder. Although this jury recommended life imprisonment, Seventh District Court Judge F.W. Keller sentenced Bebee to death.

After several appeals to the Utah Board of Pardons, Bebee managed to avoid execution. On November 22, his sentence for the cold-blooded murder of Larsen was reduced to life imprisonment. When he received news of the commutation, Bebee was in a surly mood. He threatened to attack several reporters who came to his cell in the old Sugar House prison to get his reaction. After he calmed down, Bebee told reporters that he didn't care which way the board had voted, though it was obvious that he had.

Bebee enjoyed a certain dubious celebrity status among prison inmates. Over the years, he became an avowed atheist, a member of a group called the House of David, and a practitioner of yoga. He even developed another small following based largely on his willingness to defy his keepers. Since his incarceration, he steadfastly refused to allow prison officials to cut his hair and beard. In 1949, fed up with Bebee's defiance and growing notoriety, Warden Mason Hill had the convict forcibly shorn. Bebee was furious. He claimed to have had his long hair for centuries, and that the locks contained lifegiving atoms. The loss, in any event, greatly subdued him.

Glame continued to visit her husband throughout the rest of her life, moving to nearby Draper when Bebee was transferred to the Point of the Mountain facility from Sugar House in 1952. On January 4, 1953, she made her last visit. Climbing the entrance steps near a guard tower, she collapsed and died of a heart ailment. When informed of her death, Bebee responded, "That's her problem, isn't it?"

Bebee lasted another two years, dying June 2, 1955, in the prison hospital of causes incident to age. Such was his colorful status among local news reporters that the story of his death appeared in front sections of newspapers.

Bebee was buried in the prison section of the Salt Lake Cemetery. The small red headstone marking his grave is sometimes pointed out by the uninformed as the "real" final resting place of the Sundance Kid. Meanwhile, the final resting place and memory of the unarmed lawman he killed has largely been forgotten.

Owen T. Farley
Salt Lake City Police Department
May 23, 1951

On the night of May 22, 1951, Salt Lake City police officers observed an unoccupied tan sedan parked on State Street in front of Auerbach's department store, just south of Broadway. The vehicle closely matched the description of one used earlier in the day during the robbery of an Ogden motel. Hoping that the suspects would return to the car, officers staked it out.

The following morning, Officer Walt Olson sat in an unmarked police car for hours in front of the nearby Center Theater, seeing no sign of the suspects. The lunch hour came and went and Olson radioed for someone to spell him so that he could get something to eat. All the other officers were busy, so Detective Sergeant Owen Farley walked down to the stakeout from the police station two blocks north. "He said he would relieve me for a few minutes," Olson later related. "I told him that the car I was in had vapor locked and wouldn't start."

Olson crossed State Street to the Broadway Coffee Shop, where he bought a milkshake and drank it while joking with the waitress. He was gone less than fifteen minutes. When he came back out, he looked south on State Street and was shocked to find the suspect vehicle gone. He was still trying to sort out what had happened when he noticed a crowd starting to gather around the suspect vehicle, now stalled against a row of parked cars. He ran to the scene and found Farley sprawled out of the passenger door, bleeding from a bullet wound to his stomach.

It would take a few hours to determine what happened. After Olson left, Farley apparently noticed a couple preparing to get into the suspect vehicle. He crossed State Street on foot and arrested the male suspect, Don Jesse Neal, 31, of San Francisco, California, without incident. Neal's hands were handcuffed behind his back and he was searched. The female suspect, Wilma Tully, 30, who had hooked up with Neal in Reno, Nevada, was also arrested but not handcuffed.

With the police car disabled, Farley decided to use the suspects' vehicle. Placing Neal in the middle, and the woman on the right, Farley made a U-turn and drove north on State Street toward the police station. At approximately 300 South, Neal turned his back to Farley and shot the sergeant in the stomach with an Italian-made .38-caliber automatic pistol. Farley lost control of the vehicle, which then struck a parked car and stopped at 269 South State.

Salt Lake City Sergeant Owen T. Farley had just relieved another officer for lunch when he was gunned down by an armed robber. (Salt Lake Police Museum)

Neal and Tully jumped out, followed by the mortally wounded Farley, who collapsed in the gutter. Most onlookers thought they had witnessed nothing more than a traffic accident. But Robert H. Jensen, a mail carrier, saw Neal holding the gun, and heard him say to Farley, "Do you want another? I'll give you one more."

As Neal and Tully fled, Joseph M. Anderson, another mail carrier, went to Farley's aid. The officer moaned, "He shot me. I'm a police officer. Call the department."

Farley was rushed to Holy Cross Hospital, where he died an hour and a half after being wounded. The bullet that killed him entered just above his navel, severed his spine, and exited through his back. The imprint of the gun muzzle was visible in the material of his jacket.

Born on February 4, 1914, in Salt Lake City, Farley was educated in Pleasant Grove and in Heber City, where he graduated from Wasatch High School. He married Avis Horner in 1932. Active in the LDS Church, Farley was the basketball coach for the Wells Ward Boy Scouts. The couple eventually had three sons. Farley joined the police department in 1941, serving in the uniform division until his promotion to sergeant and assignment to the auto-theft bureau several months prior to his death.

Three days after his death, Farley was buried in the Heber City Cemetery. The subsequent arrest and conviction of his killer would spark a national controversy for years to come.

After shooting Farley, Neal and Tully fled in separate directions. Neal ran across State Street and south to the intersection of Broadway. There he shoved people aside and stormed aboard a bus. With his coat bunched over his hands to conceal the handcuffs and gun, Neal ordered the bus driver to get moving. "I've already shot one man, so let's get going."

The driver complied but stopped again to pick up passengers at 500 South. Neal jumped out and tried to carjack a vehicle in the parking lot of an A&W Root Beer stand, telling the female driver, "I have a gun here, lady. I'll shoot you if you don't do what I say."

When the woman refused to get out or unlock the door, Neal ran west to Main Street and ducked into the paint shop of Streator Chevrolet. An employee spotted the killer trying to hide in a locker. Neal threatened to kill the man if he alerted the police, but the employee turned and ran for help as soon as the locker door closed. He spotted officers searching for Neal, and shouted for assistance. Neal tried to run again, but surrendered as officers converged on the paint shop. He tossed the gun into a nearby sink and waved his manacled hands in the air. "My God, my God," he screamed. "Don't shoot, don't shoot. I've got my hands up."

Olson arrived at the scene shortly after Neal's arrest. A dozen officers were dragging the suspect to a waiting police vehicle when someone announced, "Sergeant Farley's dead." Olson's temper snapped. "I hung a left one right on his face," Olson said. "Knocked him right out of the arms of the guys who were pulling him along."

Neal was taken to the police station and booked on various charges, including first-degree murder. Detectives soon learned that he was a parolee from California's Folsom Prison, wanted in San Francisco for armed robbery and passing bad checks. The killing of Farley, Neal told detectives, was an accident. All he intended to do was force Farley to release them. "I managed to reach

After he was shot, Sergeant Owen Farley lost control of the car he was driving and struck a parked car. Onlookers gather at the murder scene at 269 South State. Don Jesse Neal's car rests against the back fender of the parked car. (Utah State Historical Society, *Salt Lake Tribune* Collection)

around to my gun which was in my right pants pocket. I pushed it into his stomach and told him to let me go. The next thing I knew the car had hit some parked cars and the gun went off."

After the shooting, Tully fled to a hotel bar, knocked back a few drinks, and then hired a cab to take her to Wendover. When officers arrested her the following day at the State Line Hotel, Tully denied having been in Salt Lake or having any knowledge of the shooting. She changed her mind when she was brought back to Salt Lake, eventually becoming the state's star witness.

Neal's initial confession to the shooting was the first of many. Over the next four years, he would prove to be a prolific if somewhat unimaginative liar. The many changes in his account aggravated even those trying to help him Based on Tully's account and their own investigation, detectives determined that Farley's cursory search of the suspect vehicle failed to reveal a pistol hidden between the upright seat cushions of the front seat. With his hands cuffed behind him, Neal was able to take hold of the pistol, turn his back to the officer and fire the fatal shot. Neal then stepped through the cuffs, bringing his arms in front of him.

Charged with first-degree murder, Neal's case went to trial October 2 and lasted three days. Neal claimed that Tully took the gun from her purse and shot Farley when the officer lunged for her across the seat. The jury didn't go for it. They deliberated for two hours and fifteen minutes, returning a verdict of guilty without recommendation for leniency. Third District Judge Arthur Ellett sentenced Neal to die before a firing squad in December. When Ellett gave Neal his choice of hanging or a firing squad, Neal replied, "I don't think I'm going to die."

Cop killer Don Jesse Neal at the Salt Lake City Police Department. Seated at the table with the murder weapon is Detective J. Ross Hunsaker; standing is Detective Harold W. Clark, whose son Percy Clark also would be killed in the line of duty. (Utah State Historical Society, *Salt Lake Tribune* Collection)

Neal was right, but only for a while. An appeal to the Utah State Supreme Court resulted in a temporary stay of execution from Governor J. Bracken Lee. Neal spent the next three and a half years writing letters, hiring and firing lawyers, and placing advertisements proclaiming his innocence in newspapers. His efforts to attract attention succeeded in directing national publicity onto Utah, most of it bad.

One of those convinced of Neal's innocence was twenty-one-year-old Constance Keehn, who responded to an ad Neal placed in the *Los Angeles Times*: "California boy in trouble. God knows I'm innocent." Keehn traveled to Utah and met briefly with Neal, afterwards sending him books and pinups for his cell. She also began a letter-writing campaign of her own, and eventually managed to attract the attention of former first lady Eleanor Roosevelt, who asked Governor Lee to look into the matter. Lee complied. Following a personal meeting with the killer, during which Lee tried to get Neal's account to match the facts, the frustrated governor said of Neal, "He couldn't tell you *anything* that was the truth!"

Neal survived four execution dates, including one in 1954 that was called off at the last minute. The fifth execution date came after the U.S. Supreme Court denied a final appeal for clemency. Four weeks before his execution, a frantic Neal placed a final ad in the newspapers. "Willma Tully, for God's Sake write Governor, confess your crime or I will die July 1. Hurry, don't let

Don Jesse Neal and Wilma Tully in court. Tully eventually testified for the prosecution, helping to send Neal to prison and a firing squad. (Utah State Historical Society, *Salt Lake Tribune* Collection)

me die." If Tully saw the ad, there is no evidence that she bothered to reply. The legal proceedings over, she had long since vanished.

On the day before his execution, Neal appeared in Ellett's court for the final time. He told the judge that tomorrow would probably be his last day on earth, and that he had already "died four times out there."

At 5:00 a.m., on July 1, 1955, Neal faced a firing squad at the Utah State Prison. Strapped to a chair inside a temporary shack, he spoke briefly with a Catholic priest and Salt Lake County Sheriff George Beckstead. His final words were, "I am innocent. I have no malice toward anyone." A minute later, four rifle bullets slammed into him. The *Salt Lake Tribune* reported that the bullets "made a pattern which could have been covered by a half-dollar."

Neal's body was claimed by his foster mother, Irene O'Brien, and transported to Fort Thomas, Kentucky, for burial under an assumed name. It was the last time Utah executed the killer of a police officer.

Walt Olson retired from the police department in 1976. During his thirty-seven years with the department, four more of his co-workers were killed in the line of duty, but Farley's death affected him the most. Half a century later, in an interview before he died, Olson's eyes still filled with tears when he remembered Farley: "He took a bullet that was meant for me."

On August 6, 2003, cancer claimed the last victim of Farley's murder. Walt Olson passed away at the age of ninety-one and was laid to rest in Larkin Sunset Garden by a Salt Lake City Police honor guard.

Edwin J. Fisher

Utah Department of Corrections
June 1, 1955

Shortly after 12:30 p.m. on June 1, 1955, Utah State Prison Correctional Officer H.B. Smart received a phone call. When the prison cannery supervisor picked up the receiver, an anonymous voice said, "Fisher's been hurt in the boiler room."

Smart dashed to the boiler room, where he found Officer Edwin J. Fisher crumpled on the bloody floor of his small office. The fifty-eight-year-old boiler room supervisor had been stabbed in the arm, back, and upper right side of his chest. Smart ran next door to the laundry room for help.

Meanwhile, Deputy Warden John Turner and Captain M.F. Jensen were talking in Jensen's office, located in the same building where the murder had just occurred. A lanky prisoner came in and said that he needed to talk to

Corrections Officer Edwin Fisher quarreled with an inmate and was stabbed to death with a knife stolen from the prison kitchen. (*Salt Lake Tribune*)

Turner. Jensen noticed the blade of a knife protruding from the bottom of the prisoner's front pocket. "Wait a minute," Jensen ordered. "What have you got there?"

"I just stabbed Fisher," said the prisoner. He handed over the knife without incident.

Thirty minutes later, prison physician Dr. J.O. Jones pronounced Fisher dead, stating that the officer died of internal hemorrhaging and shock from the knife wounds. In addition to the chest wound, Jones found a small cut on Fisher's hand, a clear indication that the officer saw the assault coming and tried to defend himself. Furthermore, Fisher's blood was discovered on a crumpled newspaper in his office, evidence that the killer had calmly wiped off the knife blade following the assault.

The murder seemed out of character for the prisoner. William Walter, 21, of Stockton, California, was serving a one-to-twenty-year prison sentence for a 1953 burglary in Sanpete County, and was scheduled for parole in 1957. Although not a model prisoner, Walter was not a known troublemaker. He worked in the prison mattress factory, located in the same building as the boiler room.

In addition to his own investigation, Warden Marcell Graham called in detectives from the Salt Lake County Sheriff's Department and the office of the county attorney. With the murder of Warden Matthew Burgher in 1876

William Walter, when he was originally incarcerated for burglary at the Utah State Prison. (Utah State Department of Corrections)

long forgotten, officials believed that Fisher's death represented a singular occurrence in the history of the Utah State Prison. Despite frequent assaults on guards and an occasional riot, no corrections officer had been killed in the line of duty. Officials claimed that Fisher's murder represented a new level of violence at the prison.

Investigators set about reconstructing the murder. Walter said that he didn't know why he killed Fisher. He remembered going into the boiler room and seeing the officer behind the desk, but reported that he subsequently "blacked out" and could not remember anything until he saw Fisher on the floor. Walter admitted that he stole the murder weapon, an eight-inch boning knife, from the prison butcher shop several months before. The knife was worn out and scheduled for replacement when he took it and hid it in a mattress.

Witnesses said that Fisher left the officers' dining room about 12:30 p.m. and walked to the boiler room. Officers speculated that Fisher was alone in his office for just a few minutes before the assault occurred.

A widower and childless, Fisher had worked at the prison as a boiler engineer since 1952. Born in Covington, Kentucky, Fisher came to Utah after serving in the U.S. Navy. He had no immediate family in the area, and lived alone in Murray. His body was eventually returned to Kentucky for burial in Frankfort.

On June 3, the county attorney formally charged Walter with first-degree murder. Walter appeared in court and was ordered to face a preliminary hearing the following month. Following the hearing, he was bound over to Third District Court, where, on July 23, he entered a plea of innocent.

Walter's trial began November 2 in the courtroom of Third District Judge Ray Van Cott, Jr. Prison guards and inmates filled the seats outside the courtroom as they waited to testify. Inmate Robert L. Bingham testified how he found Fisher bleeding and leaning against his desk in the boiler room. Fisher was still breathing when Bingham lowered him to the floor and ran to call for help. Investigators related elements of their investigation, including Walter's confession.

Walter took the stand that afternoon. Rather than sticking with his original story of blacking out, he claimed to have stabbed Fisher in self-defense. Walter said that Fisher caught him with the boning knife eight months before the murder but agreed not to turn him in if Walter would become his errand boy. "Fisher told me that if I did things for him he would not tell anybody that I had a knife," Walter testified.

Walter claimed Fisher "blackmailed" him into furnishing the officer with cigarettes and coffee, an arrangement that Walter soon came to resent. Walter said on June 1 Fisher ordered him to bring some coffee into the boiler room. "I told him I would get it," Walter said. "When I brought him the coffee I told Fisher he could take the knife and turn me in."

Walter said Fisher became enraged, jumped up, and slugged him. During the scuffle, Walter said he stabbed the officer to protect himself, and then fled because he got scared.

On November 4, after deliberating for eight hours, the eleven men and one woman of the jury found Walter guilty of second-degree murder. Ten days later, Walter returned to prison with a life sentence.

Walter was part of the prisoner grievance committee during a 1957 prison riot. On August 17, 1971, he escaped from medium-security facilities by hiding under a load of lumber and trash in the back of a truck bound for the dump. A guard later saw him at the dump, but Walter got away by fleeing along the Jordan River.

Two days later, a Layton City police officer found Walter walking along Highway 106 and arrested him without incident. Returned to prison, Walter served time until the termination of his Utah sentence in 1979, at which point he was turned over to federal authorities. Walter remains incarcerated in a federal corrections facility in Victorville, California, where he is not eligible for parole until 2014.

Chapter 4 _____

1961–1980

This period was one of the most violent in modern law enforcement history. Changing social mores coincided with an increase in assaults on police officers. As a result, national police deaths skyrocketed from 96 in 1959 to 271 in 1974—nearly a 300 percent increase in fifteen years. The changes also affected Utah.

For more than fifty years, Utah Highway Patrol troopers patrolled isolated areas and apprehended some of the most dangerous criminals in the country without losing an officer to homicide. Their luck ended with the December 8, 1974, murder of Trooper William Antoniewicz.

By the 1960s the nature of law enforcement had become sophisticated enough to require mandatory training. The Utah Legislature established a police academy in 1967, but it would be more than a decade before officers were required to become certified prior to putting on a badge.

Several innovations helped reduce the number of deaths of police officers at the end of the 1970s, including better training and the invention of soft body armor. Consequently, although the number of assaults on police officers continued to escalate, the number of deaths due to homicide decreased dramatically.

Lloyd Larsen
Moab Police Department
January 5, 1961

It was cold and quiet when Officer Richard Wells arrived at the Moab City police station, just before 11:00 p.m. on Thursday, January 5, 1961. The holidays had come and gone, and the small southern Utah community was settling in for the rest of the winter. As the department's only graveyard-shift officer, Wells expected a slow night. What he got was a nightmare.

Wells had ample reason to expect an easy shift. Just before leaving home, he telephoned the swing-shift officer, twenty-one-year-old Lloyd Larsen. Larsen was in the station finishing up his reports. The two officers chatted for a few minutes, discussing the routine events of Larsen's shift. Larsen told Wells that the town was quiet.

It was still quiet when Wells walked through the front door of the police station less than fifteen minutes later. Because the door was unlocked, Wells knew Larsen was in the station. However, the young officer failed to respond when Wells called out. Wells walked to the rear of the small building and found Larsen facedown on the floor, the victim of multiple gunshot wounds.

The young officer had been shot three times: once in the back of the neck near the skull, once through the elbow, and again in the upper torso under the right arm. Larsen's sidearm was still snapped in its holster.

Stunned, Wells quickly checked the rest of the station. Except for the dead officer, the building was empty. He then called for help. Grand County Sheriff John Stocks and Moab Chief of Police Arthur Sutten arrived and began an investigation. Officers from other agencies swarmed into the small town to help search for the killer.

Investigators determined that Larsen was seated at a desk typing a report when he died. The unidentified assailant simply walked through the front door, slipped up behind the officer, and opened fire with a .38-caliber weapon. All of the bullets were fired from behind or slightly to Larsen's right. There was no sign of a struggle, nothing to indicate that Larsen was even aware of his assailant's presence. If Larsen had heard someone enter the station, he may have continued working on his report in the mistaken belief that the footsteps coming up behind him belonged to the graveyard officer.

Why Larsen was killed was a little harder to answer. Larsen joined the

Moab Police Officer Lloyd Larsen
was alone in the police station when
his killer crept up behind him. (Mike
Larsen)

department in November 1960, just six months after completing a hitch in the
U.S. Navy. Investigators had to ask themselves if the homicide had been a
random killing committed by someone with a grudge against police officers
in general, or if someone had intentionally singled Larsen out.

Outside the station, officers located a set of footprints they believed belonged
to the killer. The tracks entered the police station lot on the southwest corner
and proceeded to the back door of the station, which was locked. There the
killer would have been able to look through a window and observe Larsen
working at the desk. From the window the tracks continued around to the
front door of the station.

The tracks left the station by the front door and proceeded across the lot,
over a fence, and through the block onto Second East. There the tracks turned
north. As officers followed the tracks toward Legion Hill, suspicions about
the identity of Larsen's killer began to develop.

On the night he was killed, Larsen had been a member of the Moab Police
Department less than six weeks; yet that was long enough for him to make a
deadly enemy. Testimony offered at a later inquest revealed that Larsen had
clashed repeatedly with twenty-five-year-old Terrell Paulsen, a local barber.
The most notable confrontations occurred on December 31 and January 1,
when Larsen cited Paulsen for several traffic violations. It was then that a
furious Paulsen told Larsen he would get him before the end of the week.

Like his victim, Paulsen was not a native of Moab. He came to town from
Idaho in 1957. He married in 1960 but currently lived by himself in a trailer
on Legion Hill, earning a living operating a barbershop in Miller's Super
Market. The barber's troubles with the law were not confined strictly to Larsen.
Paulsen apparently had an affinity for alcohol and the company of minors,
two factors that had brought him to the attention of police officers. Before
receiving the traffic tickets from Larsen, Paulsen had been charged by other

An Idaho high school yearbook photo of Terrell
Paulsen. He committed suicide after the murder
of Officer Lloyd Larsen. (Author's collection)

officers with selling liquor to some minors. He also had been questioned at
length about his activities involving other minors in town. As if that wasn't
enough, only days before the murder Paulsen was then forced to post his car
as security for bail on a grand larceny charge from Grand County.

Officers continued following the footprints through the dark toward the
mobile home where Paulsen lived. Along the route they discovered four empty
.38-caliber S&W cartridges. The cartridges fit a Webley revolver, an English-
manufactured and relatively uncommon firearm, one of which Paulsen was
known to possess.

Officers closed in on Paulsen's trailer approximately two hours after the
murder. Knocking on the door failed to produce the suspect. Meanwhile, other
officers poking carefully around outside the mobile home discovered two more
S&W cartridges in a junk box, and a third on the seat of Paulsen's car. Pointing
spotlights into a bedroom window, Sutten spotted Paulsen sprawled on a bed
with a pistol in his left hand. Getting no response, officers broke down the
door. They found Paulsen still in bed clutching a .22-caliber Ruger pistol. He
was still alive despite a small-caliber gunshot wound near his left ear. Paulsen
was taken to the Moab office of Dr. I.W. Allen, where he died a short time
later without regaining consciousness.

Evidence pointing to Paulsen as the killer continued to mount after his
death. Shoes similar to those that made the tracks outside the police station
were found inside Paulsen's trailer. Clothing belonging to Paulsen found near
his bed was covered with seeds from dried plants identical to those along the
escape route from the station. Most damning of all, however, was a will
discovered on January 6 in Paulsen's barbershop. Dated the day before the

murder, the will listed Paulsen's various properties, as well as an admission to illegal acts he had committed and statements derogatory to local police officers. Written in Paulsen's hand, the document was brief, and it left to a local attorney supervision of the disposal of all of Paulsen's possessions.

Despite a lengthy search, the Webley revolver used to kill Larsen was never recovered. Investigators speculated that Paulsen may have buried the gun or tossed it into a field during his flight from the police station.

Separate inquests into the deaths of Larsen and Paulsen were held January 9, in which autopsy reports, witness statements, and police evidence were examined. The coroner's juries deliberated for three hours before officially concluding that Paulsen had killed Larsen and then himself.

On January 11, Paulsen's body was released by county officials and shipped to relatives in Idaho Falls for burial.

Funeral services for Larsen were held January 10 in the Moab LDS chapel. Born in Delta, he had graduated from Lincoln High School in Orem. At the time of his death, Larsen was married to the former Jane Bowman, a young woman he dated through high school. The son of Clifton and Pearl Twitchell, Larsen was buried in the Moab City Cemetery.

At the time of this writing, Larsen's nephew Michael Larsen is chief of police in Orem.

Marshall N. "Doc" White

Ogden City Police Department
October 18, 1963

The only African-American Utah police officer to lose his life in the line of duty, Detective Sergeant Marshall "Doc" White, 54, died October 18, 1963, three days after being shot in the abdomen by an escapee from the Utah State Industrial School in Ogden.

Born July 7, 1909, in Humboldt, Tennessee, White served in the Army Air Corps as a medical technician during World War II. He was employed as a special police officer with the Ogden City Health Department for three years prior to joining the police force in 1948. White devoted much of his time and efforts to working with the youth of Ogden. At the time of his death, he was president of the Weber County chapter of the NAACP.

On October 15, 1963, Michael Patrick Jones, 15, and Ramon Torres, 17, escaped from Ogden's state industrial school. The two were part of a supervised tomato-picking detail north of the school when they slipped away shortly before

Ogden Police Detective Marshall White unsuccessfully tried to talk an escapee from the Utah State Industrial School into surrendering. (Ogden Police Department)

noon. Their absence was reported immediately to Ogden officers, who began looking for the two boys.

Born October 19, 1947, in Berkeley, California, Jones was living in Murray when he committed a series of motor vehicle thefts and other crimes. He had previously spent time in the federal reformatory at Englewood, Colorado, and was arrested again in Las Vegas, Nevada, on a charge of carrying a pistol. Arrested again in Utah, Jones was sent to the state industrial school on August 31, 1963.

A few minutes following the escape, a neighbor of Joseph and Flora Black called police and reported seeing someone break into the Blacks' home, located at 11 Quincy Avenue, one block from the school. Officers arrived and checked the home but determined that aside from a broken pane in a basement window nothing was awry. Since the owners were not home to grant permission to search the residence more thoroughly, the officers left the scene. Unbeknownst to the officers, Jones was hiding inside the home, armed with a .32-caliber carbine he had found in a closet. He was alone because Torres had refused to break into the home with him. Torres was later apprehended without incident while hiding in an apple orchard on 12th Street.

Flora Black returned home shortly after the first search by officers. Her suspicions were aroused by the smell of fresh cigarette smoke in the home. As she unloaded groceries from her car, a neighbor told her about the visit by police. The two women were discussing this situation when officers suddenly returned to the scene. At approximately 11:45, White, Lieutenant Vaughn Anderson, and police trainee Arie P. Roth arrived and began searching the interior of the home with the permission of Mrs. Black. Entering a hallway

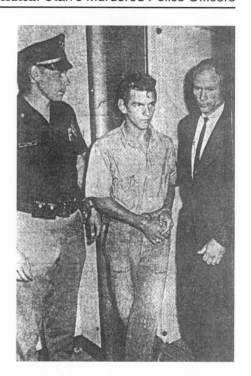

Michael Patrick Jones is escorted to
juvenile court by Ogden Officer
L.H. Yates and Detective Tim Dyer.
(*Ogden Standard-Examiner*)

running the length of the home, White was in the lead, dressed in plain clothes
and carrying his service pistol in one hand. The officers were in single file
when Jones suddenly appeared from a bedroom at the end of hall armed with
the carbine. "Come on, kid," White said to Jones. "Give yourself up."

Instead, Jones fired at White. The bullet struck White in the right side of his
abdomen just below the ribs, exited out his back, and buried itself in a kitchen
wall. Seriously wounded, White fired one round at Jones before slumping to
the floor. Roth and Anderson dragged him into the kitchen. Roth, a naturalized
American citizen and World War II combat veteran of the Dutch underground,
cornered Jones in the back bedroom. Jones and Roth each traded a shot without
hitting the other. The bullet fired by Jones blew out the kitchen window and
struck a willow tree in the front yard, causing the small crowd of onlookers
outside to scatter. Roth then told Jones to surrender. "All right," Jones replied.
"As soon as I fire one more shot."

Jones's third and final round passed through two bedroom walls, a closet,
clothing, and into a bed. Jones later told officers he wanted to fire the carbine
again because he had "never fired a rifle before." He then threw the carbine
into the hall and walked out of the bedroom with his hands on his head.

Officers rushed White to Ogden's Thomas D. Dee Memorial Hospital, where he remained in critical condition until Friday evening, when he died.

White was buried October 24 in the Ogden City Cemetery. Although he was a Baptist, White's funeral services were held in Ogden's LDS tabernacle in order to accommodate the more than fifteen hundred people who came to pay their final respects. Police Chief Harry Needham presented a memorial tribute to White's widow, Jessie, and the couple's seven children.

Jones was taken to the Weber County jail and held on a charge of first-degree murder. He signed a confession stating that he had armed himself after seeing police officers the first time. "I looked out of the kitchen window and saw police cars again. I ran back to the bedroom and grabbed the rifle. I heard someone say, 'Come out, we have you covered. We know you are in there.' I jumped to another bedroom because I was going to jump out of the window. I saw a colored man in plain clothes with a gun. As I went from one bedroom to the other the man said, 'Stop!' At the same time I pointed the gun at him and pulled the trigger."

On October 21, First District Juvenile Court Judge E.F. Zeigler bound Jones over to Second District Court to stand trial as an adult. Prior to his scheduled trial, Jones received psychiatric evaluation at Utah State Hospital in Provo. Counselors later testified that, although Jones badly needed counseling, he understood the difference between right and wrong.

Jones pleaded not guilty to the murder of Marshall White. However, on February 25, 1964, he changed his plea. After a pre-trial conference with his parents and his attorney, Jones entered a plea of guilty to a charge of first-degree murder. Although Second District Court Judge Charles D. Cowley advised Jones that such a plea could mean the death penalty, Jones repeatedly insisted that he was guilty. Instead of death, however, Jones was sentenced to life in prison.

On February 28, Jones entered the Utah State Prison to begin serving his sentence for White's murder. For the next six years he led a tumultuous existence. He escaped twice and received an additional three-to-twenty-year sentence for assault on an officer. However, beginning in 1970, the state Board of Pardons noticed a change in Jones's attitude and appearance. Over the next several years he completed six quarters of extension courses offered by the University of Utah. He maintained close ties with his family, and was eventually even allowed to marry a girlfriend while still incarcerated.

On December 14, 1976, after serving just twelve years, Jones was paroled by the state of Utah. He seemed to be on his way to better life; but it all changed when Jones and an accomplice held up a Salt Lake City grocery store.

On the morning of November 7, 1977, Jones entered Mr. J's Quality Foods, 866 East 3300 South, pulled a .22-caliber pistol on the manager, and demanded all the money from the safe. Keeping his eye on the manager, Jones failed to notice another employee slip away to call police. Taking approximately $1,900, Jones fled the store and got into a vehicle driven by his accomplice. The manager followed Jones at a distance, saw him get into the car, and gave a description to the sheriff's department.

A short time later, a woman living near 3800 South and 800 East called police dispatch and reported two strange men hiding in and around her garage. Deputies closed in and surprised the two men in the backyard, prompting a foot chase. The accomplice surrendered when deputies ordered him to halt. However, Jones kept running. Deputy Jerry Townsend fired one round at Jones from a 12-gauge shotgun. The round missed but caused Jones to stop and spin around. Deputies said Jones was reaching into his belt when Townsend fired again. This time the pellets struck Jones in the neck and head.

Critically wounded, Jones was taken to St. Mark's Hospital. Doctors determined that the shotgun blast had severed his spine. The wound left Jones permanently paralyzed below the neck. Although Jones was in fact unarmed at the time of the shooting, a review board upheld Townsend's actions.

In July 1978, after spending the previous six months between the hospital and a jail cell, Jones pled guilty to armed robbery. A judge sentenced him to one to fifteen years in prison. Still permanently disabled, Jones became a relatively free man again on March 25, 1981, when his sentence and parole were terminated. Because of his physical condition, the parole board saw little reason in spending tax money to keep him in prison. He was placed in a convalescent care center in Salt Lake City, where he died in 1984.

In 1968 the Marshall N. White Center, a community center for youth, was dedicated to the memory of White. Dedicated five years to the day after White died, the center stands at 28th and Lincoln Avenue in Ogden.

Adolph F. Bush

Ute Tribal Police
September 19, 1967

On the afternoon of September 19, 1967, Stephen Mann, a full-blooded Navajo living on the Uintah and Ouray Reservation near Roosevelt, ordered his wife to make him something to eat. When Sarah Mann refused, Stephen punched her in the face. Sarah went to a neighbor's home and called the tribal police department dispatcher in Fort Duchesne. The dispatcher contacted Officer Adolph Bush, 27, on call at his home fifteen miles south of Randlett.

Although intimately familiar with the reservation and its people, Bush had been a police officer for only two months. He was born February 5, 1940, in Fort Duchesne, and attended local schools before serving in the U.S. Army. Following his discharge, Bush returned home and married Nema Myore in 1965. Two years later, on July 7, 1967, Bush accepted a job as a police officer with the Ute Tribe. He was stationed in Ouray, living there with his wife and two small children.

Bush set out immediately for Randlett. Shortly after 3:00 p.m., he advised the dispatcher that he had arrived at the Mann residence. Ten minutes later, an unfamiliar voice called over the tribal police frequency. "This is Stephen Mann," the voice said. "I just put two plugs in Adolph Bush."

Not sure that he had heard correctly, the dispatcher asked the voice to repeat the message. "I just put two bullets in Adolph Bush," the caller said. "Come and get him." As the voice finished the second announcement, the phone rang in the Fort Duchesne police office. It was Sarah Mann, sobbing. "Stephen just shot Adolph," she said.

Officer Robert Tapoof was pulling into the parking lot of the Fort Duchesne jail when he heard the chilling broadcast. He made a U-turn and headed for Randlett at high speed, followed closely by Officer Bobby Serawop. Pulling cautiously into the yard of the Mann residence, Tapoof spotted the suspect sitting in Bush's truck, still talking into the radio mike. The officers arrested him without incident. They then entered the home and found Bush sprawled facedown in the hallway. Securing a rifle found nearby, they called for an ambulance and an investigator.

Criminal investigator John Garcia arrived a few minutes later. He asked Sarah Mann what happened. "Stephen shot him," she said. "And as he fell, he shot him again."

Sarah said that she met Bush at the front door when he arrived and showed him down the hall to the bedroom where her husband had closed the door. Bush opened the door and saw Stephen sitting on the bed with a Winchester .30-30 rifle. Before Bush could react, Mann raised the rifle and shot him in the left side of the chest. As the officer doubled over, Mann shot him again through the left shoulder. Bush fell dead in the hallway. Mann then calmly stepped over the body and went outside to use the police radio. Meanwhile, Sarah fled to the neighbors and the telephone.

As investigators secured the crime scene, patrol officers took Stephen Mann to the Fort Duchesne jail. Interviewed by FBI agents, Mann readily admitted killing Bush, describing in detail how it happened. The following day, the

U.S. Attorney's office in Salt Lake City charged Mann with first-degree murder and ordered him brought to Salt Lake City for trial.

Bush was buried in the John Harmes Cemetery in Whiterocks, following a funeral service in the Episcopal church. Unlike the murders of other Utah police officers, his death received little attention outside the reservation. Salt Lake newspapers barely mentioned it. Nor did local papers consider the incident a headline event; on September 21, the *Uintah Basin Standard* ran a two-paragraph story about the murder under an announcement for a PTA meeting.

The case against Stephen Mann seemed as solid as concrete. Investigators had a body, a murder weapon, a motive, a dozen witnesses, and a confession. However, prosecutors had not reckoned on U.S. Judge Willis Ritter. On November 16, Mann appeared in Ritter's Salt Lake City courtroom. His attorneys made a motion to suppress all statements of confession made regarding the murder of Bush. The case against Mann was seriously impaired when Ritter granted the motion and further excluded all statements made to investigators by Mann's wife. In December, lacking sufficient evidence to prosecute Mann on the original charge, the United States Attorney's office reduced the charge to voluntary manslaughter. Mann attempted to plead guilty to this charge, but the plea was rejected by Ritter, who set a date for trial.

Mann appeared for trial on January 8, 1968. Following jury selection, Ritter immediately disqualified the prosecution's Ute interpreter because of his familiarity with Mann, Bush, and the witnesses. Given the close-knit nature of the Ute community, the prosecution was unable to find another interpreter who was not familiar with the principals in the case.

Officer Tapoof took the stand as the prosecution's main witness. His testimony regarding the discovery of Mann talking on the police radio was immediately objected to by the defense and sustained by Ritter, who claimed that it would unfairly harm the defense. The case in shambles, and sensing further crippling decisions by Ritter, the prosecutor motioned for a dismissal of the charges. Ritter congratulated the prosecutor for his clear thinking and accepted the motion.

Following the dismissal, Ritter addressed the courtroom, holding forth at length on a variety of subjects, including the defendant's rights, the role of the Bureau of Indian Affairs, Native Americans in general, and his intent to solicit the assistance of President Lyndon B. Johnson to help Mann start a new life.

Mann left Ritter's court a free man but still in trouble. On January 9, the Uintah and Ouray Tribal Business Committee served an expulsion order on Mann, informing him that he would be arrested if he returned. Mann subsequently relocated to a relative's home in Tooele, where he found employment at the army depot. His wife later divorced him. Ten years later,

Ute Tribal Police Officer Adolph Bush responded to a family fight and was gunned down. His killer was later freed by U.S. Federal Judge Willis Ritter. (Viola A. Smith)

Investigator Benny Jeannott of the Ute Tribal Police reopened the case against Mann. Prosecutors were set to charge Mann again until they discovered that the jury in Ritter's court had been sworn, making the dismissal permanent.

Ritter's behavior in the case of White's murder was not a singular occurrence. Since the mid-sixties the dictatorial judge had issued a stream of decisions that could only be described as bizarre, including an order that once prevented the Salt Lake City Police Department from issuing traffic tickets. The ensuing chaos caused by this decision required an emergency order from the U.S. Tenth Circuit Court of Appeals. Ritter occasionally ordered the arrests of people for no other reason than the fact that he did not like them. He once ordered a building contractor to sit through an entire day of proceedings because the man made a noise while inspecting an air conditioner. "That will teach you to make noise in my court," Ritter told him.

At the end of his long and controversial career, Ritter's behavior had become a Utah scandal. Attorneys were in constant contact with the U.S. Justice Department about "the Ritter problem." But rather than initiate impeachment proceedings against a sitting federal judge, the appeals court elected to moderate the impact of his behavior by overruling him. Finally, in 1977, the Justice Department began an inquiry into alleged improper relationships between Ritter and some local attorneys. A petition was filed later that year to remove Ritter from all criminal cases. Before a decision could be made, however, Ritter died in 1978.

In addition to a small insurance policy, Nema Bush received assistance from the Ute Tribe. In 1991, she died of complications following surgery and was buried in the Fort Duchesne Cemetery.

Donald Wagstaff

Utah Department of Corrections
December 23, 1970

In the early morning darkness of December 23, 1970, Department of Corrections Sergeant George Roseman entered a granary on the dairy farm at the Utah State Prison and found the body of a fellow officer partially buried under a pile of feed grain. Officer Don Wagstaff, 56, had become Utah's third corrections officer to be murdered in the line of duty.

Roseman checked Wagstaff's body and discovered that the officer had apparently been bludgeoned to death. The victim's feet were bound with rope, and nearby was a 28-inch pair of metal hoof clippers stained with blood and matted hair. After assaulting him, Wagstaff's killers had then made efforts to hide his body under the grain.

Identifying possible suspects was relatively easy. Wagstaff, the dairy supervisor, oversaw eleven prison trustees working on the farm, located a quarter mile west of the prison. A quick head count revealed that two of his charges, Ronald K. Kirby, 28, of California, and Ricky Archuletta, 25, of Ogden, were missing. Kirby was three years into a five-years-to-life sentence for assault with a deadly weapon with intent to commit robbery. Archuletta had been at the prison since 1968, serving one-to-twenty years for second-degree burglary. Descriptions of the two men were broadcast to police agencies, including the fact that they were wearing identical military field jackets.

Warden John W. Turner praised Wagstaff as a "square shooter," who took little guff from prisoners. He continued, "I have no idea why he was attacked so viciously." Turner told reporters that Kirby and Archuletta were among six prisoners Wagstaff had escorted to the dairy farm for work at 4:00 a.m. Another five prisoners arrived for work an hour later. However, it was not until Roseman discovered Wagstaff's body at 6:30 a.m. that anyone knew about the crime. By then the escapees had at least a two-hour head start.

At 7:40 a.m., a man driving to work on Redwood Road picked up two hitchhikers between 11400 and 11800 South. The two said their car had broken down and asked to be taken to a phone so they could call a taxi. The driver took the men as far as his place of employment, dropping them near 3900 South. When the man walked into his office a short time later and heard a news broadcast about the murder, he immediately phoned the police.

Salt Lake County Deputy Dan Fletcher learned of the possible sighting on his radio while investigating a traffic accident near a service station at 3847

Corrections Officer Donald Wagstaff suffocated
in the prison's dairy following a beating by an
angry inmate. (Utah State Department of
Corrections)

South Redwood Road. He checked with employees there and found that two
men matching the escapees' description had just left the station in a cab.

Within minutes, Deputy Bernard Haun observed two men wearing Air Force
field jackets in the back of a taxicab traveling south near 600 West and 3500
South. Haun and several other deputies pulled the cab over. The two escapees
offered no resistance. Kirby was wearing Wagstaff's blood-spattered coat and
had the victim's wallet and watch. Seven hours after their arrests, Kirby and
Archuletta were arraigned on charges of first-degree murder. A preliminary
hearing was set for January 8. Both men were ordered held in the Salt Lake
County jail.

An autopsy revealed that Wagstaff had sustained a skull fracture in the
beating, but the final cause of death was suffocation caused by inhaling the
grain in which he was buried. Funeral services for Wagstaff were held the day
after Christmas, followed by burial in the American Fork City Cemetery.
Warden Turner praised Wagstaff's loyalty and diligence, and more than a
hundred employees from the prison formed an honor guard.

Wagstaff was born February 21, 1914, in American Fork, to John A. and
Susan Whipple Wagstaff. He attended public schools in American Fork. He
married Ruth Broadbent in Salt Lake City in 1935. The couple had two children,
and seven grandchildren. A former stockman and farmer, Wagstaff became a
corrections officer at the Utah State Prison in 1957, where he was assigned as
the dairy supervisor. An active LDS Church member, Wagstaff was serving in
the American Fork Second Ward bishopric and in the presidency of the Alpine
Stake Mission when he was murdered.

Kirby and Archuletta pleaded innocent to the murder charge. The trial began
June 7 before Third District Judge Bryant H. Croft. Prosecutors asserted that

Kirby was tired of working on the dairy farm and wanted to escape. On the day of the murder, Wagstaff apparently discovered him asleep in the granary. Angry at being wakened, Kirby quarreled with the victim and then punched him, knocking him to his knees, whereupon he was struck with a shovel with sufficient force to break the handle, then beaten unconscious with the hoof clippers. Although it was obvious that Wagstaff was still breathing, Kirby bound the guard's feet and dragged him to a grain bin, where he covered him with grain, turned out the lights, and left the prison farm with Archuletta.

On June 14, after four hours of deliberation, a jury found Kirby guilty of second-degree murder. Kirby was sentenced to life for assault with malice aforethought, and ten years to life for second-degree murder. Archuletta was found innocent and returned to prison, where he completed his sentence.

Kirby appealed his sentence to the Utah State Supreme Court. The appeal was denied in September 1972, and Kirby served time until his parole on September 13, 1983.

Donald Perry Jensen

Davis County Sheriff's Office
May 14, 1971

Davis County Deputy Attorney George Diumenti III was on his way home from the Farmington sheriff's office at 3:40 a.m. on May 14, 1971, when he made a chilling discovery. As Diumenti turned onto U.S. Highway 89-91 to go south, he saw the body of a police officer lying beside the road. Diumenti recognized the victim immediately as Davis County Deputy Sheriff Donald P. Jensen. The two men had talked at the station shortly before Jensen left to search for a vehicle stolen during an armed robbery in South Ogden. The forty-two-year-old victim had been shot six times. His sidearm and patrol vehicle were missing. A 1963 Ford belonging to the robbery victim was parked nearby.

The robbery had occurred an hour before, when two men entered the Hill Top Chevron Station at 4398 Washington Boulevard and pointed a pistol at clerk Ward Powell. When Powell displayed an empty till, one of the men beat him with a socket-wrench handle. The man drove away in Powell's car, while the other followed him in a 1961 Oldsmobile.

Barely conscious, Powell managed to call police and report the robbery. He was still on the phone when he looked out the window and saw his assailants returning. After abandoning their own car five blocks from the station, the

Davis County Deputy Donald P. Jensen did not know that the stranded motorist he stopped to help was a robbery suspect who would then kill him. (Davis County Sheriff's Office)

two men had discovered that Powell's vehicle was low on gas. Powell hid inside the station until the men left after they discovered that they could not operate the fuel pumps.

The description of the vehicle was broadcast to law enforcement agencies and received by the Davis County Sheriff's Department at 3:00 a.m. Although Jensen was supposed to go off duty then, he left the station and drove north to the Farmington Crossroads, then south on Highway 89. Shortly thereafter, he radioed the dispatcher. "There's not anything by the crossroads. I'll stay in the area."

A few minutes later, Utah Highway Patrol Trooper Roger Fordham saw Jensen's patrol car parked near some construction equipment on Tippets Lane. Jensen was sitting in the car talking through the driver's window with a white male standing outside. When Fordham contacted Jensen by radio, Jensen replied that the man was a stranded motorist and that everything was fine. Fordham drove away to continue the search for the stolen vehicle. Ten minutes later, Diumenti discovered Jensen's body.

Any of the six bullets that struck Jensen would have killed him. In addition to a bullet in the head, he was shot once through the left arm and into his side, and four times in the back. He died less than a mile from his home. Police were still trying to sort things out when they received a report that two men driving a Davis County police car had robbed a couple in Bountiful and stolen their pickup.

Boyd Herzog and Tracy Holbrook were parked in Herzog's 1970 GMC pickup on Skyline Drive when the patrol car pulled in behind them and two men got out. Holbrook said later that she thought the men were police officers because one of them was wearing a uniform jacket. She became suspicious, however, when she noticed blood on the man's pants. When she asked for identification, one of the men pulled out a pistol. "This is all the I.D. I need," the man said.

After threatening to kill the couple if they moved, the two men took Herzog's wallet, disabled the patrol car, and left in the pickup. The couple walked to town until they found a home with the lights on and called police. A description of Herzog's truck went out to all law enforcement agencies.

Near dawn, Utah Highway Patrol Trooper William Todd was working at the Echo Port of Entry west of Evanston, Wyoming. He heard the broadcast description of Herzog's pickup just as the vehicle drove past the checking station and into Wyoming. Todd contacted Wyoming authorities, who trailed the pickup to Kemmerer, where the two killers were stopped and arrested without incident. Jensen's sidearm and shotgun were found inside the truck.

The two men were Daniel Kaye Weddle, 27, of Dixon, California, and Ronald Allen May, 21, of Sacramento, California. Brothers-in-law, Weddle and May were ex-cons with extensive criminal records. They were wanted for an armed robbery three days before in Yuba City, California, where they took $163 after assaulting a female clerk and shooting the male storeowner in the chest. A second robbery of a Circle K in Boise, Idaho, occurred on May 12.

Two days after their arrest, May waived extradition and was returned to Utah for trial. Weddle initially fought extradition but eventually changed his mind. Both men were arraigned in Bountiful City Court on May 17, the same day funeral services were held for Jensen in the Davis Stake Center of the LDS Church.

A native of Coalville, Jensen was born July 10, 1928, to Parley P. and Ethel Christensen Jensen. He graduated from Davis High School in Kaysville, and married Olvie Whaite in Farmington on March 5, 1948. He was the father of two daughters and a son. Jensen had been employed by Standard Oil for eighteen years before attending the police academy at Weber State College. He joined the Davis County Sheriff's Department in July 1968, working as a jailer and a dispatcher before transferring to patrol just five months prior to his death. He was buried in the Farmington City Cemetery, on a hillside not far from his home.

At a preliminary hearing on September 23, the two suspects pleaded innocent to charges of robbery and first-degree murder.

The trial for Weddle began January 19, 1972, before Judge Thornley K. Swan. After two days of testimony from witnesses, and a refusal from Swan to lower the charge to second-degree murder, Weddle took the stand and confessed. Weddle admitted to the South Ogden robbery and said that Powell's vehicle ran out of gas near Tippets Lane. He abandoned the vehicle with the intention of hitchhiking. He used a flashlight to flag down the first set of headlights to come along. "When I saw that it was a patrol car I was too afraid to run. I decided to try and talk my way out of it by convincing the officer I was a stranded motorist and maybe get him to take me to a gas station."

However, Jensen became suspicious of the stranded vehicle and started asking about the registration. Frightened, Weddle drew a .38-caliber pistol and ordered the deputy out of the car. Instead, Weddle claimed that Jensen grabbed the barrel of the gun and began struggling for possession of it. Since one of the rounds passed thorough Jensen's left arm and into his side, prosecutors doubted that the deputy made a move for Weddle's gun.

"I just panicked," Weddle said. "I don't how many times I pulled the trigger, but I do know the gun was empty when I finished." Weddle said he opened the door and saw Jensen, still alive, attempting to draw his sidearm. He grabbed the deputy's hand and told him: "Stop going for your gun." He testified that a gun barrel appeared near his head and he heard an explosion. Jensen stopped moving. When asked who fired the shot into the Jensen's head, Weddle refused to say. Ordered by Swan to answer, Weddle said, "My brother-in-law, Ronald Allen May."

The jury deliberated for six hours, finding Weddle guilty of first-degree murder. On January 28, he was sentenced to life in prison.

May's trial began February 3, before Second District Judge Calvin Gould. A medical examiner testified that Jensen was still alive when a .22-caliber magnum bullet was fired into his brain, and that it was highly unlikely he would have had the strength to try to draw his gun after having been shot five times.

On February 7, May took the stand and told a packed courtroom that his brother-in-law had already shot Jensen several times when he approached the car with the .22 pistol. "I looked in [the car] and pulled out the .22, and the next thing I knew it went off," said May.

May testified that he was hiding behind some construction machinery when Jensen pulled up and began talking with Weddle. He claimed Weddle had forced him to carry the .22 and that he complied only after his brother-in-law threatened to kill him. He claimed to have shot Jensen by accident, but he admitted robbing the gas station and stealing Herzog's truck and driving it to Wyoming.

Called to the stand by the prosecution, Weddle refused to testify, invoking the Fifth Amendment to the Constitution. Gould found Weddle in contempt, and ordered him to serve sixty days in the Davis County Jail before beginning his prison sentence.

On February 8, the jury deliberated for five hours before finding May guilty. Leniency was recommended, and May was sentenced to life imprisonment.

Weddle served fifteen years for the murder of Jensen and was paroled January 13, 1987. He returned to California. May had a 1987 parole date as well, but he decided not to wait for it. He served his time until May 18, 1981, when he and another inmate walked away from a work detail at a business on 14400 South. May's companion was captured within a day, but May remained at large until the evening of May 22, when a Salt Lake City police officer spotted him riding in a car. May offered no resistance when he was arrested. The woman driver told officers that she had picked May up when she saw him hitchhiking on Redwood Road.

Returned to prison, May escaped again for two days in April 1987. Released the following year, he was back in prison in September 1988 for violating his parole. Paroled yet again in 1990, he was returned for a parole violation on June 7, 1993, after serving time in California for assaulting a Marysville police officer with his car and then leading officers on a high-speed chase. May later told authorities that he was drunk and angry. He spent nine months in San Quentin before being returned to Utah.

In May 2002, after earning a bachelor's degree in psychology, May was again up for parole. "You killed one officer and injured another," said parole board chairman Michael Sibbett. "It doesn't build much confidence. Someone who kills law enforcement [officers] might not ever get out." A lack of confidence notwithstanding, May was given a September 10, 2003, parole date.

Percy "Perc" L. Clark
Salt Lake City Police Department
January 11, 1973

A robbery stakeout in the quiet Avenues district of Salt Lake City on the night of January 11, 1973, ended in a gun battle that claimed the life of a veteran police detective. The murder of Detective Percy L. Clark occurred six months after the U.S. Supreme Court abolished the death penalty. It sparked an outcry from capital punishment supporters who believed that the murder occurred in large part because criminals no longer feared punishment.

Percy Lindsay Clark was born February 19, 1930, in Salt Lake City, to Harold William and Moline Lindsay Clark. He attended local schools and graduated from South High School. On January 8, 1948, Clark married Maurine

Salt Lake City Detective Percy Clark was shot in the head after ordering robbery suspects to halt. (Salt Lake Police Museum)

Peterson in Ely, Nevada. The couple lived with their seven children on Valentine Street (1100 West) in Salt Lake City.

Law enforcement was a family affair for the Clarks. In addition to his father, his cousin A.B. Clark also worked for the Salt Lake City Police Department. Clark followed in his father's footsteps, joining the department on November 16, 1951. His career assignments included patrol, vice, personnel, and training, until 1966, when he transferred to the Detective Division. At the time of his death, Clark was vice-president of the Utah Peace Officers Association, while Maurine had once served as president of the Utah Peace Officers Auxiliary.

An excellent gunsmith, Clark also was one of the top pistol shots in the state, winning numerous awards and trophies. He was sentimental about firearms. He carried an old-fashioned but finely tuned single-action Colt revolver rather than the more modern weapons used by fellow officers. Father and son shared an interest in marksmanship and ballistics. Together they took care of the police target range and built or modified old firearms. A year after his son made detective, Harold Clark retired from the police department with forty-one years of service.

On the night he died, Clark was part of a surveillance team keeping watch on the Third Avenue Pharmacy, 564 Third Avenue. An informant told officers that a group responsible for robbing the business the previous month for drugs and cash planned to hit it again. Clark had worked his regular shift during the day, gone to his part-time job as a gunsmith, then returned to the department for the stake-out. Maurine had a premonition that something would go wrong, and she tried to talk him into staying home. Other detectives involved in the stake-out were Sergeant Mel Shields, Alan Thompson, Steve Diamond, Larry

Michael Mahoney told friends that he would fire at any officer who tried to stop him. (Salt Lake Police Museum)

Hardwick, and Floyd Ledford. The team surrounded the pharmacy on the evening of January 9 and waited. On January 10, two suspects entered the business and sized it up. However, they left quietly.

The following night was cold and snowy. Shortly before 9:00 p.m., four suspects arrived near the store in a vehicle. Two of them got out and entered the business. This time, one of them pointed a handgun at the clerk and demanded the money from the cash register. After ordering the clerk to get all the more potent (Schedule One) narcotics from the back room, the men forced the two employees to the floor and left.

The original plan called for officers to apprehend the suspects once they were well away from the business. Detectives had sealed off potential avenues of escape and saturated the surrounding area with members of the department's tactical squad. It was supposed to be a well-controlled operation. Detectives knew all of the suspects, where they lived, how many were armed, and the vehicles they used. However, things immediately went wrong.

Clark's assigned position was directly across Third Avenue from the front door of the pharmacy. But when the suspects entered the business, the detective left his unmarked police vehicle and crossed the street, taking a position behind a large mailbox about fifteen feet outside the front door. Other officers protested this move by radio, but Clark ignored them. In order to cover Clark, Ledford then also crossed the street and positioned himself on the west side of the building. As the suspects came out, Clark stood up and told them they were under arrest. "Gentlemen, hold it right where you are," Clark said.

The suspect with the gun was twenty-one-year-old Michael E. Mahoney. A week before the robbery, Mahoney had participated in a ride-along program offered by the Bountiful Police Department. He told the officer that he was new to the area, out of work, and wanted "to help people." Mahoney, however, was more interested in helping himself. A resident of Bountiful, he had lived in the area for only a couple of months, moving there from Washington, where Mercer Island authorities knew him as a hardcore heroin addict. He was also the prime suspect in an earlier robbery of a Davis County convenience store. Mahoney had a criminal record for burglary, forgery, and narcotics violations and was currently awaiting sentencing in federal court for securities violations. The gun he carried, a 9mm nickel-plated Llama automatic, had been stolen from the home of Morris Gailley, the brother of his girlfriend.

When Clark told the suspects to halt, Mahoney spun around and fired one shot, striking the forty-two-year-old detective over his right eye. Clark's pistol discharged and he collapsed in the snow. Crossing the street to intercept the suspects, Diamond heard the shot and saw Clark fall. "It was an instinctive shot," Diamond said. "There was a pop, then suddenly everyone was shooting. It sounded like a battle."

As Clark fell, the two robbers fled. Mahoney ran west up the sidewalk, turning again to fire at converging officers. He went down in a hail of gunfire. An autopsy later revealed eighteen buckshot wounds in his body from a blast fired by Hardwick, but it was a .38-caliber bullet fired by Ledford that struck him in the head and killed him instantly. Ironically, Ledford's weapon was an older model single-action Colt Army revolver rebuilt by Clark.

Mahoney's companion, seventeen-year-old Brian R. Johnson, surrendered immediately, still clutching a pillowcase containing drugs and $50.36 in cash. Elwood Bown, 19, was taken into custody as he walked along Third Avenue

Michael Mahoney's hooded body sprawled in the snow after the shootout. The pillowcase with drugs and cash is visible near his left hand. Nearly buried in the snow at his feet is the 9mm pistol he used to kill Detective Percy Clark. (Salt Lake Police Museum)

toward a car parked on J Street, while a fourth accomplice, Kevin M. Tutorow, 18, was arrested inside the car. A woman, Ann James, 19, of Bountiful, was arrested later that night for her part in planning the robbery.

Clark was taken to nearby LDS Hospital. A detective rushed to Maurine Clark's work and brought her to the hospital, but it was too late. The shot that struck her husband was almost instantly fatal. Meanwhile, Mahoney was taken to University Hospital, where he was pronounced dead.

Police Chief J. Earl Jones held a brief news conference. He stated, "Percy was a good man with a gun. He tried to talk them out of it, but they wouldn't listen. He could have taken all four of them, but he didn't have a chance."

Clark was buried January 15 in the Salt Lake Cemetery, escorted to his final rest by hundreds of police officers from around the state. Governor Calvin L. Rampton and Salt Lake Mayor Jake Garn were among the 1,200 mourners who attended the funeral at the Rose Park North LDS Stake Center. Family and friends eulogized Clark, calling him a faithful man who never put himself before others. "He never looked up or down at anyone," said Sergeant John Moesser. "He was just Percy. He was really a professional policeman and what police work is all about."

A trust fund of more that $40,000 was eventually established for the Clark children. Of that total, $10,000 came from a city grant, individual members of the police department donated $8,000, while another $9,000 came from a benefit basketball game played by the Utah Stars basketball team.

Tuturow obtained immunity from prosecution by agreeing to testify against his accomplices. He was, in fact, the informant feeding information to the police about the suspects' activities.

On February 2, city judge Robert C. Gibson dismissed all charges against Bown, after Tutorow testified that Bown was merely a hitchhiker picked up while the group was en route to the robbery. When he became aware of the group's intent, Bown wanted nothing to do with it. His elder brother, a bread deliveryman, in fact had been murdered September 2, 1971, when he unknowingly walked in on a robbery at a market on Seventh East. That killer was never apprehended.

Prosecutors immediately sought to have Johnson stand trial as an adult. When a Second District Juvenile Court judge certified him as such, Johnson's attorney appealed to the Utah Supreme Court. On February 6, the high court rejected the appeal, and Johnson was bound over on charges of first-degree murder and robbery. He pleaded innocent and was held in jail until his parents posted a $25,000 cash bond.

James, who helped plan the robbery and was to be one of the drivers of a getaway car, was also charged with robbery and murder. She pleaded innocent and posted $10,000 bail. Along with Johnson, she was ordered to appear for trial on April 9. Delays postponed this court date until Johnson pleaded guilty to second-degree murder and was sentenced on May 29 to a ten-years-to-life prison term. He was subsequently sent to the state mental hospital for psychiatric evaluation.

James, who by then lived in Wyoming, pleaded guilty on August 6 to misdemeanor conspiracy. She received probation. Her new husband, Morris Gailley, sought to have his stolen gun returned by police; instead, the murder weapon was destroyed.

Melvin C. Colebrook
Salt Lake County Sheriff's Office
March 10, 1973

As America's involvement in the Vietnam War came to an end in the spring of 1973, news focused on the returning American prisoners of war. Locally, U.S. Air Force Major Don Jensen and Captain Larry Chesley arrived home after years of captivity in Hanoi.

Meanwhile, another war continued to rage in Utah. On Saturday, March 10, the Salt Lake County Sheriff's Office received a call from a distraught woman claiming that her husband was being abusive. Geraldine Roll wanted deputies to intervene in a custody dispute involving the couple's fourteen-month-old child. It was not the first time deputies had been summoned to the home in recent weeks.

Deputy Melvin C. Colebrook arrived at 3569 Warr Road, located in a fashionable neighborhood near the mouth of Parley's Canyon, just before 9:00 p.m. Deputy David J. Miller arrived moments later. Geraldine Roll met the deputies outside, telling them that she and her husband had decided to divorce, and asking them to prevent him from taking their child. The two men followed her inside.

Robert Roll, 43, a vice-president for Walker Bank and Trust Company, was in a bedroom trying to pack a suitcase while carrying his daughter in one arm. He refused to put the child down and told deputies that he was leaving. When the deputies moved to detain him, Roll allegedly put his hand to his child's throat in what was deemed a threatening manner. Miller asked Geraldine Roll if she was placing her husband under citizen's arrest. When she said "yes," Roll took a step forward and shouted, "For what?" The two deputies then grabbed Roll and a violent struggle ensued, during which the child was pulled

Salt Lake County Deputy Melvin Colebrook tried to break up a family fight and was shot in the head with his partner's sidearm. (Salt Lake County Sheriff's Office)

from his arms. The three men fell across a bed and then onto the floor, Roll being pinned beneath the two deputies.

During the altercation Roll managed to remove Miller's .38-caliber sidearm from its holster and point it upward into Colebrook's face. Miller later testified that he heard Roll say, "Hold it or I'll use it." Seconds later, Colebrook was shot in the face. The bullet struck him just behind the right eye, killing him almost instantly. Miller attempted to draw his weapon. Finding it gone, he pulled Colebrook's revolver from its holster and ordered Roll to surrender. Pinned under the dead officer's body, Roll gave up the weapon. Miller then unloaded both pistols, tossing them out of reach before handcuffing the suspect and calling for assistance.

Lieutenant Don Strong, commander of the night watch, and Deputy Ron Jenkins arrived at the scene a few minutes later. The sobbing bank executive lay on the floor at the foot of the bed, pleading with officers to kill him. "Why don't you just shoot me," Roll shouted. "I killed a man. I killed a man. It was for nothing at all."

Instead, deputies arrested Roll and booked him for first-degree murder. Roll spent less than forty-eight hours behind bars. On March 12, he was charged with first-degree murder before Third District Judge D. Frank Wilkins, who released him that same day on $10,000 bail, a move that infuriated officers and prosecutors. Salt Lake County Commissioner Pete Kutulas, a former sheriff's lieutenant, said it was unconscionable that a suspected murderer was free to move about while the jail was full of inmates charged with crimes against property. County Attorney Carl J. Nemelka attempted to have Roll's bail revoked, but the motion was denied. Nemelka appealed the decision to

Bank vice-president Robert E. Roll was acquitted of Colebrook's murder and later tried to sue the dead officer's estate. (Salt Lake County Sheriff's Office)

the Utah Supreme Court. The high court agreed with the appeal in December, specifically that bail should have been denied Roll, but the decision came too late to have any bearing on events.

Meanwhile, Utah police officers tried to cope with the murder of a second co-worker in as many months. More than fifty years had passed since a Salt Lake County deputy had been murdered. Now, Colebrook's death rocked a law enforcement community already reeling from the murder of Salt Lake City Police Lieutenant Percy Clark just two months before. Few could believe that two officers known for their easygoing manners could have been murdered.

Colebrook had been with the sheriff's office just a year when he died. The forty-one-year-old father of three children had left a twenty-two-year career with the Union Pacific Railroad to pursue a longtime dream of becoming a peace officer. It was a considerable step down in pay, but the desire to become a police officer had been strengthened by the encouragement Colebrook received from friends already employed in law enforcement.

Born December 31, 1931, in Salt Lake City, to Melvin Charles and Carolina Robbins Colebrook, the fallen officer had graduated from Davis High School. He married Jean Muffet in 1957. The couple lived with their children in Sandy. Colebrook was an avid golfer, bowler, and dedicated family man. He joined the sheriff's department in 1971, graduating from the police academy in June of that year.

On March 14, while Roll's release was being hotly debated in court, the man who only wanted to help people was laid to rest in Wasatch Lawn Memorial Park. The funeral, held at an LDS chapel near the family home, was packed with family, friends, and officers from around the state. Speakers eulogized the fallen officer as a devoted family man and hero who died trying to protect others. Following the services, a three-mile-long funeral cortege led the way to the cemetery. The American Legion Bonneville Post performed military graveside service rites.

As terrible as it was, the day came close to marking another tragedy. That evening, a patrol car driven by Salt Lake County Deputy Roger Taylor was riddled with bullets as he pulled up to the scene of a domestic disturbance in Kearns. The car was struck repeatedly by fire from a high-powered rifle, and Taylor suffered lacerations from flying glass. The Colebrook tragedy and the near murder of Taylor prompted both the county and Salt Lake City to begin sending two patrol cars out to deal with all family fights.

After considerable legal maneuvering, primarily over the issue of bail but also regarding a motion for dismissal filed by Roll's attorney, Roll finally entered a plea of not guilty to first-degree murder on July 28. Roll was ordered to stand trial in October. Roll's troubles mounted on September 27, when Jean Colebrook filed a $300,000 civil suit against him for the wrongful death of her husband.

Roll's trial began October 3, before Third District Judge Wilkins. Deputy Miller was the lead witness for the prosecution, and he testified that during the struggle with Roll he had seized and twisted the defendant's testicles in order to force him to stop hitting and kicking. Miller admitted being the initial aggressor in the struggle and stated that he saw a hand holding the gun pointed at Colebrook just before it fired.

Later, Deputy Ron Jenkins testified that Roll had admitted "shooting a man." Roll took the stand on October 10. He stated that he was terrified by the deputies and did not understand what was happening when they began assaulting him. He admitted saying to Jenkins that he had killed a man, but he claimed he said it only because he felt responsible for the events that brought the deputies to his home in the first place.

When asked who shot Colebrook, Roll said he did not know, "but I didn't." Roll said he saw a pistol pointed at his stomach and struck the barrel up. As he did this, a shot was fired, striking Colebrook. Geraldine Roll testified in her husband's defense, stating that she witnessed the incident and that her husband did not shoot Colebrook.

However, prosecution witness Sharon Rae Cracraft testified that Mrs. Roll told her previously that she had seen her husband take Miller's pistol and shoot Colebrook. Cracraft said she was confused when during a radio interview before the trial she later heard Mrs. Roll deny seeing her husband do this. When she asked Mrs. Roll about her conflicting statements, Cracraft was told: "When you hire an attorney and pay the fee that we're paying, you say and do what he wants." Mrs. Roll later denied making the statement, and called Cracraft a liar.

In his final instructions to the jury, Wilkins told the ten men and two women that because of insufficient evidence they could not find Roll guilty of first-degree murder. They must choose between second-degree murder, voluntary manslaughter, and involuntary manslaughter. Furthermore, Wilkins said the deputies had had no right to arrest Roll, who was in his own home and holding his own child. He continued to say that the deputies had been called to the home to settle a family matter, and that anyone who felt threatened by death or great bodily harm had a right to defend himself against his assailants.

On October 11, the jury deliberated just over an hour, finding Roll innocent of killing Colebrook. Ironically, on this same day, the Union Pacific Railroad, Colebrook's former employer, held a family day, during which wives and children toured the railroad's facilities to see their husbands and fathers on the job.

David Miller retired from the sheriff's office in 2000. Jean Colebrook received financial aid from the community, but the death of her husband came too early for the family to benefit from later legislation that provided financial compensation for the survivors of police officers killed in the line of duty.

The Rolls moved to California following the trial. In 1975, Roll filed a $1.5 million legal suit against the Colebrook family, citing false arrest and the violation of his civil rights. Five months later, Roll and the Colebrooks settled their respective lawsuits when Roll agreed to drop his suit and pay the Colebrook family $25,000.

William J. Antoniewicz
Utah Highway Patrol
December 8, 1974

The death of Utah Highway Patrol (UHP) Trooper William J. Antoniewicz on a lonely stretch of Interstate 80 changed forever the nature of patrolling the state's highways. In the fifty-one years since the patrol's beginning, just four troopers had been killed in the line of duty, all of them accidentally. Then, on Sunday, December 8, 1974, the twenty-seven-year-old trooper was shot to death by a man he stopped for speeding. The murder occurred just six months after Antoniewicz joined the patrol.

William J. Antoniewicz was born July 29, 1947, in New Bedford, Massachusetts, the son of Joseph and Janina Stupaishi Antoniewicz. Raised in a Catholic blue-collar family, Antoniewicz enjoyed fishing with his father and family summer vacations to the beach. He graduated from New Bedford High School in 1965 and attended Bridgewater State College for two years. During this time period a brief marriage ended in divorce. In 1972 Antoniewicz moved to Utah, where his older married sister Joyce Johnson had settled with her family in Logan. He worked briefly for Concord Motor Homes in Brigham City. Prior to leaving his home in the east, Antoniewicz had applied for a job with the Massachusetts State Patrol. He was still waiting to hear from that agency when he took the UHP test and was hired on July 16, 1974.

Antoniewicz was assigned to the Echo Port of Entry on the Wyoming border, where he checked and weighed interstate trucks. He was ordered to report to the police academy in November, but his training slot was instead given to another officer. While he waited for a new slot at the police academy, Antoniewicz continued to work at the port. This assignment required that he drive a pool car from the UHP office in Coalville to the border, a distance of approximately forty miles. Although not part of their regular duties, port troopers did occasionally stop traffic violators during this commute. Eager to be out of the port and actively pursuing violators, Antoniewicz sometimes picked up the car early and patrolled the area near Echo Junction, where he lived alone in a mobile home.

On the night of December 8 he was scheduled to meet Sergeant Darrell Shill near Echo Junction at 10:00 p.m. The two would then travel to the port together. Shill arrived and waited, but Antoniewicz failed to show. Witnesses later told officers that they saw a UHP patrol car chasing a speeding vehicle eastbound into Echo Canyon and subsequently observed a UHP trooper talking to a man in the emergency lane.

Shortly after 10:00 p.m. a Summit County dispatcher, Jean Wilson, heard an unknown male voice on the police frequency asking if anyone could hear him. When she acknowledged the call, the voice said, "I've got a trooper shot in the head," and then gave an approximate location in Echo Canyon. Wilson immediately sent backup officers and an ambulance.

The voice belonged to John W. Dodds, a truck driver. Dodds found Antoniewicz lying in the outside lane of eastbound I-80, nine miles east of Echo Junction. The patrol car, its emergency lights still flashing, was parked on the shoulder of the road, as if Antoniewicz had made a traffic stop. His .357 magnum service weapon was still snapped in its holster. Antoniewicz tried to tell Dodds what happened but died before saying anything intelligible. Dodds attempted emergency CPR, but it was too late.

An autopsy revealed that Antoniewicz had been shot once in the left chest and again in the back with a .38-caliber handgun. The head wound turned out

A scheduling problem at the police academy contributed to the murder of Utah Highway Patrol Trooper William Antoniewicz in Echo Canyon. (Utah Highway Patrol)

to be superficial, sustained when Antoniewicz's assailant apparently kicked him repeatedly in the head. The tread of a boot was visible on his face.

Investigation of the murder fell to deputies under Summit County Sheriff Ron Robinson, but there was precious little evidence to go on. Roadblocks were conducted until the following day, as well as a twenty-five-mile search of the freeway, but they failed to produce anything. Citizen-band radios were used to question passing motorists and truckers, to see if anyone had seen what happened. A westbound out-of-state motorist heard the chatter, and later called UHP dispatchers to report that he had seen a trooper talking to an unidentified man on the side of the road only minutes before hearing CB reports of the shooting.

Gradually, a sketchy picture began to emerge. Detectives determined that Antoniewicz drove past his scheduled meeting with Shill at Echo Junction because he was following a car, and that the narrow canyon blocked any attempt to notify dispatch that he would be late. It also was possible that Antoniewicz simply followed standard UHP procedure of the time and stopped the car without calling in. With no evidence to tie a suspect to the crime, the investigation crawled toward a standstill.

On December 13, Joseph and Janina Antoniewicz traveled to Utah for the funeral of their only son. William was buried in the Richmond City Cemetery. During the ceremony, UHP Colonel Roy M. Helm presented the Antoniewiczs with the first of the new-style campaign hats recently adopted by the agency. The Antoniewiczs never recovered from the murder of their only son. Both are now buried next to him. "It turned a light out in their lives," Joyce Johnson said in 1998. "They got no joy out of life after that."

Emory Dean Beck shortly before his release from prison. Beck's first trial ended in a hung jury. He pled guilty to second-degree murder rather than take his chances in a second trial. (Utah State Department of Corrections)

UTAH STATE PRISON
DRAPER, UTAH

By February, the investigation was completely stalled. All leads had been exhausted. Detectives continued to follow up on the occasional phone tip for another year, but little was obtained beyond conflicting descriptions about the man Antoniewicz was seen talking with just prior to his murder. Finally, a reward was offered for information.

In the spring of 1976, Sherrie Sundbloom, 23, came forward and told detectives that a friend had bragged to her about killing a highway patrolman two years before. The suspect, Emory Dean Beck, had been living with Sundbloom and her former husband in Lyman, Wyoming, at the time of the murder. She said Beck had demonstrated to them how the murder occurred, then threatened to kill them if they told anyone.

Although eighteen months had passed, Beck was easy to find. The twenty-four-year-old man was serving two seven-to-ten-year sentences in the Wyoming State Prison for two counts of attempting to deliver a controlled substance.

On July 2, 1976, prosecutors filed a first-degree murder charge against Beck. Utah Governor Calvin Rampton signed an extradition order the following week, bringing Beck back to Summit County. At a preliminary hearing, Beck pleaded not guilty. The trial began in Coalville on March 22, 1977.

According to Sundbloom and other witnesses, Beck went to the Evanston Police Department shortly after dark on the night of the murder and broke into the unattended station. He burglarized the evidence room, taking several guns and a large amount of drugs, and then released John W. Tague from his cell. The two men then headed for Salt Lake City, where Beck dropped Tague off at an apartment. Tague later testified for the prosecution that Beck was in a hurry to get back to Wyoming in order not to be late for work. He quoted the killer as saying that he "had to book it like hell, and God help any cop that stopped him."

Based on statements from other witnesses, Beck fired six shots at Antoniewicz, two of them passing through the trooper's jacket, and two striking him fatally. When the fallen trooper would not stop moving, Beck stomped repeatedly on his head.

Nearly all of the evidence against Beck was circumstantial. There was also a matter of credibility regarding the state's witnesses, particularly Sundbloom, who in addition to being a drug user also claimed to be a witch and a worshipper of Satan.

After two days of deliberation, the jury reported to Third District Judge Stewart M. Hanson, Jr., that they were hopelessly deadlocked. A poll of the jury revealed that eight members voted to convict, while four voted to acquit. Hanson dismissed the jury and ordered Beck to stand trial again. Whether the four jurors who voted to acquit Beck truly believed him innocent or simply felt there was a lack of evidence to convict soon became a moot point.

Rather than face another trial, Beck made a deal with prosecutors. According to Summit County prosecutor Robert Adkins, Beck did not want to be returned to the aging Wyoming State Prison. Calculating that he would serve about the same amount of time in Utah but in better surroundings, Beck entered a plea of guilty to a charge of second-degree murder on May 17. In a quiet and unrepentant voice, he told the court how he shot Antoniewicz after the trooper stopped him for speeding: "On the way back [from Salt Lake City], I was in a hurry to get back to work.... I was pulled over. Antoniewicz came up to the door and said, 'what's your hurry?' I said I was late for work. He said, 'looks like you're going to be later.' I just pulled the gun and shot him ... the next thing I knew I was back on the highway."

On August 4, Beck was sentenced to a five-years-to-life term in the Utah State Prison, the maximum penalty allowable for the charge. Beck asked Hanson for a sentence conducive to rehabilitation. Hanson replied that Beck would have to find rehabilitation on his own. Beck served twelve years for the murder of Antoniewicz. Paroled in 1989, he went to Tacoma, Washington, where he lives today.

On May 12, 2000, the Utah Highway Patrol Association erected a memorial to Antoniewicz on a hill at a rest stop near the spot where he died. A tall white cross bearing his name and badge number faces east into Echo Canyon.

Robert B. Hutchings
Department of Public Safety
July 20, 1976

Department of Public Safety Agent Robert B. Hutchings died July 20, 1976, during a "poorly run" raid on the Salt Lake City home of a suspected drug dealer. Hutchings was born on December 7, 1943, in Boston, Massachussetts, to R. Bay and Marva Cram Hutchings. The family later moved to Riverside, California, and then to Sacramento. His boyhood included camping and road trips with his family. Hutchings met Janet Pfohi at Brigham Young University, and the two were married in Sacramento in 1962. Hutchings began his law enforcement career as a deputy sheriff for Sacramento County, California. He later moved to Utah, joining the Department of Public Safety on January 2, 1974, where he worked as an agent for the Narcotics and Liquor Enforcement Division. Hutchings was an avid photographer and gun collector. The couple first lived in Taylorsville, and then moved to Provo with their six children. At the time of her husband's death, Janet was seven months pregnant.

Several days before the murder, the West Jordan Police Department contacted state narcotics agents, asking for help in a drug investigation that had expanded beyond city limits. Officers believed that Ricky Milton Larsen, a twenty-eight-year-old mail carrier, was selling cocaine from his Salt Lake City home at 588 East 1700 South. Agents had a warrant for Larsen's arrest, but decided to strengthen their case by conducting a "buy/rip" operation in which they would purchase narcotics from Larsen and then immediately arrest him.

At 6:30 p.m. on the evening of the murder, officers held a briefing at the Utah State Fairgrounds prior to the raid. Present were West Jordan Police Chief Lance Foster, his wife, Janey, West Jordan Reserve Officer Lori Glick, and state narcotics and liquor enforcement agents Robert Hutchings, Manuel "Lefty" Lopez, Grant Larsen, and their undercover agent Mark Ridley. The officers discussed how to conduct the raid. It was agreed that Ridley would enter the home, purchase some cocaine, and then say the words "It's hip" as a signal for officers waiting outside to make the arrest.

Wearing a hidden microphone, Ridley went to the home and made the purchase. Also in the home at the time were Larsen's girlfriend Rosemary Thurman and a twenty-year-old man named Joel Martin, who was in the bathroom as the transaction took place. The conversation inside the home was recorded by officers in a vehicle parked a block from the scene. When Larsen

Department of Public Safety Agent Robert Hutchings died in a badly planned drug raid. (Utah Highway Patrol Association)

asked Ridley if they could sample the drug together. Ridley agreed and then spoke the code words.

Before Larsen could open the plastic bag containing the drug, he heard a noise and got up to investigate. He peered out the door and saw plainclothes agents converging on his home. Larsen slammed the front door and locked it, breaking a glass panel in the process. As agents began kicking at the door, Larsen turned to run into a back bedroom, scuffling briefly with Ridley. When the agents managed to get the door open, Hutchings was the first one through, with Foster immediately behind him.

Larsen retreated down a hall and into a bedroom, followed by Hutchings. Foster went into the front room and covered Thurman and Martin but was distracted by the sound of gunshots. "I was covering the two on the floor when I heard 'boom' followed by 'pop, pop, pop,'" Foster recalled in 2002. "I went down the hall and saw Bob on his knees. He told me, 'I've been shot. I've been shot.'"

Investigators later determined, however, that Larsen had made it to the bedroom and armed himself with a Fox double-barreled, 12-gauge shotgun loaded with double-aught buckshot. As Hutchings entered the room, he saw Larsen with the gun and fired first with a .380-caliber Walther PPKS, hitting the man in the lower stomach. Larsen then fired and the buckshot hit Hutchings in the left side of his neck and upper chest.

In Foster's statement following the shooting, he told investigators that Larsen fired again at him when he looked into the room. However, investigators determined that Larsen fired only one barrel before being shot himself. In fact, when Foster later unloaded the shotgun and turned over the shells to investigators, there was one live round and one empty casing. No other empty casings were found.

What followed next is confusing. Maintaining that the suspect had fired at him and was preparing to shoot again, Foster stuck the barrel of his Heckler & Koch MP5A machine pistol around the corner and fired nine rounds. When he looked back into the room, the suspect was down. Although Foster claimed to have been the one to have shot Larsen, ballistic tests on the bullet later recovered from Larsen's body proved unmistakably that it had come from Hutchings's gun. "Afterward I was told by a Salt Lake detective to say that Bob killed the guy," Foster said. "But it was me. I felt like they were trying to set me up for something. I didn't trust them. But I went along with it." Several of the rounds fired by Foster tore into some cupboards in a neighboring home belonging to the parents of a Salt Lake County deputy sheriff.

Thurman began screaming for the agents not to shoot Martin, although at this point she had no idea that Foster, Ridley, and Hutchings were connected with law enforcement. During the confusion, Martin managed to escape from the house. He later told officers that he had no idea who the men with guns were, but assumed that Larsen was being robbed again.

Eventually, Thurman and a next-door neighbor caught up in the ensuing sweep of the area were detained. Martin ran until he found a man willing to give him a ride away from the scene. When they drove by the scene a few minutes later and saw the police, Martin decided to report the robbery attempt to them. It was his first clue that the shootout had been the result of a police drug raid gone horribly wrong.

Larsen died minutes after his arrival at LDS Hospital. Hutchings was taken to Holy Cross Hospital, where it was determined that he had died within seconds of being shot. At the residence, officers seized substantial quantities of drugs, including marijuana and cocaine, and approximately $3,000 in cash. Thurman and Martin were taken to the Hall of Justice, interviewed, and then released.

Funeral services for Hutchings were conducted in the LDS Provo 13th Ward on July 23. His flag-draped coffin was escorted to the Orem City Cemetery by an honor guard of more than 100 officers. Among the speakers at the funeral was Elder L. Tom Perry of the LDS Quorum of the Twelve, a friend of the Hutchings family. Hutchings was eulogized as a "tender-hearted" individual, always ready to help others, particularly family members.

Officers began sorting out what had gone wrong in the raid. Initially, Salt Lake Police Department homicide investigators believed that Larsen resisted officers by firing the first shot that killed Hutchings, and was in turn killed by a bullet from Foster's sub-machinegun. However, statements taken from witnesses, including Thurman, said the men who burst into the home did not identify themselves as police officers, and that Larsen may have legitimately believed that he was being attacked again in a home-invasion robbery.

On March 22, Larsen and a friend had been robbed, beaten, and threatened with sexual assault inside the home by thieves who broke in looking for drugs and money. The men, who were never identified, took thousands of dollars in cash, jewelry, and drugs before leaving. The beating resulted in injuries severe enough for Larsen to obtain medical treatment at the Veterans Administration Hospital. According to Martin, the officers who investigated the robbery suggested that Larsen arm himself against future attempts. The following day, Larsen bought the shotgun and told friends that he would resist any future robbery attempts by shooting the trespassers.

The recording from the wire worn by undercover officer Ridley was sent to the FBI laboratory in Washington, D.C., for examination, as was the bullet recovered from Larsen's body. The investigation took six months. On December 15, Salt Lake County Attorney Paul Van Dam called the raid a "poorly run" affair, and said that a number of mistakes by officers contributed significantly to Hutchings's death. Calling it a difficult decision, Van Dam said that Larsen was justified in shooting at the unidentified men who burst into his home.

Although officers claimed that they had identified themselves at the onset of the raid, an examination of the wire recording, including sounds of the gun battle, failed to substantiate this. Furthermore, it revealed that Hutchings had in fact fired first, probably when Larsen pointed the shotgun at him. There was no sound of a second shot fired by Larsen, as claimed by Foster.

The eight-page report issued by Van Dam's office stated, "Under the evidence in this case, a successful prosecution of Larsen for killing Agent Hutchings could not have been maintained because of the existence of a good case of the defense of habitation." It also said that future first-purchase arrests should not be used by officers unless a high probability existed that the suspect would not be located if time was taken to first secure a warrant. Van Dam's report also held that Hutchings was justified in shooting Larsen, since a felony drug-sales arrest warrant existed for the suspect.

Lance Foster resigned from the West Jordan Police Department in 1978 and moved to Montana, where he works for the Stevensville Police Department. He still maintains that it was he who shot Larsen.

Following the death of her husband, Janet Hutchings and her children moved to Ohio and then to Georgia. She eventually remarried and began working in the trucking industry. Divorced now, she has returned to Utah. On May 10, 2002, she and son Brian were present when the Utah Highway Patrol Association erected a memorial cross for their husband and father at 5700 South 360 West, Murray.

Ray Lynn Pierson
Utah Highway Patrol
November 7, 1978

On October 7, 1978, the Utah Highway Patrol narrowly escaped tragedy when Trooper Ralph Evans was shot and seriously wounded while attempting to arrest a man in Farmington, Davis County. Two suspects in the shooting were arrested only after a harrowing high-speed pursuit. Evans would have bled to death if a doctor passing by had not stopped and attended to him.

Troopers were still breathing a sigh of relief when tragedy struck again exactly one month later, this time with deadly results. Trooper Ray Lynn Pierson, 29, was shot to death during a traffic stop on Utah Highway 20, approximately thirteen miles northwest of Panguitch. He was the second UHP trooper murdered in the line of duty. The first was William Antoniewicz, shot to death four years before.

Born August 6, 1949, in Ogden, to Charles H. and Sheren Hardy Webb, Pierson was later adopted by his stepfather, Dean J. Pierson. He graduated from Piute High School and served in the U.S. Navy during the Vietnam War. He received a degree in law enforcement from Southern Utah College in Cedar City. He married Darlene Roberts in 1969. The couple had three children, although Pierson only saw two of them. Three months after the death of her husband, Darlene gave birth to their third child—a daughter.

Even as a small boy Pierson wanted to be a trooper like his father, who was a UHP sergeant at the Kanab Port of Entry. Pierson first worked as a police officer in Parowan, before joining the Utah Highway Patrol on January 7, 1974, the same year as William Antoniewicz. Pierson was assigned to the Heber Port of Entry. Two years later, he requested and received a patrol assignment to Moab. The two years Pierson spent in Moab were good ones: he enjoyed the work and grew to love the area. "We all loved him," said Grand County attorney Bill Benge, a close friend of Pierson's. "I don't believe there was a person in Moab who didn't love him."

On November 5, Pierson transferred to Panguitch. He told Benge that he wanted to move back to the area where he and his wife were raised in order to have more time to spend with family and friends.

Pierson was just starting his second shift in his new area when events began that would lead to his death. At 8:30 a.m. Beaver County Sheriff Dale Nelson received word that a motorist had fled a gas station in Cove Fort without paying for fuel. The vehicle was last seen traveling south on I-15 toward Beaver County. However, because the broadcasted description of the vehicle was incorrect, Nelson and other officers failed to locate it. Even if the broadcast of the vehicle had been accurate, Pierson would not have heard it. The frequency of the radio in his patrol car still operated on the one used in Moab. It was scheduled to have the radio crystals changed on November 7.

The vehicle in question was a 1977 Ford pickup that had been stolen in Montana, and the driver was a fugitive from an Illinois juvenile detention center. Just three weeks past his eighteenth birthday, Brian Keith Stack was carrying a stolen .357-magnum Ruger Blackhawk revolver. After speeding away from the Cove Fort gas station, he drove south to I-70, then east to U.S. Highway 89, then south again.

At 10:33 a.m. officers were searching in vain for the suspect vehicle when an unfamiliar voice was heard on the radio by the UHP dispatcher in Cedar City. "This is Deloy Emmett from Cedar City. I am about three miles west of U.S. 89 on Highway 20 and there is an officer bad shot here and it looks like he might be dead."

Emmett and another motorist had found Pierson lying in a shallow ditch on the north shoulder of Highway 20, about one and a half miles west of U.S. Highway 89. He had been shot once in the heart. On the ground beside him was his Smith & Wesson service revolver, containing six expended shell casings. The emergency lights on his patrol car were still flashing, leading officers to believe that he had stopped someone and become involved in a gun battle.

Garfield County Sheriff Keith Fackrell was the first officer on the scene. Sitting in his Panguitch office doing paperwork, he overheard the citizen calling for help on the police scanner. He jumped in his patrol car and raced to the scene. "I knew a trooper had been hurt, but I didn't know which one," Fackrell said. "Lynn had left my office about fifteen minutes before."

When Fackrell arrived he found Pierson on the ground in front of his patrol car, shot directly through the heart. "It was the worst thing that happened the entire time I was sheriff," Fackrell later said. "In the ten years I was there, we never even had a shot fired at an officer. Seeing Lynn lying there was just terrible."

Fackrell ordered roadblocks throughout the area, closing off the roads along which the killer would have to travel to get away. At a roadblock on I-15 near Paragonah, officers saw a blue Ford pickup make a quick U-turn and head back north toward Beaver. Officers were not sure if the driver was involved in the Pierson slaying but attempted to stop him anyway. Instead of pulling over, however, the driver punched the accelerator and tried to outrun them.

Utah Highway Patrol Trooper Ray Lynn Pierson
followed in the footsteps of his UHP father.
(Utah Highway Patrol)

It was Stack. Investigators later determined that Pierson had stopped him for what was probably a minor traffic violation. As the unsuspecting trooper walked up to the window, Stack turned and shot him once in the heart. Pierson was able to return fire before succumbing to his wound.

Traveling at speeds close to 100 miles per hour, Stack was pursued by UHP troopers, Parowan law enforcement officers, and other Iron County deputies. As the chase progressed, officers were alerted to the fact that the truck was stolen. Furthermore, Stack's driving was becoming increasingly dangerous. Officers fired repeatedly at the truck's tires with shotguns, pistols, and even a submachine gun. The only effect was a slight wounding of an officer when shotgun pellets bounced off the truck and struck the officer as he leaned out the window to fire. Eight miles south of Beaver the left front tire of the Ford pickup finally went flat. Stack continued driving on the rim and attempted to smash through a roadblock set up by Beaver County Sheriff Nelson, his deputies, and Beaver City officers on the outskirts of town. As Stack sideswiped a Beaver City patrol car at close to 100 miles per hour, officers opened fire. Stack lost control of the vehicle, plowed through a fence, and came to rest in a ditch. Eighty-seven bullet holes were later counted in the truck, including eleven through the windshield. Investigators eventually determined that five of the holes in the rear of the truck came from Pierson's weapon.

Stack admitted shooting Pierson and tossing the gun out the window as he fled. The pistol was later found off Highway 20, several hundred feet west of where Pierson died. A second pistol, a .25 automatic, was recovered inside the pickup. Despite the amount of fire directed at him, Stack received only a minor wound when a shotgun pellet grazed his skull. He was arrested and taken first to Beaver Valley Hospital, then two days later to the Garfield County Jail in Panguitch.

"He bragged about killing Lynn," Fackrell said. "He treated the murder the way a hunter would feel about bagging a trophy buck." Stack's mood grew more reflective by the time he was arraigned November 9 before Tenth Circuit Court Judge Lewis G. Tervor on a charge of attempted murder.

Funeral services for Ray Lynn Pierson were held the following day in the LDS Panguitch Second Ward meetinghouse. Flags flew at half-staff, and every business in town closed for an hour. UHP Trooper Phil Barney spoke to mourners, recounting a story about a ticket the fallen trooper had given in Moab. It summed up the regard in which Grand County residents had held Pierson. "That new trooper gave me a ticket," the motorist told Barney, "but he was so nice about it I was almost happy to get it."

Pierson was buried in the Antimony City Cemetery. The funeral procession to the cemetery, sixty miles north of Panguitch, was four miles long. Military graveside rites were provided by the Panguitch American Legion Post Number 25, and the Veterans of Foreign Wars Piute Post Number 7561.

Tragedy later again touched the lives of those who participated in apprehending Pierson's killer. Beaver County Sheriff Dale Nelson would be the next Utah officer to die in the line of duty. On September 8, 1980, Nelson suffocated while attempting to rescue two men who died after they were overcome by methane fumes in a manure tank on a farm west of Beaver.

Despite his initial confession, Stack pleaded not guilty to the murder of Pierson. His case was transferred to Sanpete County for trial, but Stack changed his plea to guilty before Sixth District Court Judge Don V. Tibbs on July 19, 1979. In exchange for the plea, prosecutors agreed not to seek the death penalty.

Garfield County Sheriff Keith Fackrell escorts a grinning Brian Stack to court for arraignment in the murder of Trooper Ray Lynn Pierson. (Jerrie Fackrell)

Prosecutors were unsure how Utah's death penalty statute, recently reenacted following the U.S. Supreme Court's lifting of the ban on capital punishment, would work.

Stack was sentenced to life in prison on September 4, 1979. In 1993, Stack said that he cold-bloodedly gunned down Pierson without speaking to the trooper. He pointed the gun at Pierson and hesitated until Pierson went for his own pistol, then he fired. "Gunfire erupted," Stack said. "I shot, then he shot." He remained in the Utah prison system until November 1995, when he was among inmates sent to Texas to relieve overcrowding in Utah. Authorities probably were also glad to get rid of him—Stack's disciplinary history is a long list of resisting officers, possession of contraband, fighting, escape attempts, and bribery. Despite this, he told a parole board in 1993 that he was taking college-level psychology courses, attending Alcoholics Anonymous, and had joined the LDS Church. Present at the parole board hearing was Pierson's sister, Tad Brown, then a Kanab City reserve police officer. She told the board that Stack belonged behind bars: "He has sentenced my family to a life of hurt, loneliness, and an empty place that can't be filled."

In Texas, Stack decided not to stick around. He escaped from a Pearsall, Texas, facility on January 19, 1996, but was recaptured in San Antonio two days later. Returned to Utah in October, Stack continued to be a problem before deciding that he needed to explore other venues. In 2001, Stack lost a court appeal alleging that the Utah Board of Pardons violated his rights by virtue of the fact that all board members were not present when the board denied him parole in 1994. In 2002, acting as his own attorney, Stack filed a motion before Sixth District Judge K.L. McIff to withdraw his 1978 guilty plea, claiming that he was unaware of the gravity of the situation at the time. The motion was denied on May 10, 2002. Stack remains in the Utah State Prison, with another parole hearing scheduled for 2014.

On June 3, 2000, Utah Highway Patrol troopers and friends of Pierson gathered again to honor his memory. A white twelve-foot steel cross was placed beside the road a short distance from where he died. The cross bears his name and badge number 344. Among the family members who attended the brief ceremony was Pierson's son, Clint, who was seven when his father was killed. The younger Pierson became a Garfield County deputy sheriff in 1996. "I always wanted to be a police officer," Pierson said. "My dad getting killed did not change my mind. I am doing what I'm supposed to be doing."

Darlene Pierson later married a Garfield County rancher. She lives with her family—including grandchildren Trooper Pierson never saw—in Panguitch, where she has opened an antiques store.

Chapter 5

1981–2003

Advances in technology also brought some increased risks for law enforcement officers. During the first fifty years of organized law enforcement effort in Utah, 28 percent of fallen police officers died accidentally. During the past fifty years, 55 percent of Utah police officers meeting their deaths in the line of duty did so in accidents rather than homicides. Being struck and killed by motorists is the third leading cause of death among Utah police officers.

Although changes in technology brought many new solutions to law enforcement problems, this period also saw a return to some tried and true methods, including bicycle patrols and an emphasis on community-oriented policing.

Women entered law enforcement in increasing numbers. This period marked the first death of a Utah female police officer when, on June 8, 1998, Navajo Public Safety Officer Esther Todecheene died in a single-car accident in southern Utah.

LEADING CAUSES OF LAW ENFORCEMENT DEATHS 1900–1998
(National statistics from National Law Enforcement Officer Memorial; Utah statistics by author.)

	NATIONAL	UTAH
1. Firearms	49%	60%
2. Automobile accidents	15%	14%
3. Motorcycle accidents	7%	3%
4. Struck by vehicle	7%	8%
5. Job-related illness	4%	0%
6. Aircraft accident	2%	2%
7. Stabbings	1%	1%
8. Fall	1%	3%

LEADING CAUSES OF LAW ENFORCEMENT DEATHS 1900–1998
(continued)

	NATIONAL	UTAH
9. Drowning	1%	0%
10. Beatings	1%	2%

Ronald L. Heaps
Salt Lake City Police Department
January 13, 1982

The night of Wednesday, January 13, 1982, remains one of the worst in Utah law enforcement history. Before it was over, four police officers had been shot, including Corporal Ronald L. Heaps, the nineteenth Salt Lake City police officer to die in the line of duty.

It began at 7:35 p.m., when a doctor at St. Mark's Hospital contacted the Salt Lake County Sheriff's Department to report that a man had become angry over the doctor's refusal to prescribe drugs for his back pain. Taking a pistol from his wife's purse as he left the hospital, the man said he was going to kill himself "and take anyone with him who tried to stop him."

A short time later, deputies Richard Owen, Scott Robinson, and Rich Bergan spotted thirty-six-year-old Jackie Lee Byrd walking south on 1300 East near 4100 South. As the deputies got out of their cars and approached him, Byrd spun around, firing a .22-caliber pistol. A bullet struck Owen in the left hand, while Robinson was shot once in the chest. As Bergan tackled the suspect and wrestled him to the ground, Byrd managed to fire three more times. These shots went into the ground, as did a single round fired by Robinson. Fortunately, Robinson was wearing body armor. The bullet left only a large bruise on his chest. Both he and Owen were taken to a hospital, where Robinson was treated and released, while Owen remained for surgery on his hand.

Two hours later, officers were not so lucky. At 9:25 p.m., Salt Lake City Officer David G. Robinson was dispatched to the area of 1300 South and 300 East to check out a report of a suspicious man. Before Robinson could reply, Corporal Ronald Heaps, 33, told dispatch that he would take the call because he was closer.

Heaps arrived in the area at approximately the same time as thirty-four-year-old Officer Dennis Nelson. Riding along with Nelson was Salt Lake County Reserve Deputy Douglas D. Roberts, who was armed but in plainclothes. The three officers searched the area but were unable to locate the suspicious man. However, they became aware of the noise of a loud party coming from a motor home with Idaho license plates parked behind a house on the southeast corner of the intersection. They decided to check with the occupants.

Salt Lake City Police Corporal Ronald Heaps
was scheduled to be promoted to sergeant before
he died in a gun battle with a suspect recently
named to the FBI's Ten Most Wanted List. (Salt
Lake Police Museum)

Two men answered the officers' knock on the door of the motor home.
Juan Casarez, 31, and Mario Tarazon, 33, were asked to step outside and
produce identification. Two other men, Eugene Dale Gonzales, 33, and Anthony
M. Reyes, 28, came to the doorway but remained inside the motor home.
What officers did not know was that Gonzales was just five days away from
being named to the FBI's Ten Most Wanted List. In addition to a string of
robberies, Gonzales was the prime suspect in the murder of a California
Highway Patrol officer.

A native of Colorado, Gonzales had a long and bloody criminal history,
beginning with a 1973 arrest for aggravated assault. Over the following years,
he was arrested for burglary, narcotics violations, robbery, auto theft, assault,
and carrying a concealed weapon.

On October 1, 1981, Gonzales and another man robbed a grocery store in
San Gabriel, California. Fleeing the scene in a car, the two men encountered
traffic congestion on the freeway, where two California Highway Patrol motor
officers were attempting to remove some debris from the road. Gonzales
thought it was a roadblock. As the robbers passed the officers they opened
fire, wounding Officers John Martinez and James Szabo. Martinez died the
following day. Following the shooting, Gonzales managed to avoid capture
by traveling in his father's motor home, living in campgrounds, and
occasionally altering the license plates. He kept a low profile until the night he
was questioned by Salt Lake City officers. Then he reached for a 9-millimeter
Walther P-38, stolen in the burglary of a Denver home.

When asked who owned the motor home, the men gave the officers
conflicting statements. Suspicious, the officers separated the men and continued

Eugene Gonzales, following a 1980 arrest in
Denver. (Salt Lake Police Museum)

their questioning. Nelson said later that he suddenly had a bad feeling. Turning
toward Heaps, who was talking to Gonzales, Nelson said, "Ron, there's
something wrong here." At that moment, Gonzales pulled a pistol and screamed,
"I own the f—king trailer!" and began firing.

The first bullet struck Heaps behind the left shoulder, in an area not covered
by his body armor, and passed through his heart. Despite this mortal wound,
Heaps was able to return fire three times. Before collapsing, he then stumbled
east toward another police vehicle pulling up to the scene.

Gonzales's next two rounds were fired at Nelson, who was struck in the
arm and in the leg. Nelson managed to fire three shots before falling and
dragging himself to a position of cover. Roberts also fired a shot that struck
the side of the motor home. In all, Gonzales was hit three times in the left arm
and upper chest. He died in the doorway of his motor home. The only bullet
recovered sufficiently intact for ballistics tests was later revealed to have come
from Nelson's revolver.

Roberts fired the last shot in the battle. Although unarmed, Reyes charged
over Gonzales's body during the shooting and ignored Roberts's command to
stop. The deputy fired once, striking Reyes in the center of the chest and killing
him. From beginning to end, the gunfight lasted ten seconds.

Nelson was taken to LDS Hospital and underwent surgery to repair a severed
femoral artery in his leg. Awarded the Medal of Valor, he returned to duty
following a long convalescence. He left the department in 1991. A shooting
review board upheld Roberts's actions in the death of Reyes.

Following an autopsy, the body of Gonzales was cremated and the ashes
returned to his family in Colorado. Meanwhile, funeral mass was held for

Reyes in St. Vincent's Catholic Church in Salt Lake City. Neither Tarazon nor Casarez was injured in the shootout. Both were temporarily jailed as material witnesses. Tarazon was later turned over to immigration officials and returned to Mexico.

The community responded to the tragedy with donations to a trust fund for the care and education of the Heaps children. Zion's First National Bank officer Richard Burdick told reporters, "The most touching are the ones from children. I had a little girl call who said she had 39 cents and wanted to know where she could send it."

Heaps was born January 21, 1949, in American Fork. He graduated from American Fork High School, where he starred in wrestling and football. He received an associate degree in electronics from Utah Technical College in Provo. On August 3, 1968, he married his best friend and school sweetheart, Anita Ruth McDaniels. The couple had four children. He joined the Salt Lake City Police Department on August 1, 1974.

On January 18, funeral services for Ronald Heaps were held in the LDS Salt Lake Hunter West Stake Center. More than 1,500 mourners paid their respects, including Nelson, who attended the services on a hospital gurney. One of the funeral speakers was Salt Lake City Police Captain Willard L. Heaps, an uncle of the slain officer. Citing from his nephew's personal journal, Captain Heaps said the fallen officer believed he would be promoted to sergeant by the first of the year. Shortly before his death, Heaps had passed the sergeant's examination; his promotion was awarded retroactive to January 1.

The funeral cortege to the Alpine City Cemetery was five miles long and consisted of officers from across Utah and throughout the western states. In

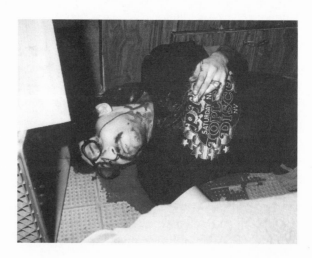

The killer of two police officers, Eugene Gonzales lies dead in his motor home. (Salt Lake Police Museum)

all, personnel from fifty-one agencies escorted Heaps to his final resting place. Among the flowers placed on Heaps's grave were those sent by the family of slain California Highway Patrol Officer Johnny Ramirez Martinez. Of the funeral it was written: "He was buried on a hill looking to the blue and white slopes of the mountains near his childhood home. The craggy tops of the mountains were hidden in clouds and the snow had been carefully removed from the grave so that the grass could be seen."

Roy Lee Stanley
Andy Begay

Navajo Department of Public Safety
December 5, 1987

Just after dawn on December 5, 1987, a fisherman spotted a burning vehicle near the Piute Farms Marina of Lake Powell. He reported it to park rangers at Glen Canyon National Recreation Area. When rangers arrived, they found two vehicles still smoldering in the bottom of Copper Canyon, a deep sandy wash emptying into an eastern arm of Lake Powell. Located some twenty-five miles from U.S. Highway 163, it is one of the most geographically isolated areas of the United States. It soon would prove to be culturally isolated as well.

Both vehicles were four-wheel-drive Chevrolet Suburban panel trucks belonging to the Navajo Department of Public Safety. Inside the prisoner cage of one were the badly burned bodies of Navajo tribal officers Roy Lee Stanley, 27, and Andy Begay, 35.

A resident of Oljeta, Roy Lee Stanley left a two-year-old son and a wife pregnant with a second child. Stanley had met his wife, Mary Lou Todecheene, when the two attended Monument Valley High School together. They were married in 1983 after Stanley finished a four-year enlistment in the U.S. Navy. He joined the police department a year before his death. Andy Begay lived in Mexican Hat with his wife, Laura, and the couple's four sons. He was a twelve-year veteran of the police department.

Because the crime occurred on the Navajo Reservation, the investigation came under the jurisdiction of the Federal Bureau of Investigation. Federal agents, tribal officers, and San Juan County deputies descended on the scene, combing the surrounding mesas and narrow canyons for clues. Rumors soon circulated that the officers might have run afoul of drug smugglers, who

Navajo Tribal Police Officer Roy Lee Stanley
was taken hostage when he tried to break up a
drinking party. Local youths were infuriated by
the officer's crackdown on liquor and had vowed
to get even with him. (Navajo Tribe)

commonly used makeshift aircraft landing strips in the remote area for
transporting drugs out of Mexico. No one wanted to believe that the crime had
a local origin.

The two officers were last seen the previous evening, when they provided
security for a basketball game at Monument Valley High School in Goulding,
Utah, a small community on U.S. 163 near the Arizona border. They had left
the gymnasium at about 9:30 p.m.

Shortly after 11:00 p.m., a police department dispatcher heard Stanley radio
Begay and advise the latter that he was going to check out a bonfire
approximately one mile west of the high school. Juveniles often built fires to
stay warm during parties that often included alcohol, and Stanley was known—
and hated—for his diligence in breaking up the gatherings.

The last radio transmission from either officer occurred just before midnight,
when a decidedly agitated Stanley requested Begay's assistance at the bonfire.
The fact that they were not heard from again that night was not considered
unusual. Monument Valley is pockmarked with "10-38 areas," law enforcement
code for dead air—places where radio communication is impossible.

Few clues were recovered with the bodies. An autopsy at the Arizona
Medical Center in Tucson revealed that both officers had been handcuffed.
Although two-thirds of the bodies had been reduced to ash, there was evidence
that Stanley had suffered a severe beating prior to his death. Bullet holes in
the vehicle and four empty casings in a recovered .357 magnum pistol indicated
that they might have been shot with Stanley's sidearm. But that wasn't what
killed them. Evidence of smoke inhalation revealed that both officers were
still alive when the vehicle burned.

Navajo Tribal Police Officer Andy Begay was lured to the scene by suspects forcing Stanley to call for help on the police radio. (Navajo Tribe)

Four days later, a funeral service for the slain officers was held in the Kayenta (Arizona) Field House. More than 1,300 mourners filled the stands, including the officers' widows. Among the eulogies were promises from officials that the investigation would proceed until the guilty were brought to justice.

Promises to the contrary, however, the investigation soon bogged down. Rumors of a gun battle with drug smugglers ceased as evidence instead led agents to what had occurred at the bonfire. When investigators examined the scene they found pools of blood, footprints, and eyeglasses and broken teeth eventually matched to Stanley.

The few Goulding residents willing to talk to police reported hearing four gunshots from the direction of the fire late in the night. Investigators now believed that the victims had been overpowered at the party, murdered, and their bodies transported to Copper Canyon for disposal. Breaking the case would require statements from Navajos willing to point the finger at other Navajos, something not easily done in an environment of clan hostility and superstition. When contacted, most reservation residents who might have known something refused to cooperate, saying they feared reprisals from the tribal police, the killers, and even witches.

On December 12, the *Arizona Republic* reported that reservation medicine men had been summoned in an attempt to crack the case. Tribal council delegate Walter Atwood said the shamans would gaze into crystals under starlight in an attempt to see images of the killers, and would also use "hand trembling" to detect them. On a more temporal level, the FBI offered a cash reward. Anyone who provided information leading to the arrests of the killers would receive $5,000. The amount was later increased to $10,000. Still, no one came forward.

By January, the investigation appeared to have stalled completely. Officials said they were still following leads but publicly admitted that Navajo distrust of white authority and cultural differences made progress slow. It was apparent to investigators, however, that some people knew who the killers were.

In late January, the FBI was forced to divert manpower away from the reservation and send it north to Marion, Utah, where a church bombing led to a thirteen-day standoff between law enforcement and the Singer family. That standoff ended tragically with the death of Utah Department of Corrections Lieutenant Fred House.

By March, agents had returned to the reservation with a decision to try to solve the murders with the help of the Navajo culture rather than in spite of it. Tribal elders were asked to make an appeal to local Navajos, encouraging them to set aside clan differences so that the guilty could be brought to justice. Witnesses began talking, and, on April 15, federal agents arrested four tribal members. Charged with first-degree murder were Monument Valley residents Thomas Cly, 22; Marques Atene, 22; his cousin Ben Atene, Jr., 24; and Vinton Bedoni, 31, half-brother of Ben Atene.

Ten days later, the four suspects faced a preliminary hearing in federal court. The courtroom was packed with family members of both the victims and the suspects. U.S. Magistrate Ronald Boyce addressed a report that some of the defendants' relatives had been "counseling" witnesses to change their testimonies. Boyce promised jail terms for anyone caught interfering with the law.

Cly, Bedoni, and the Atenes pleaded innocent to the charges, and were ordered to stand trial in July. Prosecuting the case turned out to be every bit as difficult as was the investigation. Prior to the trial, defense lawyers and prosecutors argued motions arising from allegations of FBI coercion, recanted witness statements, and perjury during a previous grand jury hearing. On July 12, U.S. District Judge J. Thomas Greene denied a defense motion to dismiss the charges, and ordered the trial to proceed.

The trial began in Salt Lake City four days later. Members of the all-white jury got their first taste of the cultural barriers that had complicated the investigation from the beginning when Rosie Cly, 65, took the stand. Cly, who could not read or write and spoke only Navajo, was so intimidated by her surroundings that at first she couldn't speak at all. Prosecutors broke the ice by asking her if she had ever ridden on an elevator, a question that brought a smile to her face. Cly's first ride on a elevator had occurred when she came to testify. Eventually, Cly said (through an interpreter) that she had heard gunshots from the direction of the bonfire, located several hundred feet from her home.

Boyd Atene, a distant relative of the accused, was the prosecution's star witness. Atene testified that he was sitting in a truck when Stanley arrived to break up the party. "The next thing I knew, Vinton tackled Roy Lee," he said.

Bedoni got the officer on the ground in a "double-chicken-wing hold," whereupon Ben Atene kicked the officer in the side. Bedoni handcuffed Stanley and led him to his police panel truck. Atene said Bedoni, who by then was holding Stanley's service revolver, told him to get behind the steering wheel of the officer's vehicle, which was still running. "I heard two shots in the back of the panel," Atene said.

A short time later Begay arrived and was also shot. Atene said he drove Stanley's vehicle to Copper Canyon at Bedoni's direction. When it became mired in the muddy creek bed, Cly produced a five-gallon can of gas and doused both police vehicles, which were then set ablaze.

Defense lawyers attacked Atene's testimony, pointing out that he had previously been charged with lying to the grand jury when he testified that he hadn't been at the bonfire. Atene admitted that a perjury charge had been dropped in exchange for his testimony, but stated he was telling the truth now.

On July 22, Marques Atene left the court a free man after prosecutors admitted they didn't have enough evidence to make a case against him. Although a witness said Atene was seen covering up evidence at the bonfire, there was nothing to tie him to the actual murders.

The case against Cly, Bedoni, and Ben Atene, Jr., continued. The defendants, along with family members, offered testimony—frequently contradictory— as to their whereabouts the night of the murders, claiming they were variously at a medicine ceremony, sick in bed, driving around in a truck, buying beer in Medicine Hat, asleep in a remote canyon, and hauling wood. Cly admitted to threatening Stanley's life during a previous alcohol arrest, telling the officer, "Your ass is mine. You're going to die later. Your badge don't mean nothing to me." However, he denied carrying out the threat.

The jury received the case on July 28, and deliberated for five days before returning guilty verdicts for Cly and Bedoni. The convictions for these two were decided upon relatively early in the deliberations, but jurors said they could not agree on the guilt of Ben Atene, Jr. When the deadlock could not be broken, Greene declared a mistrial and ordered Atene retried. He was acquitted of the murder charge at this trial in October.

Many Navajos were relieved by the convictions, believing that clan warfare would have broken out on the reservation had Cly and Bedoni been acquitted. But relatives and friends of the two denounced the verdict. A Bedoni family member protested by reading a statement from Navajo tribal chairman Peter McDonald in front of the courthouse, complaining of a "raw deal ... done totally in the white man's way."

Cly and Bedoni appealed their convictions to the U.S. Tenth Circuit Court of Appeals, claiming among other things that Native Americans were not fairly represented on the jury. On August 27, 1990, the court of appeals denied this claim. They remain in the Phoenix Federal Correctional Institution, and are not eligible for parole until 2018.

Fred Floyd House
Utah Department of Corrections
January 28, 1988

When the custodian of the LDS Kamas Stake Center in Marion arrived to plow snow from the parking lot on the morning of January 16, 1988, he found a bigger mess than anticipated. During the night, someone had set off a bomb in the church, causing $1.5 million in damages and starting a chain of events that would lead to the death of Utah Department of Corrections Lieutenant Fred House.

Fred Floyd House was born February 2, 1952, in Los Angeles, California, the fourth of six children born to Stanley and Wanda Huether House. In 1963, House's father died while trying to rescue a friend on a boating trip near Long Beach. His mother remarried two years later.

Following his graduation from Pasadena High School, House attended Brigham Young University. His older brother Tom worked for the Utah Department of Corrections, and House joined the same department in 1973. He quickly gained a reputation for unconventional methods that simultaneously caused concern and relief among his superiors. Nobody wanted to supervise House, but everyone wanted him around when things were going badly. Within five years, the martial-arts enthusiast was promoted to lieutenant.

House commanded the department's K-9 program, supervised the fugitive apprehension team, and was a member of the prison's SWAT team. Before his death, House won a gold medal during a national K-9 competition in Alabama and was awarded the Department of Corrections Medal of Merit for outstanding service. Based on a cleverly written recommendation, he also came close to having his K-9 companion named the department's employee of the year.

House married Ann Christine Whiting on December 18, 1976, in Highland, Utah. The couple eventually had three children, whom House doted on, despite some misgivings about the nature of his job and the effect it might have on his family. But it was someone else's family that would lead to tragedy for his.

Figuring out who committed the Marion bombing was easy. Tracks in the

Department of Corrections Lieutenant Fred
House tried to use non-deadly force to end the
infamous Singer-Swapp stand-off in Marion,
Utah. (Utah State Department of Corrections)

deep snow led directly to the Singer farm, a mile away. John and Vickie Singer
had had a long history of confrontation with law enforcement and neighbors
over water rights and their refusal to send their children to public school.
Fundamentalists and excommunicated Mormons, the Singers refused to allow
officials to test their children to ensure they were being adequately educated
at home and defied summonses to appear in court. In the fall of 1978 Third
District Court Judge Peter Leary ordered Summit County Sheriff Ronald
Robinson to seize the Singer children.

Aware of what the authorities intended, Singer began carrying a pistol. In
October 1978 he pulled it on Robinson when the sheriff attempted to serve the
warrant at Singer's home. Robinson wisely backed off. When three deputies
posing as news reporters attempted to arrest Singer the following week, he
produced the pistol again and forced them to leave.

Robinson was under no illusions about Singer's willingness to resist arrest
by shooting police officers. However, finding a method that would resolve the
problem without bloodshed proved to be difficult. Media attention and judicial
pressure increased until something had to give. Robinson asked for assistance
from the Department of Public Safety, and Commissioner Larry Lunnen sent
four state agents.

On January 18, 1979, officers on snowmobiles surrounded Singer as he
went to check a mailbox located on the highway a quarter of a mile from his
house. Singer again drew the loaded pistol and pointed it at officers, ignoring
their commands to drop the weapon. When it appeared that he was about to
fire, Narcotics and Liquor Law Enforcement Agent Lewis Jolley shot Singer
with a 12-gauge shotgun, killing him.

Investigations by the Summit County Attorney and the FBI upheld the officers' actions, but Vickie Singer filed a $110 million wrongful-death lawsuit. The suit was dismissed in federal court in 1982. The appeal process continued all the way to the U.S. Supreme Court, which refused to hear the case in 1985, effectively ending the legal avenue. But the battle was far from over.

Shortly after Singer's death, Addam Swapp appeared at the Singer farm. Barely out of high school, the Sanpete County youth quickly ingratiated himself into the Singer family, eventually entering into plural marriages with Vickie Singer's two daughters, Heidi and Charlotte. Over the next nine years, Swapp fathered five children.

Swapp's apocalyptic mindset was not a stabilizing influence on the Singer family. Incensed by the death of a father-in-law he never met, Swapp wrote threatening letters to anyone who offended him, including the sheriff, school district, Marion water users, and leaders of the Church of Jesus Christ of Latter-day Saints. Frustrated at being ignored by those he was calling to repentance, Swapp decided to make a bigger statement. In the early morning hours of January 16, 1988, he broke into the Kamas stake center and placed nearly ninety sticks of dynamite packed in ammonium nitrate inside the cultural hall. To announce authorship of the deed, Swapp then stuck a pole in the baseball diamond. His "spear" carried nine feathers representing the number of years since the death of John Singer, Mormon priesthood symbols, and the date of Singer's death. Then he walked home to watch the explosion with his family.

Swapp would later say that the bombing was intended to bring about the resurrection of John Singer, which in turn would start the Apocalypse and precipitate the collapse of the Mormon Church and the government. What it brought, however, was an army of federal agents and news reporters.

The House family in happier times. Ann House would later successfully sue the manufacturers of the body armor her husband wore when he died. (House family)

When the heavily armed Swapp-Singer clan failed to surrender the following morning, Summit County requested help from the Utah Department of Public Safety (DPS). Because a bomb had been used, the DPS appealed for help from the Bureau of Alcohol, Tobacco and Firearms as well as from the FBI. In all, more than a hundred officers converged on the Singer farm. Defiant, Swapp refused to negotiate. Indeed, he seemed to welcome battle with the police, claiming that John Singer would be resurrected and protect them at the very moment police attacked.

Fifteen people were barricaded in the farmhouse, three of them heavily armed adult males: Addam Swapp, his brother Jonathan Swapp, and brother-in-law John Timothy Singer, confined to a wheelchair by an old spinal injury. What concerned officers most, however, were the children, six of them under the age of ten.

On January 19, a dozen shots were fired from the Singer farm as officers erected a series of spotlights. Over the next two days, more than fifty rounds were fired at the lights. Authorities refused to return fire for fear of hitting the children and due to a reluctance to create further martyrs for the fundamentalist cult.

In an effort to motivate Swapp into communicating, all electrical power to the farm was cut by a police marksman, who shot out a transformer. Meanwhile, a federal grand jury indicted Swapp and Vickie Singer on bombing charges and shooting at officers. A copy of the indictment was dropped to the suspects from a helicopter.

The siege dragged on for thirteen days, in which media news coverage was increasingly saturated. Over that time, psychological pressure on the cult also was increased. Aircraft buzzed the farm, flares were fired overhead during the night, the water line was cut, and high-pitched electronic noise was directed at the Singer home. Although frequently fired upon, officers did not return fire. The day before the siege ended, Swapp wrote to Governor Norm Bangerter, in a letter brought out of the farm by a family friend. It said in part:

> We are INDEPENDENT and SEPARATE from your Wicked society of ever Changing laws and Dark Councils that seek to enslave the minds and souls of men.
>
> Also, if you start up your Hellish Sounds again, we will also see this as an aggressive act against us—for this form of torture can be more deadly than a bullet in the side, for it penetrates my wives and children groins …

Convinced by this that there was no further point in negotiating, authorities decided to end the siege. House, who had volunteered for security duty at the

Singer farm, proposed using police dogs to take down the Swapp brothers when they left the building to milk the family goats. The plan was accepted, and during the night of January 26, officers maneuvered near the main house and tried to get the dogs to attack the Swapps. However, the dogs became confused and the attack failed. But House still thought the plan would work and suggested they try again.

At 8:30 a.m. the following day, Swapp and his brother, both armed with rifles, left the main building. From the doorway of a home approximately a hundred yards west of the Singer home, House released a dog named Mike with the command to attack. Instead, the dog became confused. "It was a glitch," said Department of Corrections Officer Jerry Pope, the other dog handler at the scene. "We had never trained our dogs to go from the inside of the building to the outside. In the dog's mind, he was going through a doorway to the inside of a room and he checked both sides of the door for suspects."

When House stepped into the doorway to order the dog to continue the attack, he was shot by John Timothy Singer, firing from inside the Singer home. House was struck in the chest by a single .30-caliber carbine round which grazed the ceramic plate in the body armor he wore, penetrated the Kevlar material, tore into his aorta, and came out his back. It was later found on the kitchen floor of the home. House fell in the doorway and was pulled back into the building by FBI Agent Richard Intellini. Intellini later testified: "I said Fred are you OK, are you OK? And all he did was grunt. I kept talking to him because I know the last sense you lose is hearing and I didn't want Fred to die alone."

Meanwhile, the Swapp brothers pointed their rifles at other officers, who opened fire. A 9-millimeter bullet passed through Addam Swapp's arm and lodged in his chest. The wound, most likely from a shot fired by FBI Agent John Butler, was not life threatening, and Swapp ran back to the main building.

Under heavy rifle fire from the cult, two armored personnel carriers were used to extract House and other agents from further danger. During this process, the wounded Swapp came out of the main building and waved a white towel in surrender. He sat in the snow singing a hymn while his wounds were dressed. The rest of the clan surrendered as well.

House was buried four days later in the Orem City Cemetery on what would have been his thirty-sixth birthday. Funeral services were held at the LDS Orem Windsor Stake Center. Utah Corrections Department Director Gary Deland lauded House as one of the few officers with a "constant green light," referring to the lieutenant's readiness for unorthodox action that resulted in the prison's highest rate of apprehended fugitives. "I didn't always know where [Fred] was," Deland said. "I wasn't sure I wanted to know where he was. You didn't try to spoil something that was working by throwing a harness on a racehorse."

But House was remembered most poignantly for his commitment to his family, particularly as a loving father who lost a night of sleep during the Marion siege so that he could help carve his son's Pinewood Derby car for the Cub Scouts. At the end of the service, a visibly moved Governor Bangerter presented Ann House with the Medal of Honor posthumously awarded to her husband. The procession of police cars and motorcycles escorting the body of Fred House to the cemetery included officers from Utah, Idaho, Alabama, Wyoming, and Canada. A helicopter hovered overhead as House's karate mentor and friend Tsutomu Ohshima bowed to his former student and to the crowd: "Fred, you reached the level all Samurais hope to reach. I'm proud of you. I love you. Thank you. Goodbye."

The standoff at the farm was over. The one in court would last longer. On February 7, a federal grand jury indicted members of the clan and ordered them to stand trial. In May 1988, Addam Swapp was found guilty in federal court on seven charges connected with the church bombing and the later firing at agents. He was sentenced to seventeen years in federal prison. His brother and John Timothy Singer were convicted on four counts each of using firearms against federal agents, and both were sentenced to ten years in prison. Vickie Singer was sentenced on five counts of aiding in the use of a gun to resist arrest, and was sentenced to five years.

On September 7, the State of Utah charged the three male suspects with second-degree murder. They pleaded not guilty. The trial, which began in Coalville on December 2, would last nearly a month and showcase religious zealotry at its worst. John Timothy Singer readily admitted firing the rifle bullet that killed House, but he insisted that he was shooting at the dogs rather than House.

On December 22, after deliberating for two days, the jury found Addam Swapp and John Timothy Singer guilty of manslaughter, a second-degree felony. Both were sentenced to one-to-fifteen-year terms in prison. Jonathan Swapp was found guilty of misdemeanor negligent homicide.

Addam Swapp remains in a federal prison in Phoenix, Arizona, where he will complete his sentence for the bombing in 2006. He will then begin serving his state sentence in Utah. The father of six children remains adamant that he was acting through divine direction: "If I have to spend the rest of my life in prison, I will. I will not deny that what I did was inspired by God."

John Timothy Singer completed his ten-year federal sentence in 1997, and is currently spending his state prison term in an Arizona federal facility. He is scheduled to be released in 2011.

Jonathan Swapp, who married in a jailhouse ceremony while awaiting trial, completed his prison term and lives in Arizona.

Vickie Singer's prison term was reduced later for good behavior. She was released in June 1991 and remarried. She still lives on the farm where the siege occurred, and has publicly stated that House died from bullets fired by other officers.

In 1988, the Department of Correction's academy was named in honor of Fred House. In 1999, the family of Fred House settled a lawsuit for an undisclosed amount with Armour of America Inc., the manufacturer of the bullet-proof vest the officer was wearing when he died. Ann House sued the company for failure to properly warn the Department of Corrections to the fact that the vests would not stop rifle fire.

Dennis "Dee" Lund

Utah Highway Patrol
June 16, 1993

Twelve miles west of Green River, Utah, on a hill overlooking Interstate 70, stands a monument to the ninth Utah Highway Patrol trooper to die in the line of duty, and the second to be murdered. The white, twelve-foot steel cross bears the name of Trooper Dennis "Dee" Lund.

Lund was born September 25, 1955, in Brigham City, to Rodney LaVelle Lund and Nancy Lee Hedin Lund. Raised in Ogden, he graduated from Ben Lomond High School in 1973. Following an LDS mission to Holbrook, Arizona, Lund married Brenda Cooper—a young woman he met on a blind date at a church party—in 1978. The couple lived in Weber County, where Brenda worked as a licensed practical nurse, and Lund was employed as a salesman for a heating and air-conditioning company. Their first child was born in 1980. A second child was born in 1983 but died shortly after birth. Two years later, another son was born.

Lund's interest in law enforcement developed as other family members became involved in the profession. Kevin Youngberg, a brother-in-law, became an Ogden police officer, then a UHP trooper. Later, Lund's younger brother Clark also joined the UHP. Lund sometimes rode along with them. One night, while riding with his brother in Summit County, Lund observed the arrest of a drunk driver. According to Clark, it was at that moment that his older brother decided to become a police officer. "He looked over at me and said, 'You know what? I've got to do this.' I got him an application."

Utah Highway Patrol Trooper Dennis "Dee" Lund died after being shot by one of two runaway teenagers wanted for stealing fuel from a Grand County gas station. (Utah Highway Patrol)

Lund joined the Utah Highway Patrol as a security officer on April 19, 1986. He spent eighteen months in the Protective Services division guarding state facilities and providing security for government officials. The following year, he attended Peace Officer Standards and Training classes. To the surprise of family members who thought him too nice to be an officer, Lund excelled in the police academy. While going through his papers following his death, his wife learned that the irreverent prankster received top marks during the course. Following graduation on December 18, 1987, the Lund family moved to Hanksville, where the new trooper finally got what he wanted: patrol duty.

While in Hanksville, Lund served as the Deacon's quorum adviser and scoutmaster in the local LDS ward. He frequently talked about getting a pilot's license and buying a large motorcycle to tour with a club of other officers and their spouses. In 1989, Lund transferred to Green River—where the action was. Known as "Rapich's Raiders," for UHP Sergeant Steven Rapich, the Green River troopers specialized in interdicting drug shipments, high-speed pursuits, and felony arrests.

In Green River, Lund joined the volunteer fire department, and, together with his wife, served on the volunteer ambulance crew. Because of his rapport with young boys, Lund worked with the Cub Scouts in his ward.

The last time Brenda Lund saw her husband alive was the evening of June 16, as she pulled into the parking lot of the Green River city offices for an ambulance meeting. When she looked into her rearview mirror, her husband's UHP Ford Mustang was parked behind her. "We talked for a while," Brenda related. "We both worked, and it was like he was lonely for me that night. Then he left."

Twenty miles to the east, eighteen-year-old Jason Scott Pearson and sixteen-year-old George Todd Kennedy were headed into Utah on Interstate 70. Several days before, the two had fled their Indiana homes a few steps ahead of minor criminal charges. Tossing a shotgun and a rifle into a Ford Thunderbird belonging to Kennedy's mother, they headed west. Out of fuel, money, and food, they pulled into a gas station at Thompson Springs, a few miles west of the Colorado border. Filling the car with gas, they left without paying, getting back on the freeway heading west. A clerk spotted them and called police.

Grand County Deputy Steve Brownell encountered the red Thunderbird a few minutes later and tried to stop it. Instead of pulling over, Pearson punched the gas and the chase headed toward Green River. Alerted to the pursuit coming their way, Lund and fellow UHP trooper Bruce Riches put out spike strips and waited for the Thunderbird to reach them. When it did, Pearson apparently spotted the spikes and entered the median, crossing over and continuing west in the eastbound lanes.

Lund and Riches joined the chase, catching up quickly in their high-performance Mustangs. When the suspects tried to exit onto two-lane U.S. Highway 6 to Price, troopers cut them off. Fearing catastrophe if the high-speed pursuit were to continue on the narrower road, they crowded the Thunderbird back onto the wider westbound lanes of the freeway.

As the Thunderbird drove down the on-ramp, Lund passed the fleeing teenagers on the left. With a 20-gauge shotgun, Pearson blasted the right rear passenger window out of Lund's patrol car. Pellets cut through his uniform shirt, but Lund got past the suspect vehicle and sped ahead of them. By radio, the sergeant ordered Lund to pull over and shoot out the tires of the suspect vehicle as it passed. The suspects traded fire with Lund as they went by him. Lund managed to hit one of the tires, but failed to deflate it.

Lund caught up with the chase again. By then all the patrol cars had been hit by .22-caliber bullets, fired by Pearson, who had twisted out the driver's window and was sitting on the door firing over the roof.

In a patrol unit driven by Trooper Kelly Roberts, Sergeant Steven Rapich was in the backseat with a shotgun. He waited until Roberts eased into a position where he could shoot out the fleeing vehicle's tires. Suddenly, Lund screamed over the radio, "I'm hit, I'm hit, I'm hit!" Lund had been struck in the left eye by fragments of a bullet that hit the upper left corner of his windshield. The fragments penetrated Lund's head, lodging in his brain stem. The trooper's last voluntary act was to steer his patrol car off the freeway. A deputy following the pursuit stopped and found Lund slumped at the wheel.

The pursuit ran west, with Pearson continuing to fire. Seconds later, Rapich shot out a tire on the fleeing Thunderbird. Kennedy, who was steering, lost control and the vehicle rolled, ejecting both teens. Troopers pounced on them. Pearson feigned unconsciousness and was quickly handcuffed. Kennedy snatched up one of the guns, only to find he was holding a broken stock. The chase was over.

Back in Green River, Brenda heard the chase on the family's police scanner as she returned home from the meeting. A few minutes later, her ambulance pager beeped. When she arrived at the ambulance building, Brenda said to the crew, half in jest, "I hope this isn't Dee." Fear grew, however, as the ambulance neared the scene. "When someone called on the radio and asked who was on board, I got scared."

Rapich ordered Trooper Boyd Gledhill to stop the ambulance and take Brenda off. Furious, Brenda hurled some first-aid equipment against the wall. There could be only one reason for the order.

Word spread quickly in Green River. Within thirty minutes, many in the town had gathered around the clinic as the ambulance carrying Lund returned. A place was cleared for the medical helicopter from Salt Lake to land. However, instead of lifting off again with the wounded trooper, the engine was switched off. Lund died in the ambulance that brought him to town. As the crowd learned the awful truth, they converged on Rapich, filling the sergeant's hands with money for the Lund family.

On June 18, Pearson and Kennedy were arraigned in Seventh District Court on charges of capital murder and attempted murder. Kennedy was charged as

The stolen vehicle driven by Jason Scott Pearson and George Todd Kennedy rolled over after UHP Sergeant Steve Rapich shot out one of its tires. (Utah Highway Patrol)

UHP Trooper Darrell Mecham at a memorial
cross for Dennis Lund posted near Spotted Wolf
Canyon by the Utah Highway Patrol Association.
(Author)

an adult, and bail was set at $500,000 each. The families of the two Indiana
teens came to Utah to be with them during the coming trials.

Three days later, Lund was buried in West Weber. Thousands of family,
friends, and co-workers packed the Ogden LDS Tabernacle for funeral services.
Police officers from twenty-six states escorted the body to the South Weber
Cemetery, where the trooper was buried next to his son Lyle. A memorial
service was later held in Green River.

It would take two years for Pearson and Kennedy to get their days in court.
Inseparable in offense, the two fell apart in their defense. Kennedy agreed to
testify against Pearson, claiming that fear of the older boy influenced his own
actions. He pleaded guilty to murder and two counts of attempted murder and
received a sentence of five years to life. He was transferred in 1999 to a prison
in Illinois, and is not eligible for parole until 2013.

Pearson pleaded not guilty to the charge of capital murder. His trial began
June 19, 1995, in the Emery County Courthouse in Castle Dale. Pearson
tearfully admitted in Seventh District Court that he had fired at pursuing
troopers, but he insisted that he had been shooting at the vehicles rather than
the troopers in them. "I have to wake up every day for the rest of my life
knowing that I took a father from his children, a husband from his wife, a son
from his parents. I hate myself … I tore his family apart and I did not do that
intentionally." As sorry as he was, Pearson had no explanation for why he
didn't stop, or why he began firing at the troopers in the first place. He insisted
that he had been shooting at the officers just to scare them off.

On June 30, a Castle Dale jury deliberated for six hours and found Pearson
guilty of capital murder, two counts of attempted capital murder, and one

count of aggravated assault. On July 3, he was sentenced to life in prison with the possibility of parole. He remains incarcerated today in Utah, and is not eligible for parole until 2018.

The Lunds returned to South Weber. Brenda Lund eventually remarried, but divorced less than two years later.

Months after the murder, UHP Trooper Darrell Mecham and Emery County Deputy Richard Graham etched Lund's name onto a slab of sandstone and placed it upright at the location where he died. In 1999, the Utah Highway Patrol Association erected the white steel memorial cross at a rest stop near Spotted Wolf Canyon, approximately four miles west of the stone marker. During the ceremony, dark clouds loomed over the desert and threatened to pour rain on those gathered to pay tribute to Lund. While some expressed concern that Mother Nature would spoil the gathering, Mecham instead saw a glimmer of his friend's sense of humor in the coming storm. "Relax, everyone," Mecham told the crowd. "It's just Dee."

Michael Scott Welcker
Salt Lake County Sheriff's Office
February 24, 1994

Salt Lake County Sheriff's Deputy Michael Scott Welcker was born June 20, 1955, in Salt Lake City, to Lewis F. and Lois M. Welcker. The only son of a small-town pharmacist and a bank teller, Welcker was raised with his two sisters in a modest home in Magna. An avid sports enthusiast throughout his boyhood, Welcker graduated from Cypress High School, where he played football. He attended Weber State University, and eventually received a bachelor's degree in physical education from the University of Utah.

Prior to becoming a police officer, Welcker worked successfully as a landscaper and health spa instructor. His next career move led him into law enforcement at an age when most police officers are halfway toward retirement. In 1989, at the age of thirty-four, Welcker joined the Salt Lake County Sheriff's Office following his graduation from Peace Officer Standards and Training classes. His intention to attend the police academy came as a surprise to family members. "We never heard him express an interest in law enforcement before that," said his sister Kristine. "I think he saw it as a way of helping young people."

Welcker's concern for young people led him to an assignment in the sheriff's office that seemed made for him. He applied for a transfer to the Sheriff's

Salt Lake County Deputy Michael Welcker was struck by a bullet fired through a door as he and other deputies investigated an assault report. (Salt Lake County Sheriff's Office)

Assisting Youth program, and spent two years teaching at Kearns High School. Five months prior to his death, Welcker was transferred back to patrol duties.

On the morning of February 24, 1994, Welcker received his last radio call. He was dispatched to a Taylorsville apartment complex to assist other officers in the search for an assault suspect. Deputies were looking for Michael Namai Post, a twenty-five-year-old parolee from the Utah State Prison. At 8:30 a.m., Post had pistol-whipped his brother-in-law during an argument at the latter's apartment. Badly lacerated, John Earl called police.

Post was well known to police officers. A native of Thailand, he grew up in California after being adopted by an older sister and brought to the United States. His trouble with Utah law enforcement began in 1987, when he fled police on a stolen motorcycle. Arrested for that crime, Post bailed out of jail and immediately resumed stealing cars and motorcycles. Arrested again, he was sent to the Utah State Prison in October 1988. In 1990, he walked away from a halfway house and stole another car. Just days later, Post rolled the car north of Las Vegas while fleeing from the Nevada Highway Patrol. Sent back to prison in Utah, he was paroled again in May 1993. Post then worked at a local construction supply company, but abruptly quit one day.

Post told family members that police officers would never again take him alive. Toward that end, he was carrying a 9mm Ruger pistol when he stopped at his sister's apartment to give his nephew a ride to school. The pistol had been stolen during a burglary two months before, and Post used it to beat his brother-in-law after the two got into an argument.

Knowing that police would soon be looking for him, Post fled the scene and drove three miles to the apartment of another sister, located at 1747 West

Michael Post told friends he would never go back to prison. After pistol-whipping his brother-in-law, he barricaded himself in an apartment and then shot it out with officers. (*Salt Lake Tribune*)

Bowling Avenue (4620 South). There, in a back bedroom, he waited for the police.

Welcker and six other officers arrived at the second-floor apartment just before 9:30 a.m. Calls were made to a phone inside the apartment in the hope that Post would answer and a line of communication be established. Post did not respond to the call or to shouts through the door for him to come outside.

Post's sister Lamyai Sanders gave officers permission to enter the apartment. Salt Lake County Sergeant Dennis Harwood began picking the lock while Welcker and other officers, including Detective Sergeant Larry Marx, covered him with drawn weapons. As Harwood turned the lock, Post suddenly started firing through the closed door.

The first bullet hit Welcker, who was standing to one side of the door. It struck under his arm, missing the panels in his body armor and severing his aorta. He managed to stumble out onto a sidewalk before collapsing.

A subsequent round struck Marx's wristwatch, deflecting the bullet below his body armor. It tore into his lower abdomen and passed into his thigh, driving him to one knee with such force that he would later require reconstructive surgery on the joint. Marx counted himself lucky. If it hadn't first hit his watch, the bullet would have struck him in the face. "It felt like a horse kicked me," Marx said later from a hospital bed. "I knew I was hit when I saw the hole in my slacks."

Marx managed to return fire, as did deputies Mike Judd, Mike Morgan, Henry Beltran, and Roy Orton. In all, they fired more than forty rounds back through the door as they retreated "out of the kill zone." Harwood and Detective John Barker pulled Marx to safety. Morgan and Judd went to Welcker's aid.

By then the mortally wounded deputy was unconscious. Disregarding their exposure to possible return fire from the apartment, they called for medical assistance and began CPR.

A perimeter zone around the apartment was established as paramedics arrived and transferred Welcker to a medical helicopter. He was flown to University Hospital, where he was pronounced dead at 10:10 a.m. Meanwhile, Marx was transported by ambulance to LDS Hospital. Following surgery, he was listed in stable condition.

More than fifty officers participated in the two-hour standoff that followed. Repeated attempts were made to contact Post inside the apartment. When he failed to respond, a tactical team fired tear gas into a window and stormed the apartment. They found Post in the back bedroom, dead from a self-inflicted gunshot wound to the head.

Post's death ended a recent string of violent crimes in which he was a prime suspect. In the days following Welcker's murder, investigators identified Post as the man who had recently robbed two Salt Lake banks.

Michael Welcker was buried March 1 in Valley View Memorial Park. More than 2,000 mourners attended the funeral service in the Magna LDS Stake Center, including many of the teens Welcker had taught at Kearns High. Also among the mourners was Larry Marx, released from the hospital with the bullet permanently lodged in his hip.

"Mike will be remembered for his strength during moments of crisis and the love for those in his life," Salt Lake County Captain Paul Cunningham told those gathered to pay their final respects. "He loved kids and they loved him right back. He was one big kid at heart."

Marx retired from the sheriff's office in 2000. He currently works as an investigator with the Utah Department of Public Safety. Harwood retired and died of natural causes in January 2002.

In 1995, the Salt Lake County Sheriff's Office named its community police substation at 1735 West 5400 South in honor of Mike Welcker. Also, young people play in a public park at 4715 South and 4200 West that bears his name.

Cecil F. Gurr

Roosevelt Police Department
July 6, 2001

On July 2, 2001, Sandy Police Chief Sam Dawson died in an off-duty motorcycle accident. Dawson was riding his motorcycle on State Road 35 in

Roosevelt Police Chief Cecil Gurr
died trying to protect his officers
from a suspect firing at them with an
assault rifle. (Gurr family)

Wasatch County when he struck a deer. The law enforcement community was
still reeling from Dawson's loss four days later when Roosevelt Police Chief
Cecil Gurr was shot to death by a parole violator in the small community of
Ballard.

Cecil Gurr was born April 27, 1951, in Roosevelt, to Beryl and Frankie
Burton Gurr. Raised in Neola, he graduated from Union High School in 1969.
Immediately following his graduation, Gurr went to Washington, D.C., where
he worked for the FBI as a courier and office technician. He remained there
for a year, eventually deciding to return to Utah following the deaths of both
of his grandmothers.

In July 1970 Gurr volunteered for the draft and was inducted into the U.S.
Army. He spent five months at Fort Lewis, Washington, before being sent to
Vietnam. Assigned to an air assault unit, Gurr saw combat and was awarded
the Bronze Star and Army Commendation medals for valor. He finished his
tour of duty working with the Chu Lai Defense Command.

Following his discharge from the military, Gurr returned to Utah. He married Lynette Wells of Salt Lake City in June 1973. The couple had three children, and eventually four grandchildren. Gurr joined the Roosevelt Police Department in 1974 and was appointed chief of police four years later. At the age of twenty-seven, he was one of the youngest police chiefs in the nation.

In 1981, Gurr graduated from Utah State University with a degree in psychology. He was a founding member of the Uintah Basin Strike Force and was instrumental in bringing the Children's Justice Center to Roosevelt in 1996. He was considered tough but fair by both the community he policed and those who worked for him, and it was his concern for a new officer that would be a factor in his death.

In Vernal, thirty-five miles to the east, Lee Roy Wood, 35, forced a young woman into a pickup and told her to drive him to Salt Lake. Wood was angry because the woman, Kristi Pugh, had allegedly returned to Vernal from Salt Lake with less than a previously agreed-upon amount of drugs. Wood said he wanted to confront the drug contact there, but Pugh suspected that Wood intended to kill her because he suspected that she had cheated him. A parolee from the Utah State Prison, Wood had a long, confrontational history with law enforcement, with convictions for forgery, theft, assault, escape, and giving false information to a government agency.

Wood forced Pugh to drive west on U.S. 40. Reaching the outskirts of Roosevelt, she asked Wood to allow her to stop at the Maverick Store located at 1025 East 200 North. Wood agreed, following her into the store and waiting outside the door of the restroom. His behavior toward Pugh was so controlling that it made the clerk suspicious. When Pugh came out of the restroom and Wood began verbally abusing her as they left, the clerk called police.

Meanwhile, Gurr decided to see how Roosevelt Officer Henry McKenna was doing on just his fourth day as a police officer. Gurr got into his unmarked police vehicle and contacted McKenna and fellow officers Lance Williamson and Bill Garza by radio, telling them to meet him for a soft drink at a local convenience store.

Minutes later, at 8:44 p.m., the dispatcher advised the four officers of a domestic dispute at the Maverick store. As officers converged on the location, dispatch warned them that the caller was now reporting that the male suspect had armed himself with a rifle.

Outside the store, the argument between Wood and Pugh had escalated until Wood opened the truck door and pulled out a .223-caliber Norinco SKS assault rifle. He shoved the gun into Pugh's face, striking her with the muzzle hard enough to bruise the skin. Terrified, Pugh followed Wood's order to get into the truck and drive them back onto the highway. As she drove the truck

Lee Roy Wood was out of prison on parole when he murdered Chief Cecil Gurr with a borrowed rifle. (Utah State Department of Corrections)

out of the parking lot, Gurr spotted it and radioed directions to other officers. "I've got 'em back here," Gurr said, in what would be his last radio transmission.

McKenna and Williamson pulled in and blocked the path of the truck. Pugh stopped, and Wood jumped out with the rifle. He pointed the gun at McKenna and tried to fire, only to discover that he had failed to chamber a round.

As Wood struggled to load the rifle, Gurr pulled around from behind the store with the emergency police lights activated in his unmarked vehicle. He stopped and got out as Wood again pointed the rifle at McKenna. McKenna fired at Wood, missed, then held his fire when a female bystander unwittingly rode her bicycle into the line of fire. As Wood drew a bead on McKenna, Gurr shouted, attempting to distract the suspect's attention away from the new officer. Wood turned quickly and fired five times at Gurr, who returned fire twice. The fifty-year-old police chief was struck once in the forehead and instantly killed.

Jumping back into the truck, Wood told Pugh: "Get the f—k out of here. I just shot a cop." Pugh sped out of parking lot, closely pursued by McKenna and Williamson. As Wood turned in the seat to look at the officers, he briefly let go of the rifle. Pugh grabbed the gun and threw it out the window. Moments later, officers boxed the truck at a T-intersection and stopped it. Wood jumped out and advanced toward McKenna, shouting for the officer to shoot him. Instead, McKenna holstered his weapon and tackled Wood. Following a brief scuffle, Wood was handcuffed and taken to the Uintah County jail. He readily admitted trying to shoot McKenna, and, when told that he had shot Gurr, said, "Good. I should have taken more of you out."

The murder of Gurr shook the small Uinta Basin farming community to its core. Overnight, a makeshift memorial sprang up beneath a tree near the spot where Gurr died, as family, friends, and even strangers brought American flags, poems, cards, and letters.

Rain swept the basin on July 10, as the city buried its fallen police chief in the Roosevelt Memorial Park. A thousand people, including hundreds of officers from five states, escorted the twenty-seven-year veteran to his final resting place. During the funeral services at an LDS stake center, Gurr was eulogized as a humble man prone to quiet reflection.

Deseret News reporter Angie Welling attended the services and wrote: "Gurr's dedication to others is best shown in an act completed the day he died, his son said. After eating lunch with friends, Gurr noticed an elderly man with failing eyesight groping for the handrail leading into the restaurant. Without a word, Gurr took the man's hand and placed it on the railing. 'This was a story of my father,' Dax Gurr said. 'As powerful and as great as he was, he had the compassion of an angel.'"

Meanwhile, Wood remained without bail in the Uintah County jail, charged with capital murder. On October 10, Michael N. Swett, 44, appeared in U.S. District Court on charges that he supplied Wood with the rifle used to kill Gurr. Since both Swett and Wood were convicted felons, it was illegal for them to possess firearms. Two weeks later, a U.S. District Court judge sentenced Swett to ten years in a federal prison for his role in the slaying.

On September 19, 2002, Wood pleaded guilty in Eighth District Court and was sentenced to life without the possibility of parole and two five-to-life sentences at the Utah State Prison. He is currently attempting to withdraw his plea, claiming inefficient counsel, mental illness, and prosecutorial misconduct.

In March 2002, the United States Army awarded Cecil Gurr the Purple Heart, a decoration normally reserved for soldiers wounded or killed in action. Gurr was the third Utahn to receive such an award for service outside normal military actions.

Joseph Dan Adams

Lehi Police Department
August 4, 2001

Just before 11:00 p.m. on August 4, 2001, witnesses at an Albertson's express gas station at the southeast corner of 11400 South State in Draper noticed an injured man attempting to get into a red Chevrolet Corsica. The man was bleeding heavily from his abdomen. When he suddenly collapsed, pleading for help, witnesses called 911.

Lehi Officer Joseph D. Adams died in a shootout with a man he attempted to arrest for possession of cocaine. (Utah Peace Officers Association)

Salt Lake County paramedics and deputies responded to the scene and discovered that Arturo Javier Scott Welch, 23, had been shot. They also noticed a pair of handcuffs dangling from his left wrist and a bullet hole in the door of his car. An explanation was not long in coming. Officers throughout northern Utah were looking for a suspect in the murder of a Lehi police officer less than an hour before.

Welch was taken by ambulance to Alta View Hospital and then by medical helicopter to LDS Hospital, where doctors managed to save his life. He remained under guard and in critical condition.

Investigators soon pulled the pieces together. At 10:32 p.m., Lehi Officer Joe Adams, 26, stopped Welch at 2100 North 1200 West. Adams had verified that the vehicle was being operated without proper insurance and notified dispatch that he was pulling the vehicle over. Six minutes later, a Utah County sheriff's dispatcher heard Adams's last radio transmission, "Eight-J-Thirteen, I've—."

When Adams failed to respond further, the dispatcher sent Lehi officers Shawn Ferrell and Jeremy Elswood to check on him. Before their arrival, a Salt Lake County dispatcher forwarded a 911 call of an officer down at the location of Adams's stop. Adams had stopped Welch below an Interstate 15 overpass in a relatively isolated part of the city. In the car with Welch was Christopher Galvin, 22. Both men had just left the La Casa bar on State Street in Lehi, where they had been drinking and snorting cocaine. Adams approached the car and asked Welch to step out when it became apparent to him that Welch had been drinking. Welch complied and the two men stood between the vehicles while Galvin remained seated inside.

Searching Welch, Adams located a packet of cocaine. As he began handcuffing Welch, the suspect spun around, drew a .22-caliber Jennings automatic from his waistband and fired at the officer. One bullet narrowly missed Adams's bullet-proof vest, penetrated the left side of his chest, and struck his heart. A second bullet grazed the top of his back.

Mortally wounded, Adams still managed to draw his .40-caliber Glock sidearm and fire nine times, striking Welch once in the stomach. A second wound that removed one of Welch's fingers could have come from this shot or a subsequent one. As he collapsed, dying, Adams continued to fire, accidentally shooting himself in the leg.

Welch staggered to his car, got in, and told Galvin, "Let's go." Galvin, who had been talking to his brother on a cell phone at the time of the shooting, wanted no part of what had happened. He jumped out of the car as Welch sped onto the freeway and north toward Salt Lake.

The shooting was Welch's most recent contact with the law. He had been arrested for driving under the influence of alcohol in April, and was scheduled to go to trial on that charge in two weeks. In 1996, he had pled guilty to fleeing from police and possession of alcohol.

A Lehi City ambulance responded to the scene and found Adams lifeless. EMTs worked on the young officer and were able to restore a heartbeat. Adams was flown by medical helicopter to LDS Hospital but died there shortly after midnight.

While Welch recovered, a grieving community buried Adams. The services packed an Orem LDS chapel and a second meetinghouse four blocks away, where the services were telecast. Boy Scouts from Adams's ward and hundreds of police officers saluted the casket as it was carried to a hearse.

Roadside memorial for Officer Joseph Dan Adams placed by family, friends, and co-workers at the scene where he died. (Author)

Joseph Adams was born on January 3, 1975, in Provo to Thad C. and Rosemary Forsythe Adams. The second of five sons, Adams spent his early years in Pleasant Grove. At the age of thirteen he moved with his family to Orem, where he graduated from Mountain View High School in 1993. From 1994 to 1996, Adams served an LDS mission to Leipzig, Germany. Upon his return, he began dating Cydney Anderson, a young woman he met in high school. On January 4, 1997, the two were married in Lehi, Utah, a union later solemnized in the LDS Mount Timpanogos Temple.

The following year, Adams graduated from Police Officer Standards and Training classes at Utah Valley State College and went to work for the Lehi Police Department. In addition to patrol work, he was a member of the Utah County SWAT team and a drug-recognition expert. Meanwhile, his younger brother Josh followed his lead and became a police officer for the city of Orem. Seven months before his death, and on his own birthday, Joseph Adams became a father.

On September 4, Welch made his first appearance in Fourth District Court in Provo, sitting in a wheelchair. He was ordered by the court to face a preliminary hearing on October 23. At the preliminary hearing, Galvin testified that Adams asked Welch to step out of the car, and then said that "seconds later I heard gunshots." Rather than go with Welch, Galvin jumped out of the car and called 911. He cooperated fully with investigators and was not charged with any crime.

On April 29, 2002, in a move intended to spare him the death penalty, Welch pleaded guilty to aggravated murder charges and was sentenced to life in prison without the possibility of parole.

The following December, Adams's family published a book titled *A Tribute to Our Hero: The Story of Joseph Dan Adams*. All proceeds were donated to the Joseph Dan Adams Scholarship at UVSC, a fund intended to help one police officer a year graduate from the Police Officer Standards and Training course.

Ronald M. Wood
West Jordan Police Department
November 18, 2002

Five days after his brother's ambush and murder by a teenage robbery suspect, Marlan Wood told several thousand mourners that all Ronald M. Wood ever wanted to be was what he died doing. "Ever since he was a little boy, Ron wanted to be a police officer," said Wood. "He loved the law, loved to serve, and wanted to help others."

Ronald Manfred Wood was born June 12, 1963, in Salt Lake City to Blair and Birgitta Sjoberg Wood. He attended local schools, graduating from Granger High School in 1981. He served an LDS mission to Pittsburgh, Pennsylvania, from 1982 to 1984. Following his mission, Wood took classes at Salt Lake Community College with every intention of fulfilling his dream of working in law enforcement. Wood's best friend, Howard Dapp, recalled that Wood was always interested in safety and fairness. "He wasn't afraid to challenge people when he thought they were breaking the rules or endangering others," Dapp said. "At first it was kind of embarrassing that he would confront them, but later we just encouraged him because it was fun to watch."

Wood excelled in athletics, becoming an accomplished softball and basketball player as well as a proficient water skier. He ran in marathons and was planning to participate in the St. George Marathon the year he died.

Wood completed the Peace Officer Standards and Training requirements, graduating in January 1994. His hopes to be a police officer came true on April 24, 1995, when he was hired as a reserve officer by the city of West Jordan. His reserve status lasted less than a year. On November 28 he was hired for full-time work. Wood was first assigned to patrol work, transferring later to traffic enforcement and the motorcycle division. He also worked the department's Community Oriented Policing (COP) program.

In December 1999, Wood began corresponding with Maria Loremil Pulido, a woman working in the United Arab Emirates. The long-distance relationship deepened to the point that in 2000 Wood flew to the Philippines to meet her. He proposed, and the couple married on May 8, 2001, in West Valley City.

The week prior to his death, Wood was part of the police motorcycle escort in the funeral procession for Salt Lake County Sheriff's Sergeant Jon J. Wood (no relation), killed November 10 in an off-duty motorcycle accident. If Wood had any premonition that the next Utah police funeral service would be his own, he never said. He did tell family members that if the unthinkable ever happened he would not want a large funeral for himself.

Events leading up to Wood's murder on the morning of November 18, 2002, began with a string of armed robberies. During the evening of June 20 two males dressed in dark clothing and masks forced their way through the drive-up window of a McDonald's restaurant near 1800 West and 7800 South. The suspects threatened employees with a knife and gun before taking money, checks, and coupons from the safe. Four months later, on October 25, two robbers wearing similar dark clothing and masks robbed the same McDonald's in a similar manner. However, this time witnesses observed the suspects get into a car and flee the scene. They followed the car for a short time and later gave a description of it to the police. The car was located near the home of seventeen-year-old Tyler Atwood. Found inside was a small amount of blood officers suspected might be Atwood's. They sent it to be analyzed at the state crime lab.

Atwood's name struck a chord with investigators. In the early morning hours of September 19, Atwood, Justin Van Roekel, and Sean Tims were driving around, preparing to commit a home invasion robbery, when they were stopped by West Jordan police officers Robert Faircloth and Doug Saunders near 2300 West 7500 South. Tims would later confess that Atwood and Van Roekel fully intended to kill Faircloth when the officer walked up to the car, which Tims had stopped in the driveway of a home. "Apparently they decided to shoot me when I walked up to the driver's window," Faircloth said. "But for some reason I called the driver back to me and didn't approach the car."

Their plan foiled by Faircloth's failure to cooperate and the subsequent arrival of Saunders, Atwood and Van Roekel got out of the car. During the field interview, Faircloth noticed a .357 magnum on the back seat of the suspect vehicle. He scuffled briefly with Tims and then Van Roekel, before pursuing Atwood on foot into Jordan Meadows, a nearby park. Tims was arrested, but Atwood and Van Roekel (now wearing Faircloth's handcuffs on one wrist) managed to elude officers in the dark.

Recovered from the vehicle were three masks (puchased within the hour, according to a sales receipt later found on Atwood), gloves, a "Night Owl" night-vision device, a loaded Hi-Point 9mm automatic pistol, and a loaded .357-magnum revolver.

Faircloth obtained Atwood's cell-phone number from family members and later that morning managed to convince him and Van Roekel to come to the station. The two were subsequently charged with several felonies and were awaiting a court date when the murder of Officer Wood occurred.

Although detectives suspected Atwood and Van Roekel of committing the recent robberies, there was little evidence linking them directly to the crimes. However, Atwood's girlfriend worked at the McDonald's and eventually told police that he had asked her about their security cameras prior to the robberies. Atwood's mother also told officers that he was up to no good, that she was afraid of him, and that she wanted police to remove him from her home. But with no solid evidence to connect Atwood to a crime, officers could only wait for the results from the lab. In the meantime, the robbers struck again.

On November 13, two men matching the descriptions of the suspects in the previous robberies held up the Food 4 Less store near 2700 West and 7800 South, getting away with an undisclosed amount of cash.

West Jordan Officer Ronald M. Wood died at the hands of a teenage robbery suspect who later committed suicide. (Wood family)

Two days later, a counselor at West Jordan High School called the police department and said that a student being suspended for threatening to kill a teacher had just confessed to committing several armed robberies. Detectives Richard Davis and Brent Jex went to the high school and met with the counselor and Justin Van Roekel. Van Roekel was less candid with the officers, refusing to say anything about the crimes or his possible accomplices. Van Roekal's attitude was not surprising to those who knew him. Classmates said he often bragged about his crimes and drug use and said that he had nothing to live for. In addition to threatening the teacher, he previously had stated that he wanted to kill a police officer.

As Davis and Jex were discussing what to do next in another office, Van Roekel left the counselor's office and walked out of the school. The officers caught up with him in the parking lot and convinced him to come back inside and wait for his father to pick him up. As they were returning to the school together, Van Roekel changed his mind and bolted again. This time he got away. Justin's father, Robert Van Roekel, arrived at the school a few minutes later. To Jex and Davis, the elder Van Roekel's attitude was only slightly more helpful than that of the younger. "He said we would have to understand that he didn't think cops were good for anything other than investigating traffic accidents," Jex said. "It was pretty clear that he wasn't interested in helping us work with his son."

Investigators believe that Van Roekel spent the following weekend at the Atwood home near 7530 South 2800 West. He was there early Monday morning when his father Robert Van Roekel arrived to take him to school. Because Justin was in the habit of attending school only when he felt like it, the two argued. The younger Van Roekel pulled a High Point 9mm pistol and threatened to kill his father before running away.

Robert Van Roekel called 911 and reported the incident to West Jordan police, then began following his son. Several blocks away, near an entrance to Jordan Meadows (2350 West 7510 South) Justin Van Roekel ran through the park gate. Second later, Van Roekel's father saw a West Jordan Police vehicle driven by Wood and flagged it down. Wood was not the officer assigned to the "man with a gun" call, but, in typical fashion, he was one of the first officers to arrive in the area. Pointing to the gate, Robert Van Roekel told Wood that his son had just gone through it.

Had Van Roekel intended to run from police, he could not have chosen a worse adversary than Wood. City league softball teammates nicknamed Wood "Legs" for his speed, and he was well known in the police department for once having chased down on foot a fleeing motorcyclist in a field. But Van Roekel was not intent on running anymore. When he slipped through the park's gate, he turned at a right angle and knelt along the fence line with the pistol, ready for whoever had the misfortune of following him. "Given his frame of mind it probably wouldn't have mattered who walked through the gate then," said Lieutenant Bob Shober. "His father, an officer, or even a passerby—they were going to get shot."

Perhaps because he believed the suspect had continued running through the park, Wood may have wanted to see if he could establish a direction of flight for other officers responding to the scene. In any case he did not draw his sidearm, a fact that investigators do not believe would have changed the outcome. As Wood walked through the gate, Van Roekel fired three shots "gang-banger style" (the pistol held on its side so that the ejected cartridge casings fall straight to the ground instead of scattering in an arc). Detectives speculated later that the first bullet missed, causing Wood to reach instinctively for his weapon and to go into a crouch in an effort to present a smaller target. As he was ducking, the second or third shot struck him squarely in the top of the head. Wood collapsed immediately.

As Robert Van Roekel stood stunned, his son ran past the fallen officer and out through the gate, disappearing through the yards of nearby homes. Neighbor Mike Searle, 39, heard the shots from his driveway and went to investigate. He first saw the police car and then an officer on the ground inside the gate. A driver for Terry's Towing, Searle recognized Wood immediately. He ran to Wood and tried to speak to him. "He didn't say anything but he was still breathing," Searle said. "I grabbed his radio and told the dispatcher that Officer Wood had been shot."

When Wood did quit breathing, Searle began CPR, as Robert Van Roekel called 911 on his cell phone. The badly shocked Van Roekel had difficulty explaining the situation to the dispatcher, so Searle grabbed the phone away from him and explained again what had happened. By then Officer Denise Vincent had arrived and, together with Searle, began CPR again.

There was little anyone could do for Wood. He was taken by air ambulance to University Hospital, accompanied by Detective Travis Rees. Ironically, in 1986 Rees's father had become the first West Jordan police officer killed in the line of duty. With family members gathered around him, Wood was pronounced dead shortly after 10:30 a.m. in the hospital's neurocritical care unit. "I rubbed his feet, something he liked, and told him to go toward the light, that he didn't have to fight to hang on anymore. We would be alright," said his mother, Birgitta Wood.

His wife was also there at the end. Even though her husband was unresponsive, she told him that she released him from the promise he had once made to never leave her. As she spoke, tears spilled out of Wood's eyes; he died a short time later.

After shooting Wood, a frantic Van Roekel made his way to the east side of the park, where he car-jacked a vehicle driven by an elderly woman, forcing her to drive him north on 2200 West. Van Roekel used the woman's cell phone to call a friend and tell him that he had shot a cop and that he might have to shoot the woman driving the car before going into hiding. Near the intersection of 7000 South and 2200 West the woman was able to jump out of her vehicle and flee with the keys. Van Roekel got out and tried to car-jack another vehicle, but the terrified driver just sped off. Witness Brent Hildebrand later told officers what he saw as Van Roekel went from vehicle to vehicle with the pistol. "The kid was in a panic. He was in hysterics, scared to death."

Unable to commandeer another vehicle, Van Roekel fled toward some nearby homes. A few minutes later, as officers swarmed over the scene, Detective Jim Lang came face to face with the suspect. Lang was driving an unmarked police car south on 2310 West when Van Roekel walked out from behind a home near Reaper Circle. The teenager held up his hand indicating that he wanted the vehicle to stop, apparently intent on car-jacking another ride. Lang recognized Van Roekel and jumped out, holding a portable radio in one hand and a pistol in the other. Although in plainclothes, Lang wore a SWAT jacket identifying himself as a police officer.

When Van Roekel recognized his mistake, he began drawing the pistol from under his jacket. Lang fired three shots with a .40-caliber Glock 27, barely missing the killer. Van Roekel recognized that the chase was over. He placed the muzzle of the gun in his own mouth and pulled the trigger. He was dead before he hit the sidewalk.

During the chaos following the shootings, authorities expressed concern that Van Roekel's accomplices might show up and cause trouble at the school. As a result, West Jordan High School locked down for two hours. When police refused to allow a student's father to go into the school, he became combative and tried to run down an officer with his vehicle. The man fled the scene but was stopped a short distance away and taken into custody by a police K-9 unit—a situation resulting in a trip to the hospital for him.

Concerns about Atwood did not pan out. He was arrested without incident at about 4:30 p.m. while walking a few blocks from where Wood died. When he learned that his friend had murdered an officer, Atwood expressed satisfaction, accusing the police of pressuring Van Roekel until he had "no other way out." Atwood would soon find police pressure closing in on him.

A search warrant served on the Atwood home the day following the shooting resulted in the discovery of evidence linking Atwood to the robberies, including McDonald's Dollars (coupons) and customer credit-card slips dated the day of the robbery. Blood in the getaway vehicle was finally matched to Atwood, and on February 6 he pled guilty as an adult to first-degree felony robbery, kidnapping, and related weapons charges.

Van Roekel was cremated and his ashes returned to family members in New Mexico.

Grieving colleagues and family could not let Wood have the small funeral he wanted. In fact, it was one of the largest police funerals ever held in Utah. A viewing at the Welby LDS Stake Center on the evening of November 22 gave notice to what could be expected the following day. In order to accommodate all who wished to attend, the funeral was held in the auditorium of Copper Hills High School. Even so, standing room was all that was available to many of the thousands who attended. Hundreds more had to watch the service on closed-circuit television in a nearby gymnasium.

Absent at the funeral was any trace of bitterness. A statement from Wood's mother was read in which she expressed her concern for the Van Roekel family. "You will never feel anger or animosity from us, because you also lost a son. Someday, we can talk about that."

When it was time to say goodbye to his friend, Howard Dapp walked over to the casket and knocked three times on it, then returned to the microphone and said, "Gives a whole new meaning to the expression 'knock on wood.' I didn't do that to be funny," Dapp hastened to add. "Although Ron would think that was funny. I did it to create an association with Ron's name. I just forced you to remember Ron, always."

Wood was buried in the West Jordan City Cemetery. The procession down New Bingham Highway was lined with more than a thousand American flags.

The hearse arrived at the cemetery before the end of the procession had left the high school parking lot three miles away. West Jordan Detective Charles Kirby summed up the department's feeling. "Sometimes officers achieve a level of sainthood after they die in the line of duty. They get built up in our minds to be greater than they really were. But getting killed didn't make Woody a great person. He was that long before he died."

In July 2003, West Jordan City named its newest park on the New Bingham Highway after Officer Ronald Wood.

David Charles Jones

Garfield County Sheriff's Office
January 26, 2003

David C. Jones fulfilled a longtime dream when he was hired as a Garfield County sheriff's deputy at an age when most officers look forward to retirement. "I really liked his attitude," said Sheriff Than Cooper, explaining why he hired Jones over younger applicants. "Right from the beginning he was on top of things."

Instead of the action found in larger metropolitan departments, the forty-three-year-old father of five children opted for police work in one of the most isolated areas in the state. It was his attraction to the solitude of the empty desert that would contribute to his death sixteen months later.

Born April 19, 1958, in Augsburg, Germany, to Frank Edward and Ruth Mary Leiby Jones, David Jones was the youngest of seven children born into an army family. He graduated from Orem High School in 1976 and served an LDS mission to Hamburg, Germany, from 1977 to 1979. Jones attended Ricks College in Rexburg, Idaho, and married Carolyn Sabin in the Salt Lake LDS Temple on January 30, 1980. When he died, the couple's children ranged in age from six to twenty-two.

Prior to becoming a police officer, Jones served in the U.S. Army as an air traffic controller. Discharged from active duty in 1986, he was then employed by the Federal Aviation Administration in Kansas City, Missouri, where he also served in the Army Reserve.

Jones returned to Utah in 1992 and lived in West Jordan. He worked various jobs until completing Peace Officer Standards and Training courses at Salt Lake Community College in March 2000. He then worked as a TRAX enforcement officer until he was hired by the Garfield County Sheriff's Office on July 20, 2001.

Doing what he loved in the middle of nowhere
cost Garfield County Deputy Sheriff David C.
Jones his life. (*Garfield County News*)

Jones was ecstatic. Escalante was where he wanted to be, so much so that he turned down a subsequent offer from the Nevada Highway Patrol. Cooper was particularly impressed by the fact that Jones took his family to Escalante and looked the town over before he was hired. It was an indication that Jones was serious about settling in a town known for an inability to hang on to its police officers. Located 180 miles south of Salt Lake City, and considered by some to be a century removed from modern attitudes regarding firearm and alcohol laws, Escalante was usually about the last choice for law enforcement candidates.

Determined to fit in, David and Carolyn Jones bought a home near the road leading into Alvey Wash. Carolyn found work at the Canyon Country convenience store and as a physical education teacher's aide. The children enrolled in local school. If life wasn't idyllic, it was at least interesting for the town's only police officer and his family. On one occasion, while his eight-year-old son Jacob was riding with him, Jones became involved in a high-speed pursuit.

"I talked to Dave about how to handle working a small town," Cooper said. "Sometimes it's better to back off and choose your battles when it's to your advantage. What backup there is in Garfield County can be hours away." Shortly before his death, Jones single-handedly faced down a man armed with a shotgun. Cooper, the only other member of the seven-officer department on duty at the time, was sixty miles away investigating a traffic accident in which three had people died. Although the shotgun was later found not to have been loaded, the incident illustrated just how far from help Jones was if things turned bad.

Earl L. Barnes shot Deputy David Jones over a misdemeanor alcohol ticket. He pled guilty and was sentenced to life in prison without the possibility of parole. (Garfield County Sheriff's Office)

Jones's next confrontation with an armed suspect would be his last. It was a perfect winter Sunday, clear and warmer than normal. As Super Bowl fans anticipated the opening kickoff between the Tampa Bay Buccaneers and the Oakland Raiders, Jones stopped a white 1994 Ford pickup in Alvey Wash, about six miles south of town.

The truck's two occupants were William Byron Allred and Earl L. Barnes. Notoriously hard drinkers, the two men worked at Skyline Timber Resources, a sawmill on the outskirts of town. Fifty-year-old Allred was from Salina and considered a good worker at the mill, but he did have a string of drunken driving arrests. He lived with his dogs in a small camper located about a quarter of a mile from the Jones residence. Less was known about Barnes, 53, who came to Escalante from Montrose, Colorado. Officers later learned that murder was something Barnes had been working up to for years. His criminal history included arrests for assault with a deadly weapon, drunken driving, fraud, and filing false reports to police officers. When later contacted and informed of Barnes's arrest for murder, Mesa County, Colorado, officers expressed little surprise, telling Utah state investigator David Excell, "We figured he would do it someday. But we always thought it would be one of us."

Shortly after 3:00 p.m. Allred and Barnes stopped at the Canyon Country convenience store, where Carolyn Jones was just finishing her shift. It was obvious to the clerks that the two men had been drinking. Allred also had a .44-magnum Ruger Blackhawk pistol strapped to his hip. When the clerks noticed the gun, one expressed the hope that it was not loaded. In response, Allred took out the pistol and began ejecting live cartridges onto the counter, spilling them onto the floor.

When Allred and Barnes left the convenience store, they headed for Alvey Wash to do a little shooting. The wash winds through the Grand Staircase–

William Byron Allred drove the wounded Barnes away from the murder scene. (Garfield County Sheriff's Office)

Escalante National Monument and deep into the heart of the Kaiparowits Plateau. It is one of the most remote areas of the state.

Cooper believed that Jones first spotted the suspect vehicle as it drove through his neighborhood and into the mouth of the wash. As the vehicle passed by, Jones observed Barnes drinking a beer, an event later borne out by the fact that the deputy carried a tape recorder on his belt.

The stop occurred where the Smoky Mountain Road rises and makes a slight bend. Allred pulled the pickup to the far right of the road, so close to the dirt embankment that it was later difficult for Barnes to open the passenger door. Jones positioned his patrol unit, a two-door Chevrolet Tahoe, behind the pickup and approached the driver's door on foot. He explained that he had witnessed Barnes drinking. Allred agreed to submit to some field sobriety tests. When he failed them, Jones arrested and handcuffed him, taking the Ruger pistol back to his patrol car.

With the handcuffed Allred in the front passenger seat of the Tahoe, Jones then called for a wrecker from Escalante and asked Garfield County Deputy Clint Pierson to meet him at the station in town to assist with the breath test. Pierson was fifty miles away at Bryce Canyon, but he started immediately in the direction of Escalante. In a strange twist of fate, the last police officer killed in Garfield County was Pierson's father, Utah Highway Patrol Trooper Lynn Pierson, murdered in 1978 on an isolated stretch of Highway 20 near Panguitch.

From the audiotape it is clear that Barnes turned belligerent when Jones informed him that he would be issued an open-container citation and that he would have to ride back to town with the wrecker driver. As Jones returned the pistol, now unloaded, to Allred's vehicle, Barnes went back to the truck, telling the deputy that he intended to roll up the windows so that the dogs could not get out. Two rifles were hanging in the back window of the truck, a common sight in Garfield County.

It was at approximately this point that Escalante resident Jeff Gurr drove south past the stop and noticed Jones and Barnes standing between the two vehicles. Something he saw troubled him enough to wonder if there might be a problem.

Moments later, probably while sitting in his patrol vehicle, Jones saw Barnes approaching with a rifle in his hands. It is unclear at what point Jones drew his sidearm, a .40-caliber Glock Model 27. He is heard commanding Barnes to stop. "Put the gun down now," is repeated three times by Jones, followed immediately by a series of shots.

Jones fired twice, Barnes once. The bullet from the Savage 7-millimeter magnum rifle struck the deputy just below the left button of his uniform shirt, penetrated the front panel of his body armor, tore through his descending aorta and the right side of his heart, and stopped in the back panel of his armor. It was a massive wound that caused death in three to four seconds. Jones's final words were bitter and agonized curses directed at Barnes. "The tone makes it clear that Dave knew he wouldn't be going home," said Cooper. "It was an awful thing to hear."

Following the deputy's last words, Barnes is heard cursing him and ordering him to hand over the keys to the handcuffs or be shot again. Scuffled sounds of Barnes moving Jones around in an apparent search for the keys are followed by a befuddled realization that he also had been shot. He said: "God damn, Bill, I've been hit."

Barnes was struck by one round that shattered his right arm and lodged in his right lung. After removing the handcuffs from Allred, Barnes tossed them away and slumped down on the embankment, saying that he was going to die. Allred helped Barnes into the pickup and they sped away, driving deeper into the desert, following the Smoky Mountain road south toward Lake Powell. Several hundred yards from the murder, they passed Gurr, who had decided to turn around and return to the scene. Allred waved as if nothing was wrong, but Gurr noticed that Allred's hand was covered with blood. Minutes later he discovered why.

Wrecker driver Curt Richins was the first to reach Jones. At first he thought Jones had just been badly assaulted. When a closer inspection revealed the truth, Richins radioed the dispatcher with the news, including the direction of travel taken by the suspects.

Cooper, who had yet to reach the scene, believed the suspects might attempt to reach U.S. Highway 89 at Big Water. Located fifty miles south of Escalante as the crow flies, but almost triple the distance over a winding dirt road, Big

Water seemed the natural choice for a getaway. The officer began coordinating an effort to interdict all possible escape routes, asking for help from law enforcement agencies all the way to northern Arizona.

When he reached the scene, Cooper was shocked to find Carolyn Jones already there, weeping at the sight of her husband's body in the road. "[Diane Richins] came to my house and said something was wrong with Dave," Carolyn Jones later said. "We drove up to the stop and that's when I found out that he had been killed."

Allred and Barnes were not making good time in their flight from justice. Frequent stops became necessary for Barnes, who in addition to the pain from his wounds suffered periodic bouts of vomiting and diarrhea. Drunk and frantic, the two might have wandered in the desert until Barnes died. Instead, the police found them. An emergency helicopter from Classic Aviation Services in Page, Arizona, was the first to spot the white pickup traveling in Left Hand Collett Canyon in Kane County, a dirt road leading northeast to the Hole-in-the-Wall Road. Coconino (Arizona) County deputies and National Park Service rangers were landed by helicopter a half mile ahead of the vehicle. The suspects surrendered without incident as soon as they saw the officers.

The murder weapon, still loaded, was recovered from the vehicle and an empty cartridge case was found in the truck's bed. Although suffering from the effects of his wound, and later under the effects of morphine, Barnes admitted shooting Jones, confessing first to a National Park Service ranger and later to an officer from the Arizona Department of Public Safety.

Barnes was taken to a hospital in Page, Arizona, and then moved to the Flagstaff Medical Center, where doctors operated on his arm but decided that it was safer to leave the bullet in his chest. On January 27, while still in his hospital bed, he was formally charged with aggravated murder in the presence of a Coconino County judge. Two days later, Barnes signed papers clearing the way for extradition as soon as he recovered. He was returned to Utah on February 1 and incarcerated in the Iron County jail. Barnes was kept segregated from other prisoners and spent most of his days sleeping.

Meanwhile, Allred was arrested and taken to the Garfield County jail first, and later to the jail in Iron County. His first court appearance was January 28, before Sixth District Court Judge K.L. McIff, who ordered him held without bail pending the filing of formal charges. Those came a few days later, when Garfield County Attorney Wallace Lee charged Allred with aggravated robbery and aggravated escape, both first-degree felonies, and one second-degree felony count of obstruction of justice. He was also charged with drunk driving.

On February 12, Barnes was charged in Sixth District Court with aggravated murder and aggravated escape, obstruction of justice, and one class-C misdemeanor charge of traveling with an open container. Both men were ordered to appear for preliminary hearings on March 12.

The murder stunned locals in the small hamlet. Stacy Davis, an Escalante schoolteacher, said students had difficulty coming to terms with it. "I think the kids saw Dave and other police officers as someone who would try to catch them doing something wrong, but now they are talking about how he was really there to protect them."

Nearly a thousand mourners packed the Escalante LDS Stake Center on January 31 to attend the funeral services for the town's only police officer. Hundreds of police officers from Utah and adjoining states were in attendance. Paul Jones was among those who eulogized his father, summing up how many locals viewed the deputy during his short time as their protector. "My father died trying to make the world a better place for my brothers and sister. My father was a man of immense integrity."

Following the services, a long procession of police cars and motorcycles escorted Jones on a final patrol down a Main Street lined with mourners. It continued out of town toward Panguitch. Jones was buried the following day in the Orem City Cemetery.

On June 18, 2003, Barnes appeared before Sixth District Judge K.L. McIff and pled guilty to a charge of aggravated murder. He was sentenced to spend the rest of his life behind bars without the possibility of parole.

Allred pled innocent the following day to first-degree felony charges of robbery and escape, and second-degree felony obstruction of justice. He sat in jail awaiting trial until September 11, 2003, when he pled guilty to the robbery charge. All other charges against him were dropped. He was sentenced to five years to life in prison.

Addendum

Officers Killed Accidentally and
Special Sworn Officers Killed in the Line of Duty

The names of the following officers and civilian posse members also appear on the bronze police memorial in the Utah State Capitol Rotunda. They are listed here according to the chronological order of their deaths.

Salt Lake County Sheriff's Deputy **Rodney Badger**, 30, drowned in the Weber River April 29, 1853, while attempting to rescue an immigrant family stranded in a wagon. Badger successfully rescued four children and the mother. While swimming to shore with the last two children, Badger was swept under the water. His body and those of the children were recovered six months later from a sand bar about a mile and a half downstream.

Salt Lake City Police Sergeant **Alonzo M. Wilson**, 54, died April 12, 1894, five hours after being struck by a bullet fired from a gun dropped by a new patrolman. Wilson underwent surgery for the removal of his right leg but failed to rally from the procedure and died minutes before his wife reached his side. Their daughter was born the following day.

Bingham City Special Officer **J.C. Morrissey** died July 6, 1895, after being accidentally shot by another officer during the arrest of an intoxicated man. When the other officer struck the suspect with his pistol, it discharged, and the bullet struck Morrissey in the heart.

Wyoming civilian posse member **Edward N. Dawes** died July 30, 1895, after a shootout with two suspects in the attempted murder of a Utah peace officer. Dawes and Echo City Constable Thomas Stagg died approximately seven miles northwest of Evanston, Wyoming. The suspects were later captured, tried, and convicted. The shooter was executed by a firing squad.

Springville City Marshal **Silas E. Clark**, 43, was accidentally shot by one of his deputies on the night of November 22, 1897. Clark and his deputy were in the marshal's office preparing to go on patrol when a pistol the deputy was loading discharged. Struck in the abdomen, Clark lived an agonizing four days before succumbing to his wound.

A member of a Grand County posse, deputized civilian **Sam Jenkins** and Grand County Sheriff Jesse Tyler were gunned down while searching for rustlers in the Book Cliffs near Thompson Springs. Their alleged killer, Kid Curry, died four years later in a botched train robbery in Colorado.

Provo City Police Officer **Frank Tucker**, 35, was killed June 16, 1904, when he accidentally dropped his automatic pistol while preparing to go on patrol. The weapon fired when it hit the floor, the bullet striking Tucker in the abdomen.

Park City Officer **Albert Holindrake**, 43, was killed January 12, 1908, in the city marshal's office. Holindrake, who had been an officer for just six days, was examining his new revolver when it discharged, the bullet striking him in the face.

On October 5, 1909, Special Residential Officer **Charles C. Riley** was shot and killed in Salt Lake City by a robbery suspect he was escorting to the police station. Riley's killer was later arrested in Arizona and returned to Utah, where he was sentenced to prison.

Midvale Special Officer **William "Billie" Nelson** died December 25, 1912, of a gunshot wound to the head while working the city's annual "Christmas guard." Nelson was attempting to subdue individuals shooting guns into the air when a suspect crept up behind him and fired the fatal shot. His killer was never identified.

Salt Lake County civilian posse members **Thomas Manderich** and **J. Douglas Hulsey** were killed November 29, 1913, while attempting to force police killer Rafael Lopez from a mine in Bingham Canyon.

Ogden City Police Officer **Albert G. Smalley**, 20, died April 7, 1920, from injuries received in a motorcycle accident on November 9, 1919. On the day of the accident, Smalley was patrolling near the mouth of Ogden Canyon when his motorcycle was sideswiped by a passing car.

Salt Lake City Patrolman **Gustave J. "Gus" Lund**, 61, was killed August 25, 1924, when he was struck by a vehicle near 2100 South and 1100 East. Lund, who directed noontime traffic at the intersection, died when he stepped between a passing brick truck and the trailer it was pulling.

Salt Lake County Deputy Sheriff **Oscar Fullmer**, 50, died August 26, 1928, when his patrol vehicle plunged off the road in Bingham Canyon. Fullmer and his passenger, a Latino interpreter, were in the process of investigating a murder. While driving down the canyon after dark, Fullmer failed to negotiate a hairpin turn. Both men were killed.

Salt Lake City Patrolman **Carl J. Carlson** died March 9, 1929, approximately twelve hours after sustaining a basal skull fracture during a South Temple Street vice raid. Carlson and other officers were moving a barrel of mash when it landed on Carlson's foot, causing him to jump back and strike his head against a wall. He died a short time later in the hospital.

Utah Highway Patrol Trooper **George "Ed" Van Wagenen**, 46, died May 23, 1931, of injuries suffered while investigating a report of a stolen car. Van Wagenen stopped at a beet processing plant near Provo to question the owner of the car. As he was leaving, he slipped on a pile of loose lumber and fell into a saw blade.

Salt Lake City Patrolman **Blaine L. Baxter**, 28, was killed in a motorcycle accident on September 4, 1935, while chasing a speeding vehicle. Upon entering the intersection of 200 North 300 West, Baxter was forced off the road by another vehicle that turned in front of him. He struck the side of a building and died of his injuries a few hours later, with his wife at his bedside.

Carbon County Sheriff **S. Marion Bliss**, 70, was killed April 23, 1945, while attempting to capture a murder suspect one and a half miles northeast of Price. Approaching the cornered suspect in a dry wash, Bliss was accidentally struck in the chest by a bullet fired by a posse member. The suspect was killed an hour later during a pitched gun battle with officers.

Ogden City Officer **Clarence M. Bean**, 41, died May 1, 1945, of injuries received some months earlier during the arrest of an intoxicated serviceman on July 22, 1944. After he was kicked in the abdomen by the suspect, Bean's health rapidly declined. An autopsy revealed extensive internal injuries caused by the blow.

Salt Lake City Police Sergeant **Thomas W. Stroud**, 34, was killed January 5, 1951, after being struck by a bullet from his own weapon. Stroud was assisting with the preparation of a children's party at the police department. While unloading soft drinks from a vehicle, Stroud's automatic pistol fell from its shoulder holster and fired when it hit the sidewalk. The bullet hit Stroud in the heart, killing him instantly.

Salt Lake City Police Officer **Harold A. Peterson, Sr.**, 54, was killed October 27, 1954, while on routine motorcycle patrol. Peterson was struck by a vehicle that made an illegal turn in front of him in the intersection of 1300 South and 1300 East. The elderly driver of the car was not charged.

Salt Lake County Deputy Sheriff **MacKay C. Jewkes**, 28, died June 28, 1959, when his patrol car collided with another vehicle in the intersection at 6400 South State. Jewkes, who had worked for the sheriff's department for only five months, was attempting to stop a violator when he entered the intersection against the light. The driver of the other car was seriously injured.

Logan City Police Officer **Edwin L. "Ted" Edwards**, 26, died August 27, 1959, in an automobile accident. Edwards and Cache County Deputy Sheriff **Alma P. Sorenson**, 54, were transporting four juveniles to the industrial school in Ogden. The accident occurred on U.S. Highway 91, seven miles northwest of Ogden, when one of the juveniles attempted to grab Sorenson's gun. Sorenson lost control of the patrol car and collided head-on with another vehicle. Both officers and two of the juveniles were killed.

Utah Highway Patrol Trooper **Armond A. "Monty" Luke**, 54, was killed December 3, 1959, when his patrol car plunged into the Sevier River. The single-car accident occurred on U.S. Highway 89, six miles south of Circleville. Luke drowned after he struck his head while being thrown from the car. Investigators speculated that the accident occurred while Luke was pursuing a speeding vehicle, and that he had swerved to avoid deer crossing the road.

Utah Highway Patrol Trooper **George D. Rees**, 41, died at the wheel of his patrol car July 2, 1960, after it was struck head-on by two suspects in a stolen car. The accident occurred near Lagoon, at the junction of U.S. Highways 89 and 91. The two suspects, who were being chased by other officers at the time of the collision, also died.

San Juan County Sheriff **Seth F. Wright**, 53, was killed October 14, 1960, in a plane crash near Monte Vista, Colorado. Wright and the pilot of the aircraft were returning from Texas with a prisoner when the plane struck the rim of Black Canyon, ten miles northeast of Monte Vista. All three men died.

Division of Wildlife Resources Conservation Officer **Charles Gilbert "Gil" Porter**, 59, was killed May 2, 1970, when he was struck by a train. Porter was checking fishing licenses along the Weber River near Stoddard. Witnesses said Porter apparently failed to hear the train coming because another train was passing on a parallel track.

Utah Highway Patrol Trooper **John R. Winn**, 36, was killed September 22, 1971, while working on a radio tower on Lake Mountain in Utah County. Winn was operating a loader on a steep grade when it rolled over, crushing him.

Cache County Lieutenant **James R. Merrill**, 39, died January 5, 1974, from head injuries suffered in a fall on a county road south of Smithfield.

Tooele County Sergeant **Lauren E. Dow**, 27, lost his life August 26, 1975, from burns received while fighting a brush fire east of Stockton. Dow and Tooele City Animal Control Officer Danny James, 19, were driving a fire vehicle near the 300-acre blaze when winds abruptly pushed the flames in their direction. Both men were overcome and later died of their injuries.

Beaver County Sheriff **Dale E. Nelson**, 51, died September 8, 1980, of suffocation while attempting to rescue a father and son overcome by methane fumes in a concrete manure tank. The accident occurred on a dairy farm two miles west of Beaver. The three men died, while two other rescuers were injured.

Utah Highway Patrol Trooper **Daniel W. Harris**, 33, was killed August 25, 1982, while chasing a speeding vehicle in Parley's Canyon. Pursuing a white Corvette at high speed, Harris lost control of his motorcycle and was killed when he struck a delineator post. The driver of the Corvette has never been identified.

Cache County Deputy Sheriff **Charles H. Dickey, Jr.**, 30, died March 18, 1984, of injuries suffered in a one-car accident. Dickey was responding to a family fight in Benson when he failed to negotiate at high speed a turn at 3400 North 2400 West. Dickey was killed when the patrol car overturned.

Park City Police Officer **Rodney W. Schreurs**, 33, was struck and killed July 4, 1984, while directing traffic following a fireworks display. Schreurs was in the intersection of U-224 and Pay Day Drive when he was hit by a pickup truck.

West Jordan Police Officer **Thomas M. Rees**, 32, died February 23, 1986, two hours after he was accidentally shot by another officer during a training exercise. Rees and the officer were demonstrating techniques used to prevent suspects from taking officers' weapons away from them when the accident occurred.

Duchesne County Deputy Sheriff **Gerry Ivie**, 51, died July 2, 1987, after he was accidentally shot by a fellow deputy. The shooting occurred two miles west of Roosevelt as officers were attempting to take a man into custody at a roadblock.

Murray City Police Officer **Jackson D. Elmer**, 29, died November 14, 1987, after being struck by the car of an intoxicated driver. Shortly before midnight, Elmer and another Murray City officer were investigating a traffic accident near 5530 South State when a passing vehicle struck them. The second officer received minor injuries; Elmer was killed instantly. The driver of the vehicle fled the scene but was later arrested.

Emery County Deputy Sheriff **Wade A. Hansen**, 26, was killed September 24, 1987, in an automobile accident. Hansen was driving on U.S. Highway 6 near Green River when he inadvertently crossed the centerline and collided head-on with a semitrailer truck. Hansen died at the scene. The truck driver was not injured.

Wasatch County Deputy Sheriff **Blake V. Wright**, 38, died August 26, 1990, while fighting a large brush fire in the mountains above Midway. Together with another Wasatch County employee, Wright was constructing a firebreak with a bulldozer when the flames swept over them. Both men were killed.

Utah Highway Patrol Trooper **Joseph S. "Joey" Brummet III**, 24, died December 11, 1992, after he was struck by a vehicle while investigating an accident in Salt Lake County. The accident, which occurred on Interstate 15 near 2800 South, had caused a traffic jam, and Brummett was helping to clear the freeway when he was struck by a pickup truck. The suspect fled the scene but was later apprehended and charged.

Twenty-four years after being shot in the head by the driver of a stolen car, Utah Highway Patrol Sergeant **Charles "Chuck" Warren** died May 16, 1994, as a result of his wounds, which had left him partially paralyzed. The shooting occurred September 2, 1969, near Springville. The suspect was captured, convicted of attempted murder, and later paroled from prison.

Utah Highway Patrol Sergeant **Doyle R. Thorne**, 52, died July 30, 1994, while piloting a Department of Public Safety helicopter during a search for a missing girl in Duschene County. Thorne, who was alone in the helicopter, was returning to Salt Lake City when the helicopter suffered an engine failure near Strawberry Peak. Searchers found Thorne's body in the wreckage three days later.

Utah Highway Patrol Trooper **Randy K. Ingram**, 39, died at the wheel of his patrol car on October 5, 1994. Ingram was stopped in the emergency lane of Interstate 15 near Nephi when he was struck from behind by a semitrailer truck, killing him instantly. The driver of the truck later pleaded guilty to negligent homicide.

Provo City Police Detective **Norman Kim Nisson**, 39, died in a traffic accident January 11, 1995, while serving court papers in American Fork. Nisson was waiting to make a left turn at 620 South 500 East when his vehicle was struck from behind by another vehicle, forcing it into the path of a third oncoming vehicle.

Spanish Fork Officer **Larry C. Penrod**, 54, died February 5, 1997, from injuries suffered seven years before. In April 1990, Penrod was struck and critically injured by a motorist while on duty.

Navajo Division of Public Safety Officer **Esther Todecheene**, 24, died June 8, 1998, in a one-car accident while on patrol in southern Utah. Todecheene was responding to assist another officer when her vehicle rolled several times, ejecting her.

Juab County Sheriff's Deputy **Tracy Davidson**, 28, was killed July 25, 1998, when his vehicle accidentally left the highway and struck a cement culvert. Davidson and two citizens were returning from a search for a missing man in Utah's west desert.

Utah Highway Patrol Lieutenant **Thomas S. Rettberg**, 58, died February

11, 2000, in the crash of a UHP helicopter. Rettberg and a civilian mechanic were performing a test flight when the engine failed, killing them both.

Salt Lake City Officer **Michael J. Dunman**, 30, was killed July 17, 2000, after being a struck by a vehicle. Dunman was on bicycle patrol near 1500 South State, when a reckless driver lost control of his vehicle and it jumped the curb. The suspect was apprehended and charged.

Salt Lake City Sergeant **James E. Faraone**, 48, died September 18, 2001, when his police vehicle was struck by another vehicle. Faraone had stopped to assist a disabled motorist on Interstate 80 near Salt Lake International Airport. His car, with its emergency flashers operating, was parked behind the disabled vehicle when it was struck from behind.

Iron County Deputy **Edward N. Dare**, 54, died in an automobile accident on September 24, 2002, while responding to back up officers from a neighboring agency. Dare's vehicle left the roadway and landed partially submerged in a drainage ditch. The accident was discovered an hour later by a passing citizen.

Salt Lake City Officer **James W. Cawley**, 41, was accidentally killed March 29, 2003, while temporarily serving with the United States Marine Corps in Iraq. Cawley died after being struck by a Humvee during a nighttime engagement with the enemy.

Emery County Deputy **Jeremiah K. Johnson**, 30, died May 27, 2003, when his patrol car crossed the centerline of Utah State Road 10 near Orangeville and collided head-on with a coal truck.

Sources

COOKE

Brooks, Juanita, ed. *On the Mormon Frontier: The Diary of Hosea Stout, 1844–1861.* Salt Lake City: University of Utah Press, 1965.

Calder, Davis Orson. Letter dated October 22, 1858. Letterpress copybook. Historian's Office, Church of Jesus Christ of Latter-day Saints.

Holmes, Kenneth L., ed. *Covered Wagon Women: Diaries and Letters from the Western Trails, 1840–1890,* Glendale, CA: A.H. Clark, 1985.

Larson, Karl, and Katherine Miles Larson, eds. *Diary of Charles Lowell Walker,* vol. 1. Logan: Utah State University Press, 1980.

Maughan, Ila Fisher. *Pioneer Theatre in the Desert.* Salt Lake City: Deseret Book, 1961.

Moorman, Donald R. *Camp Floyd and the Mormons: The Utah War.* Salt Lake City: University of Utah Press, 1992.

Moss, Nina Folsom. *History of William Harrison Folsom, 1815–1901.* Salt Lake City, 1973.

Romney, Edith. Typescript-MS 2737 of Church Historian's Journal – CR 100/38, Box 26, Folder 2, vol. 1, pp. 467–723. Historian's Office, Church of Jesus Christ of Latter-day Saints.

Scott, Patricia Lyn. *Worth Their Salt, Too.* Logan: Utah State University Press, 2000.

Smith, George A. to T.B.H. Stenhouse. Letter Book, XIV, p. 51. Historian's Office, Church of Jesus Christ of Latter-day Saints.

Utah Territory, Third District Court; Civil Case No. 1795. "Case of Sarah Ann Cook and Lot 2, Block 78." Utah State Archives and Records Service.

Deseret News, October 13, November 3, 1858.

Valley Tan, December 17, 1858.

Zion's Watchman, March 15, 1855, pp. 30–31.

Note: McDonald, a teamster with the Hobbs wagon train, also went by the name Cunningham. His first name is unknown.

STORY

117 Year History of Story Lodge No. 4, 1872–1989. Unpublished manuscript assembled and written by the Story Masonic Lodge History Committee.

Bevan, John Alexander, An Early History of Tooele (1912). Filed under "Tooele History," pp. 61–62. Brigham Young University.

History of Battery B, 2nd Illinois Light Artillery. Civil War Soldiers and Sailors. Washington, D.C.: National Archives and Records Administration.

Deseret Evening News, May 3, 4, 1870.

Mormon Tribune, May 4, May 7, 1870.

BOWEN

Early History of Provo 1849–1872, vol. 2. Minutes of Bishops and Lesser Priesthood Meetings, November 9, 1869, p. 79.

First District Court, Utah County. Minute Book 1, 1873–1880.

Hunter, Betty. Interview with author, 1994.

Jones, Albert. Diary 1839–1925. Microfilm 1534, p. 2. Historian's Office, Church of Jesus Christ of Latter-day Saints.

Layton, Stanford J. "Fort Rawlins, Utah, A Question of Mission and Means." *Utah Historical Quarterly* 42:68–83.

Madsen, Brigham. *Exploring the Great Salt Lake: The Stansbury Expedition of 1849–50.* Salt Lake City: University of Utah Press, 1989.

Provo City Council. Records, October 20, 1873; July 1872–September 1878, pp. 98, 99, 102, 140, 172, 359, 447.

Ward, Margery W., ed. *Autobiography of Mary Jane Mount Tanner*. Salt Lake City, 1980.

Deseret News Weekly, October 16, 18, 23, 1873.

Salt Lake Daily Herald, December 14, 1873, January 11, 1874, November 28, 29, 1874, June 23–24, 1876.

Salt Lake Daily Tribune, October 16, 21, 29, 1873.

Utah County Times, November 26, 1874.

BURGHER

Brooks, Juanita R., and Robert G. Cleland, eds. *A Mormon Chronicle: The Journals of John D. Lee, 1848–1876*. Salt Lake City: University of Utah Press, 1983.

Record of Service of Michigan Volunteers in the Civil War, 1861–1865. N.p.: John K. King Books, 1998.

Deseret Evening News, March 15–18, 20, 21, 1876.

Pittsburgh Daily Gazette, March 17, 1876.

Pittsburgh (PA) City Directory, 1861–1876.

Salt Lake Daily Herald, March 15–18, 20, 1876.

Salt Lake Daily Tribune, January 5, March 16, 17, 18, 21, 1876.

Utah Evening Mail, March 15–17, 20, 27, April 13, July 8, 1876.

Notes: Burgher's name appears in various accounts and records as Berger, Burger, and Bergher. For this work, the spelling in Ohio and Michigan census records is used. Burgher's obituary in the *Salt Lake Tribune* states that he was a captain in the 9th Michigan Cavalry, a claim not supported in Michigan's official record of the Civil War.

BURT

Gerlach, Larry R. Vengeance vs. The Law: The Lynching of Sam Joe Harvey in Salt Lake City. Brigham Young University Special Collections.

Romney, Edith. Typescript-MS 2737 of Church Historian's Journal – CR 100/38, Box 24, Folder 3. Historian's Office, Church of Jesus Christ of Latter-day Saints.

Seifrit, William C. "Charles Henry Wilcken, an Undervalued Saint." *Utah Historical Quarterly* 55 (1987): 308–21.

Tullidge, Edward W. *History of Salt Lake City*. Salt Lake City: Tullidge, 1886, pp. 894–95.

Salt Lake Daily Herald, August 26–29, 1883.

Salt Lake Herald, May 13–15, 1885.

Deseret News, August 29–31, 1883.

BURNS, J.

Longdorf, Hilda Madsen. *Mount Pleasant: 1859–1939*. Provo: Community Press, 1989.

Watson, Kaye C. *Life under the Horseshoe*. Spring City: Daughters of Utah Pioneers, 1987. Copy at Harold B. Lee Library, Brigham Young University, Provo, Utah.

Daily Enquirer, July 13, 1895.

Deseret News, September 27–29, October 1–3, 8, 9, November 29, 1894.

Manti Messenger, September 28, October 5, November 30, 1894.

Provo Enquirer, December 14, 1894.

Salt Lake Herald, September 27, 1894, March 9, 1897.

STAGG

"A Taste for Strawberries Led Patrick Coughlin to His Death." *The History Blazer*, June 1995.

Burroughs, John Rolfe. *Where the West Stayed Young*. Murrow & Co., 1967.

First District Court, Rich County, Criminal Case Files 1896, File 7.

Gillespie, L. Kay. *Unforgiven*. Salt Lake City: Signature Books, 1991.

Thomson, Mildred, comp. *Rich Memories—Some Happenings in Rich County from 1863 to 1960*. Springville, 1962.

Thomson, Steven L., Jane D. Digerness, and Mar Jean S. Thomson. *Randolph—A Look Back*. Randolph, 1981.

Uinta County: Its Place in History. Uinta County Library, Evanston, Wyoming.

Utah Board of Pardons, Pardon Application Case Files, 1892–1949, Series 328, File 263. Utah State Archives and Records Service.

Utah State Prison. Inmate Registrations, 770 and 772.

Cheyenne Daily Sun, July 31, August 1, 1895.

Deseret News, July 31, 1895.

Evanston Post, May 23, 1985.

Ogden Daily Standard, October 31, 1895, December 18, 1896.

Park Record, July 27, 1895, February 21, 1936.

Salt Lake Tribune, July 29, August 5–6, 1895, December 18, 1896, December 24, 1967.

BROWN

Encyclopedia of World Crime: Criminal Justice, Criminology and Law Enforcement, vol. 3. Wilmette, IL: CrimeBooks, Inc., 1990, pp. 2092–93.

First Judicial District Court State of Utah, Box Elder County, Minute Book, May 11, 12, 16, 1899.

Roberts, Richard C., and Sadler, Richard W. *A History of Weber County*. Salt Lake City: Utah State Historical Society, 1997.

Utah Board of Pardons, Pardon Application Case Files, 1892–1949, Series 328, File 2702. Utah State Archives and Records Service.

Utah State Prison. Inmate Registrations 1123 and 1358.

Ogden Standard, May 1–3, 6, 8–10, 1899, August 15, 1900, January 22, 1918.

Salt Lake Herald, May 1, July 12, October 8, 12, 1899, June 5, 1900.

Salt Lake Tribune, May 2, 1899, October 11, 1903.

Tri-Weekly Journal (Logan), September 23, 26, 28, October 1, 3, 5, 8, 10, 1901.

STRONG

Fourth District Court. Minute Book 1898–1903, Book 9.

Fourth District Court, Utah County. Record of Indictments and Informations, Book 1, pp. 46, 105.

Provo City Council. Minute Book, 1899, p. 179.

Utah Board of Pardons, Pardon Application Case Files, 1892–1949, Series 328, File 928. Utah State Archives and Record Services.

Utah State Prison. Inmate Registration 1165.
Daily Enquirer, June 27, 1899.
Deseret News, October 10, 1899.
Provo Herald, May 2, 8, 12, 16, 1911.
Salt Lake Herald, April 1, 1892, June 27–30, July 9–12, August 6, 8, 16, 20,
    23, September 4, 17, 27, 29, 30, October 1–3, 1899, October 4, 1903.
Salt Lake Tribune, June 27–30, 1899, October 12, 15, 1912.
Springville Independent, June 29, July 19, 1899.

TYLER
Baker, Pearl. *The Wild Bunch at Robbers Roost*. Lincoln, NE: Bison Books,
    1989.
Eardley, B.J. "The Death of a Sheriff," *Canyon Legacy* (Dan O'Laurie Museum,
    Moab, Utah) 15:4–5
Encyclopedia of Frontier Biography. Lincoln, NE: Bison Books, 1988.
Firmage, Richard A. *A History of Grand County*. Salt Lake City: Utah State
    Historical Society, 1996.
Lamb, F. Bruce. *Kid Curry: The Life and Times of Harvey Logan and the Wild
    Bunch*. Boulder, CO: Johnson Books, 1990.
Seventh District Court. Minute Book A, 1896–1910, Case File 13.
Grand Valley Times, October 14, 1898, June 1, 2, 8, 29, 1900.
Salt Lake Herald, May 28–31, June 1, 2, 4, 1900.
Salt Lake Tribune, May 28, 1900.

FORD
Salt Lake Third District Court. Criminal Case Files, 1896–Present, Series 1471,
    File 1868. Utah State Archives and Records Service.
Utah Board of Pardons. Pardon Application Case Files, 1892–1949, Series
    328, Files 3202, 1006, 1080. Utah State Archives and Records Service.
Deseret Evening News, May 13, 1908, May 28, 1919.
Salt Lake Herald, December 15, 1907, March 20, 1908.
Seattle Daily Times, May 7, 8, 10, 13, 1908.
Seattle Post-Intelligencer, May 10, 11, 14, 1908.

CLARK, S.
Ogden Standard, November 28, 30, December 1, 2, 3, 5, 9, 11, 1908, February
    5, April 6, 1909.
Salt Lake Herald, February 6, March 18, 1909.
Salt Lake Tribune, February 6, 1909, March 7, 1913.

JOHNSTON

Salt Lake Third District Court. Criminal Case Files, 1896–Present, Series 1471, File 2716. Utah State Archives and Records Service.

Utah Board of Pardons. Pardon Application Case Files, 1892–1949, Series 328, Files 1535, 2853, 1974, 2308, 3156. Utah State Archives and Records Service.

Utah State Prison. Record entry 2980.

Deseret Evening News, July 5, 6, 8, 1911.

Intermountain Catholic, July 15, 1911.

Salt Lake Herald-Republican, July 5, 6, 13, December 7, 8, 10, 12, 14, 15, 20, 1911, March 9, 23, February 7, 1914.

Salt Lake Telegram, October 25, 27, 28, 1913.

Salt Lake Tribune, December 8, 9, 10, 12, 13, 14, 15, 16, 1911, September 29, 1912.

COLCLOUCH

Salt Lake Third District Court. Criminal Case Files, 1896–Present, Series 1471, File 3011. Utah State Archives and Records Service.

Utah State Supreme Court. Records, Series 1471, File 3005. Utah State Archives and Records Service.

Deseret Evening News, August 8, 10, 12, 19–21, 1912, January 6, 1913.

Salt Lake Herald-Republican, August 8–14, 19, 20, 29, 1912, March 29, 30, April 1–5, 1913.

GRIFFITHS

Salt Lake Third District Court. Criminal Case Files, 1896–Present, Series 1471, File 3341. Utah State Archives and Records Service.

Utah Board of Pardons. Pardon Application Case Files, 1892–1949, Series 328, Files 3034, 3085. Utah State Archives and Records Service.

Utah State Prison. Inmate Registration 3341.

Deseret Evening News, June 25–28, July 1, 7–9, December 18, 1913.

Salt Lake Herald-Republican, June 26–28, December 17–21, 24, 25, 1913, January 1, 2, 23, April 10, May 23, 1914.

The Sun (Price, Utah), November 28, 1919.

GRANT

Bailey, Lynn R. *Old Reliable: A History of Bingham Canyon*. Tucson, AZ: Westernlore Press, 1988.

———. *The Search for Lopez*. Great Western and Indian Series, vol. 54, Tucson, AZ: Westernlore Press, 1990.

Bristow, Allen P. "The Great Underground Manhunt." *International California Mining Journal* 65, no. 8 (April 1996).

Frost, H. Gordon, John H. Jenkins, and Gordon Frost. *I'm Frank Hamer*. Austin, TX: Pemberton Press, 1968.

Governor's Executive Orders and Proclamations, 1896–1976, Series 85039, December 9, 1913. Utah State Archives and Records Service.

Higgs, Gerald B. "Ghost with a Gun." *Saga* (August, 1951).

Lish, Randy. Interview with author, February 2003.

Van Wagoner, Richard. "Lehi's Yesteryears." *Lehi Free Press*, January 29, 1992.

Deseret Evening News, October 25, 1919, October 24, 25, 1922.

Salt Lake Tribune, January 6, 21, 1914, October 25, 26, 1919.

ROBERTSON

Juab Fourth District Court. Criminal Case Files, Series 7712, File 173. Utah State Archives and Records Service.

Utah Board of Pardons. Pardon Application Case Files, 1892–1949, Series 328, Case 3216. Utah State Archives and Records Service.

Eureka Reporter, December 10, 1915.

Juab County Times, December 10, 1915, June 9, 1916.

Provo Post, December 7, 1915.

Salt Lake Herald, December 7, 8, 9, 1915.

Salt Lake Tribune, December 7, 1915.

MELLENTHIN

McPherson, Robert S. *A History of San Juan County*. Salt Lake City: Utah State Historical Society, 1996.

Mellenthin, Rudolph. Letter to Lottie Mellenthin Potter, April 16, 1918, copy in possession of author.

Peterson, Charles S. *Look to the Mountains: Southeastern Utah and the La Sal National Forest*. Provo: Brigham Young University Press, 1975.

Utah Board of Pardons. Pardon Application Case Files, 1892–1949, Series 328, Cases 4150, 4342. Utah State Archives and Records Service.

Utah State Prison. Inmate entries 3667, 3668.

Grand Valley Times, September 6, 13, 20, 1918, May 30, June 6, 13, 20, 1919.

Moab Times-Independent, October 12, 1925, December 21, 1961.

Salt Lake Tribune, August 24, 25, 1918, June 12, 1919.

HAMBY

Diamond, Steve. Interview with author, April 1999.

Salt Lake Third District Court. Criminal Case Files, 1896–Present, Series 1471, File 4181. Utah State Archives and Records Service.
Utah Board of Pardons. Pardon Application Case Files, 1892–1949, Series 328, Files 3722, 3692. Utah State Archives and Records Service.
Utah State Prison. Record of Inmates 3876, 3877.
Salt Lake Telegram, November 29. 1933.
Salt Lake Tribune, February 9, 11, 10, 12, 1921.

MANZEL
Second Judicial District Court, Weber County. Criminal Case File 1472 (1921).
Utah Board of Pardons. Pardon Application Case Files, 1892–1949, Series 328, File 3916. Utah State Archives and Records Service.
Utah State Prison. Inmate Registration Files 3916, 3969.
Deseret News, May 9, 1921.
Salt Lake Tribune, May 3, 10, 1921.
Standard-Examiner, May 9–17, 20, June 18–25, July 28, 29, 30, 1921, June 8, 1955.

STUART
Boberg, Jack. Correspondence with author, January 28, 2002.
Gerlach, Larry R. *Blazing Crosses in Zion: The Ku Klux Klan in Utah*. Logan: Utah State University Press, 1982.
Gillespie, L. Kay. *Unforgiven*. Salt Lake City: Signature Books, 1991.
Salt Lake Third District Court. Criminal Case Files, 1896–Present, Series 1471, Files 6301, 6309. Utah State Archives.
Seymour, Dorcas. Interview with author, January 27, 1997.
Curry Coastal Pilot (Brookings, OR), March 1971.
Deseret News, April 15, 17–21, May 10, 20, June 12–19, July 19–22, 1922, May 14, 18, 21, 26, 30, June 5, 25, August 31, November 17, 19–29, 1923.
Ogden Standard-Examiner, August 31, 1923.
Salt Lake Tribune, April 15–26, 30, May 9–12, 1922, May 19, July 8, August 30, 31, September 1, 1923, January 29, February 9, 1924.

PIERCE
Gillespie, L. Kay. *Unforgiven*. Salt Lake City: Signature Books, 1991.
Salt Lake Third District Court. Criminal Case Files, 1896–Present, Series 1471, Files 6759, 6569A. Utah State Archives and Records Service.
Utah Board of Pardons, Pardon Application Case Files, 1892–1949, Series 328, Files 4207, 4304. Utah State Archives and Records Service.
Utah State Prison. Inmate Register 4207.

Salt Lake Telegram, November 30, 1933.

Salt Lake Tribune, November 27–29, December 2, 6, 7, 9, 1922, March 26, 28, 29, May 1, 19, 20, July 6, 1923, January 7, 16, 25, 29, 1924, February 20, 21, 1925.

CROWTHER

Gillespie, L. Kay. *Unforgiven*. Salt Lake City: Signature Books, 1991.

Salt Lake Third District Court. Criminal Case Files, 1896–Present, Series 1471, File 6937. Utah State Archives and Records Service.

Salt Lake Police Museum.

Utah Board of Pardons. Pardon Application Case Files, 1892–1949, Series 328, Files 4406, 4769. Utah State Archives and Records Service.

Utah State Prison. Inmate Registers 4443, 4444.

Salt Lake Telegram, December 1, 1933.

Salt Lake Tribune, October 15–27, November 1, 1923, March 20, 21, 27, 28, April 1, 2, 1924, January 14, 1926.

HONEY AND HUNTSMAN

Salt Lake police firearms information from Salt Lake Police Museum.

Deseret News, February 16, 18, 21, 22, 25, 26, 1924.

Salt Lake Telegram, December 4, 1933.

Salt Lake Tribune, February 16–26, March 1, 1924, June 6, 1963.

San Francisco Chronicle, February 17, 1924.

BURNS, M.

Gerlach, Larry R. *Blazing Crosses in Zion: The Ku Klux Klan in Utah*. Logan: Utah State University Press, 1982.

— — —. "Justice Denied: The Lynching of Robert Marshall." *Utah Historical Quarterly* 66 (1998): 355–64.

Mt. Pleasant Pyramid, June 19, 1925.

News-Advocate, June 18, 25, July 30, August 20, September 10, 1925.

Salt Lake Tribune, June 15–19, 1925, March 15, April 5, 1998.

The Sun, June 19, 1925.

DAHLE

Cache Valley Daily Herald, May 3, 1929.

Herald-Journal, April 27, 1964.

Journal (Logan), May 6-8, 1929.

Ogden Standard Examiner, May 5, 1929.

WESTWOOD

Eardley, B.J. "The Last Day: The Murder of Dick Westwood." *Canyon Legacy* 15 (1992): 6–8.

Johnson, Lamont. "Manhunt on the Colorado." *Startling Detective,* March 1941.

Seventh District Court. Minute Book A-1 1910–1930, Case file 106.

Utah Board of Pardons, Pardon Application Case Files, 1892–1949, Series 328, File 7284. Utah State Archives and Records Service.

Westwood, Dick. *Growing Up In Moab: Chompin' at the Bit.* Moab: Westwood, 1986.

Westwood, Jean. "Richard Dallin Westwood: Sheriff and Ferryman of Early Grand County." *Utah Historical Quarterly* 55 (1987): 66–86.

Westwood, Richard E. Jr., ed. *Westwood Family History* vol. 1. Provo: Stevenson, 1973, p. 251,

Utah State Hospital. Medical Records, Micro reel 29, entry 67-41.

Utah State Prison. Record entries 5290, 5291.

Moab Times-Independent, September 2, 1926, September 12, 19, 1929.

QUIGLEY

Brown, Edith Mae Allred Quigley. Journal 1902–1991. In possession of Glenna Quigley Baker.

Ogden City Board of Commissioners. Minutes May 6, July 15, July 20, August 14, 1935, September 30, 1936.

Second Judicial District Court, Weber County. Criminal Case File 3588, 1935.

Utah Board of Pardons, Pardon Application Case Files, 1892–1949, Series 328, Files 7569, 6470. Utah State Archives and Records Service.

Utah State Prison. Entries 6482, 6483.

Ogden Standard-Examiner, May 13, July 12–14, 22, 1934, October 4, 6–11, 15–17, 1935.

Salt Lake Tribune, September 30, 1942.

Note: Family information courtesy of Glenna Quigley Baker, 2001.

BLACK

Geary, Edward A. *A History of Emery County.* Salt Lake City: Utah State Historical Society, 1996.

Rasmussen, Ruth J. Interview with author, Provo, July 24, 1997.

Seventh Judicial District Court, Emery County. Criminal Case File 312 (1936).

Utah Board of Pardons, Pardon Application Case Files, 1892–1949, Series 328, File 7300. Utah State Archives and Records Service.

Utah State Prison. Record Entry 6587.

Deseret News, August 26, 1936.

Emery County Progress, August 28, September 4, 11, 18, October 9, November 6, 13, 20, 27, 1936.

Ogden Standard-Examiner, June 4–7, 11, 14, 24, 26, 1943.

Salt Lake Tribune, August 22–29, November 13–21, December 1, 1936, January 4, 18, 1942, June 5, 6, 12, 17, 1943.

GATES

Avery, Walter Robert. Signed confession to Ogden police detectives, February 12, 1941. Copy in author's files.

Gillespie, L. Kay. *Unforgiven*. Salt Lake City: Signature Books, 1991.

Roberts, Richard C., and Richard W. Sadler. *A History of Weber County*. Salt Lake City: Utah State Historical Society, 1997.

Second District Court, Weber County. Criminal Case File 4018.

Deseret News, February 12, 1941.

Ogden Standard Examiner, February 12, March 5–13, 1941

Salt Lake Tribune, February 12, 13, April 23, 1941, February 4–6, 1943.

LARSEN, A.

BeBee, Glame. Signed statement, Salt Lake City, April 15, 1946. Copy in author's files.

Drago, Gail. *Etta Place: Her Life and Times with Butch Cassidy and the Sundance Kid*. Plano: Republic of Texas Press, 1996.

Hurst, Donna B. *Sundance, My Uncle*. College Station, TX: Early West Creative Publishing Co., 1992.

Kirby, Edward M. *The Rise and Fall of the Sundance Kid*. Austin, TX: Western Publications, 1983.

Meadows, Anne. *Digging Up Butch and Sundance*. New York: St. Martin's Press, 1994.

Seventh District Court, Sanpete County. Criminal Case File 687 (1946).

Utah State Supreme Court. Cases 6955, 7098.

Utah Board of Pardons, Pardon Application Case Files, 1892–1949, Series 328, File 9314. Utah State Archives and Records Service.

Watson, Kaye C. *Life Under the Horseshoe*. N.p.: Spring City, 1987.

Deseret News, October 16–20, 1945.

Deseret News and Telegram, January 5, 1953, June 2, 1955.

Mt. Pleasant Pyramid, October 19, 1945.

Ogden Standard Examiner, June 2, 1955.

Salt Lake Tribune, October 16–20, 1945, February 6, 8, 14, 15, 17, 1946, June 27, 28, 1947, November 23, 1948.

FARLEY

Gillespie, L. Kay. *Unforgiven*. Salt Lake City: Signature Books, 1991.

Lythgoe, Dennis. *Let 'em Holler: A Political Biography of J. Bracken Lee*. Salt Lake City: Utah State Historical Society, 1982.

Olson, Walt. Interview with author, January 8, 2003.

Salt Lake Third District Court. Criminal Case Files, 1896–Present, Series 1471, File 13814. Utah State Archives and Records Service.

Supreme Court of the State of Utah. State of Utah v. Don Jesse Neal, No. 7813.

Utah State Prison. Inmate Registration 9018.

Salt Lake Tribune, May 24–26, 1951, October 3–5, 17, 1951, July 1–3, 1955.

Wasatch Wave, May 25, June 1, 1951.

FISHER

Federal Bureau of Prisons. Inmate Roster 00294-041.

Graham, Warden Marcell. Letter to Board of Corrections, June 9, 1955.

Salt Lake Third District Court. Criminal Case Files, 1896–Present, Series 1471, File14841. Utah State Archives and Records Service.

Deseret News, June 1–3, 1955.

Salt Lake Tribune, June 2–4, 6, 7, 24, November 1–5, December 13, 1955, August 17, 18, 26, 1971.

LARSEN, L.

Deseret News, January 6, 10, 1961.

Idaho Falls Post-Register, January 12, 1961.

Moab Times-Independent, January 12, 1961.

Salt Lake Tribune, January 7, 1961.

WHITE

Jones, Michael P. Written confession, October 15, 1963.. Copy in author's files.

Second District Court, Weber County. Criminal Case File 7422.

Townsend, Sergeant Jerry. Telephone interview with author, March 4, 2002.

Ogden Standard-Examiner, October 16–24, 1963.

Salt Lake Tribune, October 16–23, November 13, 19, 1963, January 28, February 25–28, 1964, November 1–3, 1977, April 23, 29, July 21, 1978.

BUSH

Jeannott, Assistant Chief Bennie (United States Bureau of Indian Affairs). Correspondence with author, 1994.

Smith, Viola A. Letter to author, April 25, 1996.

United States Department of the Interior. Bureau of Indian Affairs Case File U&O 68-08.

Salt Lake Tribune, September 20, 22, 1967, January 9, 1968.

Uintah Basin Standard, September 21, 1967.

WAGSTAFF

Supreme Court of the State of Utah. Case 12651 (1972).

Third District Court, Salt Lake County. Criminal Case File 23005.

Provo Daily Herald, December 23, 24, 31, 1970.

Salt Lake Tribune, December 24, 25, 1970, January 2, April 13, June 6, 9–11, 18, 1971.

JENSEN, D.

Cunningham, Jan. Interview with author, January 6, 2003.

Franchina, David R. Letter to author, January 27, 1994.

Payne, Kenny. Interview with author, June 22, 2001.

Second District Court, Davis County, Farmington. Criminal Case Files 1708-1600 (1970–1972), Case File 1683.

Supreme Court of the State of Utah. Cases 12928 and 13009 (1973).

Deseret News, January 7, 20, 21, February 4, 7, 8, 1972.

Salt Lake Tribune, May 15, 16, 18, 26, June 10, 13, July 13, 24, 28, 29, 31, August 20, September 24, 25, October 6, 16, 29, November 24, December 15, 30, 31, 1971, January 18–23, 28, 29, 31, February 1–5, 8, 12, April 19, 1972, May 19, 24, 1981, May 31, 2002.

CLARK, P.

Diamond, Steve. Interviews with author, June 18, August 20, 2001.

Salt Lake City Police Department. Case Files 72-46892, 73-1502.

Smith, J.L. "He Called Them Gentlemen and They Killed Him." *Utah Peace Officer,* Summer 1997.

Salt Lake Tribune, January 12–19, 24, 25, 30, February 3, 6, 10, 15, 19, 22, March 19, April 10, June 19, 20, 23, July 7, 10, 17, August 7, October 4, 1973.

COLEBROOK

Strong, Don. Interview with author, April 16, 2001.

Deseret News, March 12–15, October 9–12, 1973.

Salt Lake Tribune, March 11–21, April 21, May 26, June 13, July 4, 21, 26, 28, September 28, October 2, 4, 6, 11, 12, 18, December 15, 1973.

ANTONIEWICZ

Adkin, Robert. Interview with author, January 17, 2003.

Eley, Fred. Interview with author, November 10, 1998.

Johnson, Joyce Antoniewicz. Interview with author, November 13, 1998.

Langford, Les. "History of the Highway Patrol." *Utah Peace Officer*, Summer 1997.

Reid, Robert J. Interview with author, January 28, 2003.

Third District Court, Summit County. 1977 Criminal Case File 734.

Salt Lake Tribune, December 9–13, 19, 1974, January 21, February 2, 1975, July 2, 10, August 7, September 12, 14, 15, 18, 30, October 2, 5, 9, November 3, 9, December 7, 8, 1976, March 25, 26, 29–31, April 29, May 18, December 10, 1977.

Summit County Bee, December 12, 1974, May 20, August 12, 1977.

Notes: Beck's first name appears on official records as "Emery" and "Emory." In October 1994, I received a phone call from a woman who identified herself only as "Linda." She claimed to have met Beck while both were in the Utah State Hospital and that she later was engaged to him. She stated that Beck earned college credits and saved thousands of dollars from producing handicrafts while in prison. She broke off the engagement the day before the wedding at the prison. According to her, Beck was remorseful about the murder. However, a call to the Tacoma Police Department in 1998 revealed an "officer alert" advisory associated with Beck's name, a condition that occurred after he allegedly bragged to police officers there about the murder.

HUTCHINGS

Diamond, Steve. Interview with author, May 24, 2002.

Foster, Lance. Telephone interview with author, May 15, 2002.

Hutchings, Janet. Interview with author, May 10, 2002.

Salt Lake City Police Department. Case File 76-53521.

Versluis, Vic. Interview with author, June 3, 2002.

Salt Lake Tribune, July 21–24, 27, 1976.

PIERSON

Fackrell, Keith. Interview with author, January 4, 2003.

Garfield County Sheriff's Office. Case 78-121.

Hunt, J.J. (as told by former UHP Sergeant Elroy Mason). "Retirement Suits Them Well." *Utah Peace Officer*, Spring 1999.

Pierson, Clint. Interview with author, February 2003.

Utah Sixth Judicial District Court, Panguitch. Criminal Case File 791602724.

Beaver Press, November 9, 1978.

Deseret News, November 7–10, 1978. *Garfield County News*, November 9, 16, 1978.

Salt Lake Tribune, November 9–11, 16, December 2, 7, 1978, January 9, 23, 24, February 23, April 7, 10, June 1, July 20, September 5, 1979, January 22, November 1, 1996, June 5, 2000.

HEAPS

Denver, Colorado, Police Department. SID 16410.

Federal Bureau of Investigation. Record 121 428 E.

Salt Lake City Police Department. File 82-3736.

Deseret News, January 14–20, 1982.

Los Angeles Times, October 2, 3, 1981, January 15, 1982.

Salt Lake Tribune, January 14–19, 1982.

STANLEY AND BEGAY

Federal Bureau of Prisons. Inmate Roster, January 10, 2003.

Arizona Republic, December 6–8, 10, 12, 1987.

Deseret News, December 6, 8, 1987.

Phoenix Gazette, December 7, 1987.

Salt Lake Tribune, December 6–10, 13, 22, 1987, February 15, March 1, 12, April 16, 17, 26, 30, June 7, 20, July 7, 9, 12–16, 19, 20–24, 28, 30, 31, August 2, 3, 5, 7, September 30, October 19, 1988, November 15, 1989.

Tucson Citizen, December 7, 1987.

HOUSE

Federal Bureau of Prisons. Inmate Roster, January 1, 2002.

House, Tom. Interview with author, March 18, 2002.

Langford, Les. "Building a Modern Patrol." *Utah Peace Officer*, Summer 1996.

Pope, Jerry. Interview with author, March 17, 2002.

Powell, Alan Kent, ed. *Utah History Encyclopedia*. Salt Lake City: University of Utah Press, 1994.

Deseret News, January 11, 1998.

Salt Lake Tribune, January 19, 27, 29, 30, February 4, 5, 9, 10, 13, 17–19, 25, 27, March 1, 4, 18, 23, 29, 30, April 2, 6, 7, 9, 14, 15, 19, 20, 23, 29, May 3, 5, 6, 10, 14, June 7, 11, 29, 1988, September 9, 1990, January 7, 16, 1998, March 25, 29, 1999.

LUND

Emery County Sheriff's Office. Homicide Incident Case Report 93-2980.

Interviews by author with Utah Highway Patrol Lieutenant Steven Rapich, Sergeant Darrell Mecham, Sergeant Bruce Riches, Sergeant Boyd Gledhill, Sergeant Richard Haycock, Trooper Clark Lund, Trooper Kelly Roberts, February and March 2000.
Lund, Brenda. Interview with author, February 2000.
Utah Department of Corrections. Inmate 78682 and 84360.
Utah Highway Patrol. Internal Affairs Case 93-113.
Utah Highway Patrol. Incident Report 099301282.
Deseret News, August 26, 1993, February 16, 1994, June 19, 22, 1995.
Salt Lake Tribune, May 15, July 27, August 2, September 21, 24, December 23, 1994, April 6, June 19, 23, 24, 30, July 1, 1995.

WELCKER
Marx, Larry. Interview with author, March 4, 2002.
Welcker, Kristine. Interview with author, March 2, 2002.
Salt Lake Tribune, February 25–27, March 10, 11, 1994.

GURR
Letter to author from Cecil Gurr family, March 11, 2002.
Hansen, Shalon Gurr. Interview with author, March 25, 2002.
Wallentine, Ken. Interviews with author, March–April 2002.
Deseret News, July 7–12, 2001.
Salt Lake Tribune, July 7–9, 15, August 7, 18, 25, October 11, December 5, 2001, February 15, 2002.

ADAMS
Adams, Josh. Interview with author, May 9, 2002.
Monson, Jerry. Interview with author, March 7, 2002.
Smith, Chad. Interview with author, May 15, 2002.
Daily Herald, August 14, 2001.
Deseret News, December 4, 5, 2001.
Salt Lake Tribune, August 5, 9, 11, 15, 18, September 5, 15, October 24, December 22, 2001, February 15, 2002.

WOOD
Davis, Richard. Interview with author, February 12, 2003.
Kirby, Chuck. Interview with author, January 4, 2003.
Searle, Mike. Interview with author, February 20, 2003.
Shober, Bob. Interview with author, February 12, 2003.
West Jordan Police Department. Case File 02H028193.

Wood family. Interview with author, February 16, 2003.

Deseret News, November 18–21, 24, 27, 2002.

Salt Lake Tribune, November 19–24, 2002, January 3, February 4, 2003.

Note: On November 20, 2003, two days after a memorial oak was planted on the spot where Ronald Wood was shot, Tyler Atwood's younger brother Bryce committed suicide. A note explained that he missed his brother and Van Roekel.

JONES

Cooper, Than. Interview with author, February 18, 2003.

Davis, Stacy. Interview with author, February 23, 2003.

Excell, David. Interviews with author, February 23–27, 2003

Garfield County Sheriff's Office. Case 0019864

Jones, Carolyn. Interview with author, February 28, 2003.

Roberts, Carol Jones. Interviews with author, February 22, 24, 2003.

Deseret News, January 27, 28, 2003.

Salt Lake Tribune, January 27–29, February 1, 4, 2003.

Index

The author in Grantsville, summer 1978.